INSTITUTIONAL DISABILITY

ROBERT A. KATZMANN

INSTITUTIONAL DISABILITY

*The Saga of Transportation Policy
for the Disabled*

THE BROOKINGS INSTITUTION
Washington, D.C.

Copyright © 1986 by
THE BROOKINGS INSTITUTION
1775 Massachusetts Avenue, N.W., Washington, D.C. 20036

Library of Congress Cataloging-in-Publication data:

Katzmann, Robert A.
　Institutional disability.
　Includes index.
　1. Physically handicapped—Transportation—Law and
legislation—United States.　2. Physically handicapped—
Transportation—Government policy—United States.
I. Title
KF480.K37　1986　353.0087'5'002408　85-73176

ISBN 0-8157-4834-5
ISBN 0-8157-4833-7 (pbk.)

1　2　3　4　5　6　7　8　9

THE BROOKINGS INSTITUTION is an independent organization devoted to nonpartisan research, education, and publication in economics, government, foreign policy, and the social sciences generally. Its principal purposes are to aid in the development of sound public policies and to promote public understanding of issues of national importance.

The Institution was founded on December 8, 1927, to merge the activities of the Institute for Government Research, founded in 1916, the Institute of Economics, founded in 1922, and the Robert Brookings Graduate School of Economics and Government, founded in 1924.

The Board of Trustees is responsible for the general administration of the Institution, while the immediate direction of the policies, program, and staff is vested in the President, assisted by an advisory committee of the officers and staff. The by-laws of the Institution state: "It is the function of the Trustees to make possible the conduct of scientific research, and publication, under the most favorable conditions, and to safeguard the independence of the research staff in the pursuit of their studies and in the publication of the results of such studies. It is not a part of their function to determine, control, or influence the conduct of particular investigations or the conclusions reached."

The President bears final responsibility for the decision to publish a manuscript as a Brookings book. In reaching his judgment on the competence, accuracy, and objectivity of each study, the President is advised by the director of the appropriate research program and weighs the views of a panel of expert outside readers who report to him in confidence on the quality of the work. Publication of a work signifies that it is deemed a competent treatment worthy of public consideration but does not imply endorsement of conclusions or recommendations.

The Institution maintains its position of neutrality on issues of public policy in order to safeguard the intellectual freedom of the staff. Hence interpretations or conclusions in Brookings publications should be understood to be solely those of the authors and should not be attributed to the Institution, to its trustees, officers, or other staff members, or to the organizations that support its research.

For my family

Foreword

AMERICANS depend upon their governmental institutions to help define policy alternatives and resolve differences. Because the issues confronting policymakers are usually complex, the decisionmaking process cannot always be neat or the outcomes unambiguous. Thus many issues do not receive the deliberate consideration that should ideally guide public policy. The case of transportation policy for disabled people illustrates the kind of flaws in policymaking that have led many to believe that government is not working as it should.

In this study Robert A. Katzmann, a lawyer and a political scientist who is a senior fellow in the Brookings Governmental Studies program, examines how three institutional processes—legislative, administrative, and judicial—dealt with the problems of mobility for the disabled over a twenty-year period. During this time policy shifted constantly, confusing state and local governments, the transit industry, and the disabled community.

Katzmann concludes that an important source of the confusion and vacillation was the failure to define the problem precisely and to choose between two different approaches to its solution. One approach emphasized rights of equal access for the disabled; the other emphasized mobility by cost-effective means. This failure was compounded by the increasing fragmentation of governmental institutions: a legislature with undisciplined processes, an executive branch with competing bureaucracies, and a judiciary with conflicting views of legislative intent.

In undertaking his research, Katzmann benefited greatly from discussions with many people in the federal agencies, Congress, the transit industry, and advocacy groups representing people with disabilities. In particular, he is grateful to Douglas B. Gurin of the Department of Transportation for allowing him to review his files. In addition, the author wishes to thank for their insightful comments Alan A. Altshuler, Eugene Bardach, Lawrence D. Brown, John E. Chubb, Martha Derthick, Christopher K. Leman, R. Shep Melnick, Terry M. Moe, Paul E. Peterson, Paul J. Quirk, Barry G. Rabe, A. James Reichley, Martin M. Shapiro, Gilbert Y. Steiner, and James L. Sundquist. He also appreciates the support given him by Mark A. Goldberg, Stephen Hess, Herbert Kaufman, and R. Kent Weaver.

He is grateful to Nancy Davidson for editing the book; to Pamela D. Harris, Janet A. Hathaway, Nancy K. Kintner, and Judith H. Newman for secretarial support; to Diane Hodges for administrative assistance; and to Daniel E. Hall for verification assistance. The Brookings library staff, headed by Laura Walker, was most helpful.

The views expressed in this book are solely those of the author, and should not be attributed to the trustees, officers, or other staff members of the Brookings Institution.

BRUCE K. MACLAURY
President

May 1986
Washington, D.C.

Contents

A good government implies two things:
first, fidelity to the object of government,
which is the happiness of the people;
secondly, a knowledge of the means
by which the object can be best attained.

The Federalist Papers, Number 62

CHAPTER ONE

The Problem

THE ARCHITECTS of our constitutional framework envisioned the mutual interaction of many diverse elements, working within and without government to achieve national purposes. Although each element would act according to its own interests and incentives, together those parts would create a balanced system assuring domestic tranquillity and national security. Governmental institutions were to be the medium through which energies were absorbed, ideas refined, and outcomes realized, consistent with the popular will.

It is the judgment of many Americans today that the governmental system in practice is but a distant relation to the founders' design. For some, the difficulty is that particular institutions are not working: their vision is one of irresponsible legislatures, unmanageable bureaucracies, and imperial courts. For others, the problem is that each institution is, in fact, acting in a manner that is consistent with its incentives and interests but is ultimately adverse to the system as a whole.[1] Those who view these perceived flaws as intractable call for a diminished governmental role.[2] Still others, who concede that imperfections exist, argue that the solution lies in refashioning the structures and incentives of institutions so that they operate to secure national purposes.[3]

This book is a saga of both institutional fragility and the problems of

1. On this point, I have benefited over the years from discussions with Richard E. Neustadt of Harvard University.

2. See, for example, George F. Will, *Statecraft As Soulcraft: What Government Does* (Simon and Shuster, 1983). Government, in Will's view, should be used to enhance the vigor of intermediary institutions—family, church, voluntary associations.

3. See, for instance, Lloyd N. Cutler, "To Form a Government," *Foreign Affairs,* vol. 59 (Fall 1980), pp. 126–44. On constitutional change, see James L. Sundquist, *Constitutional Reform and Effective Government* (Brookings, 1986).

governance in a particular arena—transportation for the disabled. In the past fifteen years, at the same time that many have claimed that government should be doing less rather than more, institutions at the federal level have steadily become more concerned with a whole range of issues affecting disabled people, including not only transportation, but also education and mental and physical health.

With respect to transportation, the problem, at least on the surface, seems obvious. A segment of the population is thwarted from using publicly financed transportation because it is not built to take their special needs into account. Is this to be written off as another case of "life is unfair," or can government provide some remedy? That provisions should be made is today a matter of little controversy; but how and at what level are issues that have stirred much debate. One view maintains that each individual has a right to be fully integrated into society and thus public transportation—buses and subways—must be made accessible to everyone. Barrier-free transit is a right, impervious to considerations of cost. Another perspective regards the question of providing transportation not as one of rights, but as one of cost effectiveness—securing the most out of a given input. In principle, such separate, specialized services as taxis and minivans would be acceptable. In one respect, then, the fundamental debate is about values—the trade-offs between equity and efficiency.[4]

In 1970 Congress decreed as national policy that "elderly and handicapped persons have the same right as other persons to utilize mass transportation facilities and services, that special efforts shall be made in the planning and design of mass transportation so that the availability to handicapped persons of mass transportation which they can effectively utilize will be assured."[5] Since then, Congress has on other occasions reiterated the commitment of the federal government to the handicapped; for example, it declared in section 504 of the Rehabilitation Act of 1973 that "no otherwise qualified handicapped individual in the United States . . . shall solely by reason of his handicap, be excluded from participation in, be

4. See Arthur M. Okun, *Equality and Efficiency: The Big Tradeoff* (Brookings, 1975).

5. 84 Stat. 962, 967. Today, the term "handicapped" is viewed quite critically by many disability groups, although it once was commonly used and generally accepted. In this book, the word "handicapped" is used when it is found in such documentary materials as legislation, legislative history, statutes, administrative regulations, or court decisions, or used by groups describing themselves. Otherwise, I have attempted to use the terms "disabled" or "disability."

denied the benefits of, or be subjected to discrimination under any program or activities receiving Federal financial assistance."[6]

In the wake of these acts, a whole array of institutions became involved in policy for transportation of the disabled: various parts of the executive branch, many congressional committees, the courts, and state and local agencies. At first glance, a consensus seemed to exist that programs for disabled persons should be continued and expanded. Congress enacted several major measures with virtually no opposition. Three cabinet-level departments conducted seemingly exhaustive rulemaking proceedings, consistent with the spirit of the Administrative Procedure Act. Despite this history, for more than a dozen years it was surprisingly difficult to state concretely the content of national policy on transportation for the disabled. Though filled with activity, the intervening period has also seen uncertainty and constant changes in policy direction—shifts that baffled state and local governments and disability groups as well.

If frustrations were deeply felt, it was because the affected interests perceived the stakes to be high. Thus local governments branded 1979 equal accessibility regulations requiring the retrofitting of old subways as prime examples of "regulation gone amok," intrusive, wasteful, costly federal action, and a "mandate millstone" that "threaten[s] both the initiative and financial health of local governments throughout the country."[7] For disability groups, those same regulations were symbolic of the federal government's commitment to assure their entrance into society's mainstream.

This book examines why the outcome thus far has been marked by such confusing twists and turns. In part, the confusion resulted from an inability to choose between conflicting approaches: a rights-oriented approach and a concept of "effective mobility." In addition, the institutional processes themselves—legislative, administrative, and judicial—were not always well suited for the tasks before them. Congress could not define the problem clearly and coherently enough for the administrative agencies charged with implementing its will. The legislative branch did not guide the executive when administrators sought legislators' aid. In spite of fidelity to administrative procedures designed to facilitate rational decisionmaking, the interplay of bureaucracies with different missions and professional

6. 87 Stat. 355.

7. Timothy B. Clark, "Regulation Gone Amok: How Many Billions for Wheelchair Transit?" *Regulation,* vol. 4 (March–April 1980), p. 47; and Edward I. Koch, "The Mandate Millstone," *The Public Interest,* no. 61 (Fall 1980), p. 42.

norms exacerbated the difficulties in fashioning administrative policy. Courts acting autonomously throughout the land struggled to make sense of vague legislative histories and to rationalize policy.

Defining the Problem

There are varying estimates of the population of disabled persons who have difficulty using public transportation. Methodological controversies have complicated the efforts to determine the universe of handicapped persons; doubts about the validity of data bases have clouded discussions about how best to respond to the concerns of the disabled. Today most transit districts base their projections on a 1978 study by the Grey Advertising Company thought by its critics to underestimate the number of handicapped persons.[8] But even that disputed report indicates that the population is considerable. About 13.4 million persons have problems using public transit. Nearly 7.4 million of that population live in urban areas; of this group, 1.4 million are unable to use transit at all, while the rest can do so only with great difficulty.[9]

The federal response to the problems of immobility is of relatively recent vintage. The Architectural Barriers Act of 1968 sought to ensure that buildings financed with federal funds are designed and constructed to be accessible to the physically handicapped.[10] Two years later Congress recognized for the first time the obstacles to the use of mass transportation by the elderly and handicapped. It declared in the Urban Mass Transportation Assistance Act that "special efforts" were to be made in the design of transit systems so that the disabled could use them. An amendment to the Federal-Aid Highway Act in 1973 authorized grants and loans to private nonprofit groups to assist in providing for the special needs of the elderly and the handicapped for whom mass transportation is inappropriate or unavailable.[11] Section 504 of the Rehabilitation Act of 1973, quoted above,

8. Grey Advertising, *Summary Report of Data from National Survey of Transportation for Handicapped People,* report for the U.S. Department of Transportation, Urban Mass Transportation Administration (DOT, 1978). For a criticism of the study, see, for example, Dennis Cannon and Frances Rainbow, *Full Mobility: Counting the Costs of the Alternatives* (Washington, D.C.: American Coalition of Citizens with Disabilities, 1980).

9. Grey Advertising, *Summary Report.*

10. 82 Stat. 718.

11. 87 Stat. 250.

prohibited discrimination against the handicapped in any program or activity receiving federal aid.

These statutes, following the form of much recent social legislation, do not direct those charged with implementing them to proceed in any obvious or particular way. They are cast either as entitlements or prohibitions. Entitlements identify a segment of society suffering from some problem and vest those so afflicted with rights to benefits that will presumably enable them to satisfy their particular needs.[12] The "special efforts" provision of the Urban Mass Transportation Assistance Act of 1970 is patterned after legislation creating legal entitlements in individuals. The prohibitory mold of legislation is patterned after title VI of the Civil Rights Act of 1964, which bans discrimination on the basis of race, color, or national origin in federally aided programs.[13] Acts of this sort are framed in terms of absolute rules and appear to provide legal relief to those who are victims of the prohibited discrimination.[14] Section 504 of the Rehabilitation Act of 1973 is of that stripe.

Even where agreement exists as to ends, the absence of programmatic direction—common to both entitlements and prohibitions pertaining to the disabled—generated conflicts over means and disputes over how to formulate the appropriate approach. For example, the term *special efforts* used in the 1970 legislation is nowhere defined in law; the nature and level of the activities required are not self-evident. The mandate of section 504 is equally unclear; until recent judicial decisions, there was much uncertainty as to whether section 504 was merely a nondiscrimination statute or one that mandated affirmative action.

How a problem is defined importantly shapes the options considered and the weight given to them.[15] Some have argued that government should not be deeply involved in providing transportation services for disabled

12. See, for instance, the Older Americans Act of 1965, 79 Stat. 218; and the Developmentally Disabled Assistance and Bill of Rights Act of 1975, 89 Stat. 486 (restrictively interpreted by the Supreme Court in *Pennhurst State School and Hospital* v. *Halderman*, 451 U.S. 1 [1981]).

13. 78 Stat. 241, 252.

14. Other such examples include title IX of the Education Act of 1972; see Peter H. Schuck, "The Graying of Civil Rights Law: The Age Discrimination Act of 1975," 89 *Yale Law Journal* 27 (1979).

15. On the impact of the idea of disability on another policy, see Deborah A. Stone, *The Disabled State* (Temple University Press, 1984). On the way societal norms affect problem definition and legal development, see Lawrence M. Friedman, *Your Time Will Come: The Law of Age Discrimination and Mandatory Retirement* (Russell Sage, 1984).

Table 1. *Selected Policy Actions Affecting Transportation for the Disabled, by Government Branch, 1968–86*

Year	Legislative	Administrative	Judicial
1968	Architectural Barriers Act	...	...
1970	Urban Mass Transportation Assistance Act, sec. 16(a)	...	...
1973	Federal-Aid Highway Act / Rehabilitation Act, sec. 504	...	...
1974	Rehabilitation Act Amendments, committee reports / Appropriations act	...	...
1975	...	UMTA announces Transbus policy	...
1976	...	DOT issues regulations implementing sec. 16(a) / Executive order gives HEW authority to issue governmentwide guidelines implementing sec. 504 / UMTA drops Transbus	*Cherry v. Mathews*
1977	...	DOT Secretary Adams revives Transbus	...
1978	Surface Transportation Assistance Act	HEW issues sec. 504 guidelines	...
1979	CBO issues report criticizing DOT sec. 504 regulations / Appropriations act	DOT issues sec. 504 regulations	*Southeastern Community College v. Davis*
1980	...	Transbus dies for lack of bids	...
1981	Mass transit bill fails to pass	DOT suspends sec. 504 regulations	...
1982	Surface Transportation Assistance Act	...	*APTA v. Lewis*
1983	...	DOT issues notice of proposed rules	...
1986	...	DOT issues final regulations	...

people, but rather should improve their general welfare. Under this view, it would be more efficient to give added income to disabled persons and let them determine how best to spend the money.[16] But generally, the federal government has assumed a direct role, wavering between two different policy conceptions, which I have defined as effective mobility and full or equal accessibility. The former seeks to provide transportation for the handicapped by any presumably practical mode. Examples include special paratransit services, user subsidies, and such demand-responsive systems as dial-a-ride services to preregistered clients. The equal accessibility approach strives to allow the disabled to use transportation facilities alongside the able-bodied, thereby requiring the retrofitting of subways, the installation of lifts and ramps on buses, and the development of new technologies and such devices as reserved seating, lowered bell cords, improved stanchions, and handrails.

In addition to pragmatic factors such as the relative cost and feasibility of different options, purely normative judgments may apply. Some have argued that the disabled have a right to be integrated into society and that without equal access to transportation facilities they will suffer the discrimination that those who are segregated inevitably endure. Even if the equal accessibility approach were the more costly—an assumption that its proponents reject—they perceive it as necessary in order to obtain a fundamental right. Others counter that equal accessibility is a utopian goal and that its impracticality and costliness would secure for those who would seek to attain it nothing more than a hollow victory.

The policy course followed by the federal government can in some sense be understood as reflecting changing perspectives about such normative judgments. (For an overview of selected policy actions taken by each branch, see table 1.) In 1976, pursuant to the 1970 "special efforts" clause, the Urban Mass Transportation Administration (the Department of Transportation office charged with implementing the legislation for the handicapped) issued regulations favoring the effective mobility approach. In 1978 the Department of Health, Education, and Welfare (HEW) promulgated governmentwide guidelines that interpreted section 504 of the

16. John R. Meyer and José A. Gómez-Ibáñez, *Auto Transit and Cities* (Harvard University Press, 1981), pp. 230–53. For an examination of the equity issues involved in providing transportation for disadvantaged persons, see Alan A. Altshuler with James P. Womack and John R. Pucher, *The Urban Transportation System: Politics and Policy Innovation* (MIT Press, 1979), pp. 252–316; and Sandra Rosenbloom and Alan Altshuler, "Equity Issues in Urban Transportation," *Policy Studies Journal*, vol. 6 (Autumn 1977), pp. 29–40.

Rehabilitation Act to require equal accessibility. In response, the Department of Transportation (DOT) issued regulations that reflected the HEW view. The Reagan administration, bolstered by a 1981 opinion of the D.C. Court of Appeals rejecting the DOT and HEW interpretation of the Rehabilitation Act,[17] issued interim regulations that summer that returned to the effective mobility formula of the 1976 regulations. Five years passed before the DOT completed a rulemaking proceeding that sought a final resolution of these policy questions. The resulting regulations reaffirmed the Reagan presidency's endorsement of the effective mobility approach.[18]

As a consequence of these dramatic changes in direction, the transit industry has been unsure about what it must do, and the disabled community has been anxious. These radical twists and turns over a brief period of time not only yielded a "policy" that was far from coherent, but also had a numbing and confusing effect on state and local governments responsible for implementing federal regulation. The most recent rulemaking docket, not surprisingly, was filled with statements from those entities, alluding to the muddle and asking for a consistent and certain course.[19]

Transportation policy for disabled people involves difficult questions; before any such policy can be fully implemented in a manner likely to achieve its objectives, it requires, among other things, time, careful planning, and nurturing. At bottom, state and local governments are dependent on rather constant direction over time from the federal policymakers from whom they take their cues. They need reasonably clear signals and statements of objectives from Congress, as well as guidance from a single bureaucracy to which they are accountable and whose experts are knowledgeable about their problems. Such stability, in fact, largely characterized intergovernmental relations as late as the mid-1960s.[20] Not surprisingly, then, the frequent shifts in federal direction in the past dozen years made it virtually impossible for state and local governments to fashion and implement a coherent transportation policy for disabled individuals. All this suggests that the nature of those institutional arrangements has changed.

17. *American Public Transit Association* v. *Lewis*, 655 F.2d 1272 (D.C. Cir. 1981).

18. 51 Fed. Reg. 18994–19038 (1986).

19. See Department of Transportation, "Nondiscrimination on the Basis of Handicap in Programs Receiving Federal Assistance from the Department of Transportation," Docket no. 56b (1983–86).

20. See Martha Derthick's analysis, *The Influence of Federal Grants: Public Assistance in Massachusetts* (Harvard University Press, 1970).

Understanding the Problem

A variety of factors could explain why there has been so much vacillation and confusion. Perhaps the policymaking process itself makes uncertainty inevitable. Conceivably the difficulty may stem from the way in which the problem is defined. Or it may derive from the internal workings of the institutions involved or the ways in which these institutions interact. Or the vacillation may be a consequence of the system's virtues—openness and responsiveness—or of the difficulty of choosing between competing but worthy arguments, values, and interests.

This book explores legislative, administrative, and judicial processes, all of which—individually and in interaction—have shaped transportation policy for the disabled across the nation at the state and local level. Much of the literature concentrates on select parts of the policymaking process—conceptual problems or breakdowns in the executive, the legislature, the courts, or the state and local levels—to explain the difficulties of devising and implementing programs.[21] Such works are valuable contributions, but their selective focus, by definition, limits perceptions of the decisionmaking process. Policymaking is dynamic and complex; it can be conceived as a continuum of institutional processes, sometimes acting independently, but often interacting in subtle and perhaps not always conscious ways to influence the behavior of other processes. It is the product of individuals with different incentives and professional norms, operating inside and outside government. If results are to be properly assessed and prescriptions made, it is essential to examine the issue networks—those institutional arrangements whose interaction yields outcomes.[22] Only such a focus can fully account for the incoherence in transportation policy for disabled people by explaining the way issues and claims become problems, how

21. On conceptual problems see, for instance, David Dery, *Problem Definition in Policy Analysis* (University Press of Kansas, 1984); on the executive, see Hugh Heclo and Lester M. Salamon, eds., *The Illusion of Presidential Government* (Westview, 1981); on Congress, see Morris P. Fiorina, *Congress: Keystone of the Washington Establishment* (Yale University Press, 1977); on the judiciary, see Donald L. Horowitz, *The Courts and Social Policy* (Brookings, 1977); and on subgovernments see, for example, Jeffrey Pressman and Aaron Wildavsky, *Implementation,* 3d ed. (University of California Press, 1984).

22. On this point, see Hugh Heclo's analysis, "Issue Networks and the Executive Establishment," in Anthony King, ed., *The New American Political System* (Washington, D.C.: American Enterprise Institute, 1978), pp. 87–124.

problems are defined, and the way those definitions are linked to institutional arrangements that do not always encourage clarity of purpose or execution.

I approach the study by focusing on each institution separately, examining its internal operations and interaction with other institutions. My hope is that such an approach will have the virtue of shedding light on the particular workings of each institution as it deals with policy problems and will offer some perspectives about how institutional arrangements affect the result.

The Legislative Process

This inquiry begins with an examination of the legislative process—those elements working to influence congressional outcomes. For some, Congress's fundamental task is to set the basic objectives and standards guiding governmental activity based on a broad community interest. For others, its duty is to aggregate and reconcile parochial group or individual interests. By either conception, Congress did not fulfill its responsibility. I argue that the legislative process was a major cause of the confusion over transportation for disabled people.

Congress did not define the problem precisely. Its difficulties stemmed in part from a highly differentiated committee structure and a haphazard process that allowed measures to be appended to larger, unrelated bills and to be voted upon with virtually no discussion. Congress added to the confusion in its oversight of the administrative process. Even when the executive branch sought guidance, Congress was unwilling or unable to provide it.

For present purposes, the story will be described quickly. A problem for policy was that the relevant legislation did not specifically focus on the problems of immobility, but rather dealt with mass transit generally or the rehabilitation of the handicapped and elderly. Transit legislation has for the most part been the bailiwick of congressional committees and subcommittees that over time have embraced the effective mobility approach. Rehabilitation measures, on the other hand, have been subject to the jurisdiction of rights-oriented committees and subcommittees that have favored the equal accessibility approach. In the first instance, however, the provisions on the handicapped in the Urban Mass Transportation Assistance Act of 1970 and the Rehabilitation Act of 1973 were not the products of committee deliberation. Rather, they were added to bills at a late stage of the process, proposed by someone not on the committee. As incidental provisions, they were subject to little debate and sparked no controversy. But once enacted, these sections were to become the linchpin of attempts to provide transportation for the handicapped.

Sponsor Charles Vanik, a House Democrat from Ohio, could not have predicted that section 504 of the Rehabilitation Act of 1973 would become the basis of an ambitious regulatory scheme involving a wide range of agencies. But the staffs of the relevant subcommittees and bureaucrats in HEW seized upon it as a vehicle to engage the federal government in a program to assure civil rights for the disabled. A conference committee report on the Rehabilitation Act Amendments of 1974 asserted that Congress intended that HEW issue regulations and governmentwide guidelines pursuant to section 504 and coordinate the activities of all agencies that were mandated to conduct their own rulemaking proceedings. What makes the report all the more remarkable is that none of this was discussed in Congress at the time of the passage of the Rehabilitation Act of 1973, and the 1974 amendments in no way altered the nondiscrimination provision of the 1973 act.

The secretary of the Department of Health, Education, and Welfare, David Mathews, believed that the regulations, developed by HEW's Office of Civil Rights, went beyond the intent of section 504, and he asked Congress for guidance. The key committee leaders involved did not provide any, but urged the issuance of the regulations without further delay so that the handicapped might exercise their rights. In the aftermath, HEW set forth guidelines affecting such spheres as transportation, housing, and education. It required the Department of Transportation to issue regulations that would assure equal accessibility.

Consistent with HEW's directives, the DOT did publish rights-oriented section 504 regulations. But the DOT regulations spurred the transit lobby to action. Aided by a critical report from the Congressional Budget Office, they sought, in effect, to change the DOT regulations through legislation. The lobby made its case principally before the House Subcommittee on Surface Transportation. A compromise was achieved, but the congressional session ended before legislation could be enacted. Ultimately, the equal accessibility regulations were suspended as a result of court action. Within Congress, there was concern among some members that the Reagan administration's Department of Transportation would be less than committed to providing services for the disabled. Two Democratic senators, Alan Cranston of California and Donald Riegle of Michigan, proposed as an amendment to the Surface Transportation Assistance Act of 1982 that the Department of Transportation be required to issue regulations providing minimum criteria for transportation services to handicapped and elderly individuals and that it establish procedures for monitoring compliance. The Surface Transportation Assistance Act had virtually nothing to do with the problems of the disabled, but was in large measure concerned with the financing of highway and transit systems. The amendment passed after little discussion. In response, the Department of Transportation took nearly four years to devise regulations consistent with congressional intent, however ill defined it may have been.

The Administrative Process

Congress's failure to define the problem clearly was a primary source of the difficulties faced by administrative agencies charged with implementing the legislative will. But the character of the administrative process itself increased the burdens of devising sensible policy. The interplay of two bureaucracies with different professional orientations and norms—the Department of Transportation and the Department of Health, Education, and Welfare (particularly its Office for Civil Rights)—significantly affected the course of events. At first the Department of Transportation (more precisely, its Urban Mass Transportation Administration) was virtually the sole actor. Very much influenced by the transit industry, it approached the problem of transportation for the disabled in terms of effective mobility. Matters became more complicated when President Gerald Ford issued an executive order vesting HEW with responsibility for formulating section 504 guidelines that other departments—the DOT among them—were to follow. With their rights orientation, the attorneys of the Office for Civil Rights concluded that section 504 required full accessibility. The HEW mandate increased the leverage of those in the DOT (especially at the secretary's level) who were sympathetic to the equal accessibility conception. HEW thus changed the nature of the debate and the balance of power within the DOT. Adding to the confusion were the mixed signals emanating from the White House, whose regulatory analysis unit opposed the equal accessibility regulations. The ineffectiveness of the White House group raises questions about presidential control of departmental behavior—a problem that chief executives (most recently, Ronald Reagan) have sought to resolve.

Apart from revealing the ways in which competing forces affect policy, study of bureaucratic behavior can reveal something about the premises underlying rulemaking. In theory, the rulemaking process should facilitate the rational formulation of policy in a fair, open, and efficient manner. It seeks to assure a role for all participants. Presumably, information secured through the public avenue of "notice and comment" should enable decisionmakers to reach sound judgments. The assumption of the proponents of rulemaking is that technically skilled experts will reach judgments after a careful assessment of the data. It is questionable, however, whether that describes reality, at least with respect to the rulemaking proceedings that the DOT conducted. The judicialization of decisionmaking can shift ultimate influence to lawyers whose responsibility is to insulate the regulations from legal attack and take it away from those bureaucrats with substantive knowledge of the problems. Those who control the writing of the regulations are most likely to affect their content. Moreover, the public aspects of the process may tend to lock the affected parties into rigid positions and to exacerbate conflict; it is often difficult for representatives to offer compromise in the open without risking the wrath of their constituents, especially when the issues are highly visible and emotional. The absence—in fact, prohibition—of informal negotiation precludes bargaining, which is often essential to reaching a satisfactory agreement. Furthermore, the information secured, dependent as it often is on self-interested parties, is not always reliable. Time constraints may make it difficult to consider carefully all of the comments submitted to the rulemaking document.

This examination also includes analysis of administrators as technology forcers, focusing on the DOT's ill-fated efforts to mandate a vehicle— Transbus—that would make mass transit accessible to those confined to wheelchairs. The DOT had sought to force technological development and in the process marry commercial purpose and social objective. Transbus became a symbol to the disabled community of the government's commitment to facilitate access to society's mainstream, but it ultimately fell victim to uncertain and changing government policies and the unwillingness of risk-averse manufacturers to change their corporate plans.

The Judicial Process

It is axiomatic that political disputes often become judicial ones as disaffected parties seek redress from the courts. In recent years, much has been made of the "imperial" judiciary, of unconstrained courts ready to impose their preferences in support of big government. The judiciary is frequently viewed as the institution that thwarts the will of the executive and the elected legislature. I contend that the reality is more complicated with regard to transportation policy for the disabled. Federal courts have been less the eager participant than an instrument used by all sides—the disabled and the transit industry—to secure desired ends. The courts have strengthened one side, then the other, and in so doing have affected the influence of competing factions within the bureaucracy. Judges have played an important role in shaping events at critical points. It was a lower court decision, requiring the secretary of HEW to issue section 504 regulations, that legitimated the department's attempts to impose substantive enforcement standards on such other agencies as the DOT. To that extent, this case study adds support to the notion of an "iron triangle," consisting of agency, court, and interest group. Congress creates a statutory right, but then retreats. An interest group then files suit in court, seeking enforcement of the right. The judiciary interprets these rights expansively and requires the executive to implement them—regardless of the president's policy preferences.

Ultimately, however, this is an account of judicial contraction. It was the Supreme Court that limited the scope of section 504 in an opinion essentially rejecting HEW's broad interpretation of what that statute mandated. A subsequent opinion of the U.S. Court of Appeals for the D.C. Circuit Court facilitated the suspension of the full accessibility regulations. Across the country, courts have increasingly been reluctant to delve into the technical aspects of transportation policy for the disabled.

Apart from concluding that the impact of the judiciary's decisions has been to restrain sweeping federal regulatory efforts, what can be said about the way it has reached its judgments? How capable have the courts been in interpreting legislative histories, in making sense of the labyrinth of rules and regulations? The record is decidedly mixed as courts have struggled to deal with claims brought by private parties seeking to enforce their vision of section 504 and the "special efforts" provision.

Conclusion

Having discussed these institutional frailties, the book concludes with an examination of possible remedies. Can the structures and incentives of institutions be changed so that policy processes and outcomes are less confused? If so, at what cost? Or if the vacillation and confusion are byproducts of the system's virtues, should they be tolerated if to do otherwise risks doing violence to those values?

CHAPTER TWO

The Legislative Process

LEGISLATIVE policymaking is often presumed to be deliberative and purposive. That is, decisions supposedly follow from a process that involves certain fundamental steps, including the definition of problems, the specification of alternatives, the making of an authoritative choice among those options, the monitoring of executive implementation, and the refinement of initial congressional judgments based on experience.[1] The assumption is that Congress, through its committees, subcommittees, legislators, and staffs, is institutionally capable of performing those tasks.[2] Drawing upon Madison and Mill, William K. Muir, Jr., has likened a responsible legislature to a school, an institution that teaches its members to govern well. A good legislative school has to have "a diverse student body, testing by floor debate, some exemplary legislators, manners grounded in the norm of reciprocity, well-informed lobbyists working openly, and leadership concerned about process." Legislators have to understand the circumstances of all their constituents and "learn to manage legislation and discipline themselves to do it fairly, openly, and in the face of opposition." They also have to develop an expert competence for a discrete segment of the legislative workload.[3]

1. For a review of congressional policymaking in terms of stages of program development and execution, see Charles O. Jones, *The United States Congress: People, Place, and Policy* (Dorsey Press, 1982), pp. 352–408; for an examination of agenda setting generally, see John W. Kingdon, *Agendas, Alternatives, and Public Policies* (Little, Brown, 1984); and Lawrence D. Brown, *New Policies, New Politics: Government's Response to Government's Growth* (Brookings, 1983). For a discussion of the varying roles and uses of legislatures in political systems, see Nelson W. Polsby, "Legislatures," in Fred I. Greenstein and Nelson W. Polsby, eds., *Handbook of Political Science*, vol. 5: *Governmental Institutions and Processes* (Addison-Wesley, 1975), pp. 257–320.

2. For an examination of congressional procedures, see Walter J. Oleszek, *Congressional Procedures and the Policy Process*, 2d ed. (CQ Press, 1984).

3. William K. Muir, Jr., *Legislature: California's School for Politics* (University of Chicago Press, 1982), pp. 1–8.

15

To be sure, Congress can and does perform responsibly.[4] But the reality, as I will show in this study of transportation policy for disabled people, can be far different from this idealized scenario.

Having identified a problem, the legislative branch defined it imprecisely, wavering between the two approaches of rights-oriented full accessibility and transit-oriented effective mobility, and then, not knowing what to do about it, left it to the administrative process for resolution. Apart from conceptual frailties, difficulties stemmed from aspects of the legislative process itself. Congress's highly differentiated committee structure led to fragmentation in the way the problem was conceived and addressed. Transportation for disabled persons could be viewed as a matter of assuring that they reach their destination. If the issue was before a committee with jurisdiction over transportation policy, it would be considered against the backdrop of transit programs generally, with attention given to such factors as costs and technology. But if the bill was before a committee concerned more with rights than with resource allocation, then cost became irrelevant. The existence of these committees with different orientations, each capable of spawning legislation, led to a less than coherent congressional vision.

Legislation was not always the product of much deliberation at all; entrepreneurial legislators tacked amendments onto larger bills that were voted upon with little or no discussion. Uncertain about what to do in the midst of such confusion, agencies turned to Congress. But even when the bureaucracy sought guidance or clarification about legislation, Congress was generally unwilling, for political or other reasons, to supply it. Finally, policy confusion had roots beyond the legislation itself and stemmed from Congress's oversight of the administrative process. The interplay between committee staffs and bureaucrats affected policy in ways not contemplated by the legislation.[5] To understand all this, I offer some observations to

4. See James L. Sundquist, *The Decline and Resurgence of Congress* (Brookings, 1981). Another analysis of a deliberative congressional process can be found in Martha Derthick and Paul J. Quirk, *The Politics of Deregulation* (Brookings, 1985).

5. Discussions of legislative staffs can be found in Michael J. Malbin, *Unelected Representatives: Congressional Staff and the Future of Representative Government* (Basic Books, 1979); Kenneth T. Kofmehl, *Professional Staffs of Congress* (Purdue University, 1962); Harrison W. Fox, Jr., and Susan Webb Hammond, *Congressional Staffs: The Invisible Force in American Lawmaking* (Free Press, 1977); and Michael Pertschuk, *Revolt against Regulation: The Rise and Pause of the Consumer Movement* (University of California Press, 1982).

guide the analysis that follows—not as hard and fast truths, but as suppositions that might have explanatory power.

The legislature is especially tested when it also assumes the role of the executive in proposing complex legislation. It is usually best equipped to participate in the policymaking process as a partner of the executive, that is, when the presidency initiates measures. Typically, the president proposes legislation after the executive agencies have defined problems and collected and analyzed large quantities of information—tasks these agencies are thought suited to do, given their resources and structure. But for Congress, such undertakings tend to be more difficult, though often instrumental in raising issues that the executive has not considered or is reluctant to address. It is not simply that the legislative process can be untidy or at times lacking in order. More fundamental is the failure to define problems precisely and to make conscious and definitive trade-offs among competing approaches. The difficulty may be due partly to the inherent complexity of the issues. But, as I will seek to show, it may also have to do with the way issues and claims become problems, the manner in which problems are defined, and how those definitions are related to institutional structures and processes that can frustrate coherent policymaking.

The legislative process can recognize or identify problems, but the identification of a problem does not necessarily lead to precise definition.[6] If problems, as initially conceived, are framed in general terms, questions of scope, means, and costs are obscured; consequently, their ramifications are not very well appreciated.

A problem is framed in general terms either because not enough is known to style it more precisely or because it is easier to secure support for ambiguously worded measures that can mean all things to all people. Indeed, in some circumstances there may be little incentive for a legislator to define the problem acutely if to do so would draw attention to its costs and thus reduce its support. Moreover, a problem can be conceived in a way that precludes cost considerations. Thus, if it is termed and viewed as

6. On problems, see Aaron Wildavsky, *Speaking Truth to Power: The Art and Craft of Policy Analysis* (Little, Brown, 1979); and Kingdon, *Agendas, Alternatives and Public Policies,* pp. 115–19. As Kingdon notes (p. 115), drawing upon James Q. Wilson, "There is a difference between a condition and a problem. We put up with all manner of conditions every day: bad weather, unavoidable and untreatable illnesses, pestilence, poverty, fanaticism. . . . Conditions become defined as problems when we come to believe that we should do something about them."

a right, it is absolute and must be honored, regardless of the fiscal consequences.

Once a problem is identified or recognized, interests within and without Congress push for an interpretation consistent with their policy preferences, regardless of whether it is faithful to the original legislative intent. To the extent that the problem is ambiguously worded, these interests have greater freedom to maneuver in efforts to shape the terms of the policy debate and its outcome even in ways not envisioned by the legislative drafters.

Contributing to the difficulty of defining and resolving problems is the structural character of Congress itself. Generally, Congress is limited, by reasons of resources and organization, in its capacity to assume the leadership role of the executive in gathering and analyzing large quantities of data. Congressional organization leads to fragmentation. The legislature is divided into authorization and appropriation committees and subcommittees, each charged in theory with jurisdiction over particular policy areas.[7] In fact, because issues are crosscutting, several committees may claim that an area is within their domain. The orientations of committees differ, reflecting, among other things, the diversity of policy environments and member goals.[8] Consequently, committees dealing with the same issues may initiate legislation based on differing and even incompatible premises. The lack of effective congressional consultative or coordinating mechanisms means that Congress is often not cognizant of these differences and inconsistencies in approach and thus does not make conscious trade-offs among alternatives. The result is that the legislature sends confusing and conflicting messages to the administrative agencies charged with divining the congressional "will."

The legislative process itself provides points of opportunity for legislative entrepreneurs, eager to promote their professional and personal goals, to push through measures and policy preferences largely free of close congressional scrutiny, without hearing or extended discussion.[9] Amend-

7. On subcommittee work, see Roger H. Davidson, "Subcommittee Government: New Channels for Policy Making," in Thomas E. Mann and Norman J. Ornstein, eds., *The New Congress* (Washington, D.C.: American Enterprise Institute, 1981), pp. 99–133.

8. See Richard F. Fenno, *Congressmen in Committees* (Little, Brown, 1973); Steven S. Smith and Christopher J. Deering, *Committees in Congress* (CQ Press, 1984); and David E. Price, *Who Makes the Laws? Creativity and Power in Senate Committees* (Schenkman Publishing Co., 1972).

9. See David R. Mayhew's interesting examination of what he calls credit claiming, advertising, and position taking, in *Congress: The Electoral Connection* (Yale University

ments are added on the floor to bills only peripherally related to them. Such measures, if framed in seemingly noncontroversial ways, tend to escape tough examination because legislators focus on the larger bill at hand. Low-visibility mechanisms, such as committee reports that accompany bills, allow legislators and staffs to press for policy preferences generally immune from observation by the full chamber. Through such means as conference committee reports, they may require executive action not compelled in the legislation itself, causing confusion in the agencies charged with implementing the laws.

As I test these observations, it is altogether fitting that I begin with the legislative process. For it was in Congress—not, as is usually the case in most policy arenas, the executive—where bills concerning transportation for disabled persons were initiated. Those measures were generally parts of legislation that dealt either with mass transit or the rehabilitation of the disabled and the elderly. Transit legislation has been at various times in the recent past the domain of the House Committee on Banking and Currency, the House Committee on Public Works and Transportation, and the Senate Committee on Banking, Housing, and Urban Affairs. Those committees have tended to adopt an effective mobility conception. Rehabilitation measures have been the province of the rights-oriented House Committee on Education and Labor and the Senate Committee on Labor and Human Resources, which have favored the equal accessibility approach. Because the transit and rights-oriented rehabilitation legislation often involved distinctly different routes and environments, each will be examined separately before they are assessed together. Among the key features of the process were an inability to define objectives clearly, legislative entrepreneurship, legislation without debate, staff efforts to create legislative history after the fact, and congressional reluctance to assist in legislative interpretation.

The Hodgepodge of Transit-Oriented Legislation

From the late 1960s through much of the next decade, most of the transit legislation concerning the problems of disabled people lacked conceptual coherence. Most measures were responses to discrete problems, rather than elements of an overarching policy. They had in common the

Press, 1974), pp. 49–77. For an insider's view of the forces that affect a legislator's decisionmaking, see Stephen J. Verdier, "What Makes a Congressman Tick?" *Independent Banker* (February 1985), p. 58.

view that the needs of the disabled were legitimate, that something practical should be done—though they were uncertain about what should be done or how it should be accomplished. Institutional arrangements and conceptual weakness produced a hodgepodge of legislation. Out of that disjointed activity of the early 1970s both the effective mobility approach and the rights-oriented conception eventually emerged. Each train of thought proceeded along a different track, seemingly oblivious of each other, only to collide by the end of the decade.

A Beginning and Unanswered Questions

Congressional attention to the transportation problems of disabled people is in a sense the logical extension of a more general concern with physical barriers confronting handicapped individuals. In this age of sidewalk curb cuts and ramps, it is striking to reflect that not until 1968 did Congress even address the problem of architectural barriers at all. That legislative effort was not the initiative of an interest group, technical experts, or government agencies. Rather it owed much to Hugh G. Gallagher, a legislative aide to Democratic Senator E. L. Bartlett of Alaska. And its conception is testament to the view that legislation, whatever its ultimate effect, is not always born out of grand or ambitious design, but often arises out of the need to confront basic, elemental problems—in this case, mobility. At the same time, the events culminating in the Architectural Barriers Act of 1968 support the proposition that problems, at least as initially conceived, tend to be framed in general terms that obscure questions of scope, means, and costs.

Confined to a wheelchair after polio struck, Gallagher had to contend with many inaccessible buildings.[10] But inducing authorities, even public ones, to eliminate barriers was not a simple task. What especially rankled Gallagher was that he was denied access to those treasures in the nation's capital that presumably belonged to all Americans. A typical Saturday morning would find him at work in Bartlett's office; ideally, he would have liked to have spent afternoons in the National Gallery of Art and the Library of Congress, not far away. Yet both buildings were inaccessible. The National Gallery, Gallagher recounted, initially turned down his request for a ramp, asserting that it would ruin the architecture. Only a direct appeal by Senator Bartlett to the board of directors of the gallery led to a

10. Interview with Hugh Gallagher, December 10, 1981.

decision to install a ramp. The Library of Congress reluctantly agreed to put in a ramp, principally because Bartlett, as chairman of the subcommittee that reviewed library appropriations, could exert influence.

For a time, Gallagher left his Senate job and worked in the Bureau of the Budget on legislative clearance matters. Because the Executive Office Building was inaccessible, Secret Service officers had to lift Gallagher up the stairs. Narrow doorways made the restrooms there inaccessible to him. The wasted energy expended to circumvent these physical barriers prompted Gallagher to think about a legislative solution. His view was that any bill should be simply drafted, broadly setting policy and leaving to the executive the task of writing specific regulations. At the time that he conceived of a legislative approach, a National Commission on Architectural Barriers had independently begun to study how best to deal with environmental barriers (see chapter 3); the commission's existence suggests that the problem of architectural barriers was one whose time had come and it would have eventually been placed on the congressional agenda, apart from Gallagher's efforts. But Gallagher believed that the work of the commission was unnecessary and he did not wait for its report and recommendations. His first concern was to find a way to put the matter on the congressional agenda, that is, to interest some committee in the problem. He would then draft the bill so that it would fall within the jurisdiction of that committee and thus be referred to it for consideration.

The Senate Committee on Labor and Public Welfare was Bartlett's and Gallagher's first choice. But many in that committee preferred not to act until the commission completed its work and the Johnson administration proposed its own legislation. Bartlett did find support in the Public Works Committee, whose chairman, Democratic Senator Jennings Randolph of West Virginia, had long been concerned with social welfare issues. So that the measure would be sent to the Committee on Public Works, specifically its Subcommittee on Public Buildings and Grounds, the bill was rewritten with the words "public building" featured prominently. Gallagher conferred with the Office of Legislative Counsel of the Senate and drafted "a bill to insure that public buildings financed with Federal funds are so designed and constructed as to be accessible to the physically handicapped."

As introduced by Senator Bartlett, the bill would have simply authorized the head of the General Services Administration to prescribe regulations establishing standards for the design and construction of public buildings to ensure accessibility to the physically handicapped. In testimony before the Subcommittee on Public Buildings and Grounds of the Senate

Committee on Public Works, Bartlett emphasized the limited purpose of the enterprise: "What this problem area needs is a logical and justifiable start, not [an] all-encompassing, 'solution to the problem.'" He stated that he would oppose any amendment requiring alteration of existing buildings as being "too expensive." He rejected the view that the legislation should incorporate standards, preferring "to trust the [GSA] Administrator's good judgment in establishing regulations."[11] In keeping with this measured approach, the bill provided for no enforcement mechanism. Underscoring the measure's modesty, Bartlett commented that it

> contains no seeds of controversy, carries with it no appropriation, and will cost the taxpayers of this country only a nominal amount. Its advantages for one segment of our country's citizens are not counterbalanced to any extent by disadvantages for another, nor does it have any accompanying appropriation—or the prospect of appreciable costs in the future—over which we, as Members of Congress, must agonize.[12]

The Senate committee heard testimony from a number of organizations and government entities, including the National Commission on Architectural Barriers, the President's Committee on Employment of the Handicapped, the National Federation of the Blind, the Easter Seal Society, the National Rehabilitation Association, the Vocational Rehabilitation Administration of HEW, the Department of Housing and Urban Development, and the General Services Administration.[13] Reaction was most favorable, though some suggested strengthening the bill's provisions, and others, mainly governmental representatives, argued that it was preferable to wait for the national commission to complete its work before acting on the legislation. Further, the commission itself suggested that the responsibility for devising the standards and regulations should be assigned not to the General Services Administration, but to the Vocational Rehabilitation Administration (VRA) of the Department of Health, Education, and Welfare[14]— not surprising, given that Mary Switzer and Kathaleen Arneson, the driving forces of the commission, were the key officials of the VRA.

Only once during the Senate committee hearings did the issue of transportation accessibility for the handicapped arise. While testifying about the work of the American Institute of Architects, Edward H. Noakes, a hos-

---

11. *Accessibility of Public Buildings to the Physically Handicapped,* Hearings before the Senate Committee on Public Works, 90 Cong. 1 sess. (Government Printing Office, 1967), p. 3.
12. Ibid.
13. Ibid., pp. 25–29, 40, 52–54, 64, 70, 82–85, 90–93.
14. Ibid., p. 51.

pital architect and director of a project on architectural barriers, declared that the needs of the disabled are those that the "designers of our communities, their structures and their transportation systems can easily cater to."[15]

The revisions of the bill made in committee reflected the testimony at the hearings, and some would eventually bear upon matters having to do with transportation for the handicapped. The most important modification required unqualifiedly that all public buildings be "accessible and usable" to the physically handicapped, rather than "reasonably accessible," as stated in the Bartlett bill. Further, the committee provided that the GSA administrator consult with the secretary of HEW in prescribing regulations—a position advocated by the national commission.[16] The amended bill reached the Senate floor on August 25, 1967, and sailed through the chamber. It was so lacking in controversy that it sparked no debate at all. Indeed, Senator Bartlett was the only legislator to make remarks about the measure on the Senate floor, and he commended the Committee on Public Works for "marking up and reporting out a fine bill."[17]

The legislative process then moved to the House of Representatives, where Representative Charles E. Bennett, Democrat of Florida, introduced a bill identical to the Bartlett proposal. Bennett, like Bartlett, emphasized that there would be "no extra cost" in constructing accessible buildings. Senator Bartlett testified before the Subcommittee on Public Buildings and Grounds of the House Committee on Public Works and reiterated that budgetary constraints led him to conclude that legislation should apply only to new buildings; "Otherwise," he said, "at this juncture in history, our efforts might be doomed to failure."[18] The tenor of the House hearing was much the same as that of the Senate; the individuals, organizations, and agencies testifying before the Senate subcommittee were represented at the House deliberation. All agreed upon the need for legislation that would mandate accessible federal buildings.

The House hearings were noteworthy because they explicitly addressed the question of whether the legislation would require that transportation systems be free of barriers. Democratic Representative Jerome Waldie of

15. Ibid., p. 89.
16. *Design and Construction of Public Buildings Financed with Federal Funds to be Accessible to the Handicapped*, S. Rept. 90-538, 90 Cong. 1 sess. (GPO, 1967), p. 1.
17. *Congressional Record* (August 25, 1967), p. 24133.
18. *Building Design for the Physically Handicapped*, Hearings before the Subcommittee on Public Buildings and Grounds of the House Committee on Public Works, 90 Cong. 2 sess. (GPO, 1968), pp. 5, 7.

California wondered if the Bay Area Rapid Transit System (BART), which was constructing a system with some federal funds yet would be inaccessible to the handicapped, would be compelled to remove architectural barriers as a condition for receiving such support. He estimated the cost of eliminating such obstacles at between $4 million and $8 million for each barrier and noted that BART's board of directors had resolved to address the problem only "if the Federal Government would pick up the bill." William McCahill, executive secretary of the President's Committee on Employment of the Handicapped, later asserted that he suspected that the costs of making the San Francisco system accessible would be a minimal percentage of the total cost. He declared that the proposed legislation should cover transportation systems: "We are not interested in exceptions, we are interested in inclusions."[19] Subcommittee chairman Kenneth Gray, Democrat of Illinois, later responded to such concerns on the House floor by explicitly stating that "if constructed with Federal public funds such [transit] facilities would be covered."[20]

Once in committee, the Bennett bill was changed in much the same way as the proposed Senate measure introduced by Bartlett. On the House floor, there was virtually no discussion and the comments made were all supportive of the legislation. Of interest, particularly in view of the subsequent concerns about the budgetary implications of the act, was the perception that the legislation would not impose any substantial costs at all. No representative voted against the legislation; 303 members supported it; and 130 did not participate in the roll call.[21]

As enacted, the Architectural Barriers Act authorized the administrator of general services, the secretary of housing and urban development, and the secretary of defense, each in consultation with the secretary of health, education, and welfare, to prescribe standards for buildings within their respective jurisdictions so as to ensure that physically handicapped persons would have ready access to, and use of, such buildings. "Building" was defined to include any structure constructed or altered by or on behalf of the United States, leased in whole or in part by the United States, or financed in whole or in part by a grant or loan made by the United States.[22]

Neither the drafters of the legislation nor the other actors involved in

19. Ibid., pp. 16, 70.
20. *Congressional Record* (June 17, 1968), p. 17431.
21. Ibid., pp. 17432–33.
22. 82 Stat. 718.

the disability groups, the national commission, or the congressional committees thought very much about accessible transportation for the handicapped. Rather, they focused for the most part on the physical barriers facing handicapped persons seeking to enter public buildings. In some ways, the act was quite modest, conceived as a simple instrument to attack a problem. It was, after all, to apply only to structures built after the act's passage; barriers in existing buildings would not be modified. Projected costs would presumably be minimal. Further, the legislation neither prescribed standards nor provided for an enforcement mechanism to monitor efforts to design and construct accessible buildings. It was hardly a contested measure; it did not need the impetus of interest group activity or other efforts to secure enactment. The legislation fit well with the dominant political currents of the time, with the notion that technology forcing could be simple and cheap if only government expressed its will.

But the ramifications of problems generally defined are not always appreciated. However mild the legislation seemed at the time, its enactment would serve as a prologue for the ensuing years of controversy concerning accessible transportation for the handicapped. Fundamental questions, for the most part not considered at the time, would later surface: how to define "handicapped" and "accessible" in operational terms; what standards and criteria should be used to measure compliance; who would determine when those standards had been breached; whether accessibility would require that a transportation system accommodate any and all handicapped persons; whether all modes (for example, buses, subways) in a transit system would have to be accessible; and whether every transit vehicle in each mode would have to be accessible.

The First Focus on Transit Facilities

Committees and their members, who sponsor legislation and take credit for its passage, seek to ensure executive compliance. For their part, interests affected by legislation press for an interpretation consistent with their policy preferences. Both of these propositions were borne out in little more than a year after the passage of the Architectural Barriers Act. Prompted by the President's Committee on Employment of the Handicapped, the Subcommittee on Public Buildings and Grounds of the House Committee on Public Works sought to compel the Washington Metropolitan Area Transit Authority to make its planned transit system accessible to the physically disabled.[23] District authorities claimed that the Architectural Barriers Act did not cover its system.[24]

A bill in the form of an amendment to the Architectural Barriers Act of 1968, explicitly requiring the Washington Metro to be accessible to the physically handicapped, was introduced by committee chairman George H. Fallon, Democrat of Maryland. The subcommittee conducted a hearing on the bill on the same day of the groundbreaking for the new system. The comments and testimony at the hearing were illuminating because the session marked the first time that a congressional body had to address explicitly the competing claims of handicapped persons and transit operators. This presaged the debate that would occur at the end of the decade. The Public Works Committee's natural jurisdiction included neither mass transit nor handicapped and elderly matters; thus, presumably, it could act relatively free of constituent interests.

Differences arose about how to define the problem, the magnitude of the problem, the size of the handicapped population, and the appropriate response. For the transit operators, the issue of providing transportation for the handicapped was tangential to building a new system and one they obviously would have preferred not to address. In fact, they conceived of the problem as providing transportation for the able-bodied. Officials at the House hearing noted that Congress had not provided guidance as to who was to be classified as handicapped. The transit officials defined it to include only those who were not confined to their homes—approximately one-tenth of 1 percent of the population. Given that the projected patronage was so small, the transit representatives asserted that the costs would be exceedingly high. Indeed, they claimed that they did not have the resources to make the system fully accessible.[25]

23. Interviews with Edmund Leonard, December 8, 1981, and Bernard Posner, December 7, 1981, both of the President's Committee on Employment of the Handicapped.

24. Because the Washington Metropolitan Area Transit Authority (WMATA) was a regional agency created by compact, rather than a federal agency, and because its buildings or structures were not subject to standards for design or construction issued under authority of law authorizing a federal loan or grant, the General Services Administration questioned whether transit officials were bound to comply with the Architectural Barriers Act. *Design and Construction of Federal Facilities to be Accessible to the Physically Handicapped*, Hearings before the House Subcommittee on Public Buildings and Grounds of the House Committee on Public Works, 91 Cong. 1 sess. (GPO, 1970), p. 21. (Hereafter *Design Hearings*.)

25. They estimated that the costs of installing elevators would be $1 million to $3 million for each of the eighty-six subway stations. To lessen the cost, the operators advanced several suggestions, such as requiring that only a few "key" stations be accessible. *Design Hearings*, pp. 11–18.

Countering these views were representatives of the handicapped, including the president's committee and the Paralyzed Veterans of America, the United Cerebral Palsy Association, and the National Easter Seal Society. William McCahill, executive secretary of the president's committee, argued that the new system should be accessible in all respects, that through a barrier-free environment the handicapped will find a "new freedom." He asserted that lack of an accessible transportation system was the "biggest deterrent" to entry into the labor market. In language that would become popular a few years later, Peter Lassen of the Paralyzed Veterans of America called for the establishment of a constitutional right of the disabled to full use of transportation facilities. McCahill claimed that the benefited population would be substantial, including elderly persons aged sixty-five and over, pregnant mothers, and mothers with small children. The cost of providing such transit would be relatively insignificant, about 0.001 percent of the total.[26] The disability groups also emphasized the technical feasibility for realizing their objectives, pointing to the potential of such devices as the "inclinator" (an inclined elevator providing vertical movement of passengers from the surface to the station mezzanine).

For the most part, members of the subcommittee did not explicitly consider the merits of these differing positions. They all agreed that something had to be done. Representative Henry C. Schadeberg, Republican of Wisconsin, stated that the problem was "not very complicated." Subcommittee chairman Gray rejected the idea of making only key stations accessible, asserting that the system should be "uniform."[27] In the end, the House, with the Senate following suit (but without hearings), enacted legislation requiring the Washington Metropolitan Area Transit Authority to make its buildings and structures accessible to the handicapped. Although Congress exempted such rolling stock as subway cars and buses, the committee reports expressed the hope that transit officials would make such vehicles accessible to the physically handicapped.[28]

Congress, through its public works committees, had thus explicitly broadened the definition of the problem needing redress. An issue whose

26. Ibid., pp. 8, 9, 10, 11, 18. Lassen cited figures indicating that the provision of elevators in every station would require a capital investment of $5 million—a total far below that suggested by the transit operators. (Ibid., p. 20.)

27. Ibid., p. 10, 15.

28. As the report of the Senate Committee on Public Works noted, "There would be little purpose in having the subway stations accessible to the physically handicapped if they could not board the subway car when they reached it." *Accessibility to Physically Handicapped of Certain Public Facilities,* S. Rept. 91-658, 91 Cong. 2 sess. (GPO, 1970), p. 2.

focus was once public buildings now included public transit as well—with vehicles probably next. The public works committees did not have jurisdiction over mass transit and thus knew little about its complexity. But the logic seemed inescapable that if public buildings should be barrier free, then so should transit systems. The legislative branch had thus dealt with one dimension of the matter of providing transportation for disabled people, though it was far from enunciating a definitive policy.

The Fruits of Legislative Entrepreneurship

The first mass transit provision specifically addressing the transportation problems of the handicapped did not emanate from committee deliberations; nor was it even debated in Congress itself. The measure was tacked on as an amendment on the House floor by a freshman legislator looking for an issue he could call his own. It survived the conference and was enacted as part of a funding program for mass transportation. Despite the absence of studied deliberation, the amendment would later assume primary importance as the basis of the effective mobility approach. The measure would lead to the Department of Transportation's first regulations to deal with elderly and handicapped people and would frame future legislative efforts of the transit committees. Its passage supports the proposition that the legislative process provides points of opportunity for congressional entrepreneurs to push through measures largely free of close congressional scrutiny, without hearing or extended discussion.

Mass transit was the bailiwick of the Senate Committee on Banking and Currency and its House counterpart, known by the same name. The problems of the handicapped were not the concern of the Subcommittee on Housing and Urban Affairs of the Senate Committee on Banking and Currency, which met in early 1970 to consider the plight of urban mass transportation. Witness after witness from state and local governments focused upon the need to rehabilitate old systems and to build new ones. The disabled were mentioned only in passing, when Secretary of Transportation John Volpe stated that "there is the need to provide an adequate transportation system for the young, the old, the handicapped and the poor . . . in short, those who must rely on public transportation."[29] But the secretary did not propose any measures that directly addressed the problems of the

29. *Mass Transportation–1969*, Hearings before the Subcommittee on Housing and Urban Affairs of the Senate Committee on Banking and Currency, 91 Cong. 2 sess. (GPO, 1970), p. 321.

disabled, and the bill that emerged from committee and the Senate did not include such a provision. Perhaps this is not all that surprising, given that not a single representative of the disabled community testified during the Senate deliberations.

Such testimony was also absent on the House side.[30] No legislator specifically discussed ways of identifying and satisfying the concerns of aged and disabled people until Representative Mario Biaggi rose to speak. A freshman Democratic congressman from the Bronx, Biaggi was in search of causes to champion.[31] The problems of the elderly and the handicapped were such an issue.

Biaggi and his staff were impressed by a study showing that most people at some time in their lives suffer some disability, however temporary, which makes mobility difficult. Biaggi, not a member of the transportation committee, introduced an amendment on the House floor; it "declared to be the national policy that elderly and handicapped persons have the same right as other persons to utilize mass transportation," that "special efforts" be made in the planning and design of mass transportation facilities and services so that the elderly and handicapped can use them, and that all federal programs offering assistance in mass transportation contain provisions implementing that national policy. "Handicapped" was defined to include any individual suffering from some permanent or temporary incapacity or disability who is unable without special facilities or special planning or design to utilize mass transportation facilities and services as effectively as persons not so affected.[32] The secretary of transportation was authorized to make grants or loans to state and local public bodies seeking to meet the needs of the elderly and the handicapped. Further, 1.5 percent of the funds were to be set aside and used exclusively to finance research and development projects for the handicapped.

Speaking on behalf of the amendment, Biaggi emphasized that it would

30. However, spokespersons for the National Council on Aging did link the problems of the elderly with transportation policy. See *Urban Mass Transportation,* Hearings before the Subcommittee on Housing of the House Committee on Banking and Currency, 91 Cong. 2 sess. (GPO, 1970), pp. 550–64. John Martin, commissioner on aging of the Department of Health, Education, and Welfare, speaking as an individual and not as a representative of the administration, recommended that the Urban Mass Transportation Act earmark at least a small percentage of funds for research and demonstration studies on the transportation needs of the elderly and that it require grantees to use some fraction of the money specifically for programs for the aging. (Ibid., pp. 427–30.)

31. Interview with Peter Ilchuk, administrative assistant to Mario Biaggi, February 7, 1985.

32. *Congressional Record* (September 29, 1970), p. 34180.

not drain the treasury, that it would involve "very little if any additional costs." He declared: "We are not talking about appropriating additional funds here. We are not talking about specialized programs or adding to the Federal bureaucracy. We are simply talking about granting equal rights to a large segment of our population to use public facilities with the same ease as everyone else." With respect to the kinds of services envisioned, Biaggi specifically rejected taxicabs or limousines for reasons of cost and because they would further serve to "segregate" the elderly and the handicapped from society. It was time, he said, that Congress saw to it that "equal rights to transportation facilities" were extended to the aged and disabled.[33] He supplied no data to support his assertion that specialized transportation was more expensive than providing integrated services. Nor did any of his colleagues seek such information or question his rejection of specialized transportation. Indeed, only a few members besides Biaggi had anything to say at all.

Intended to address a basic problem, the Biaggi amendment was of uncertain programmatic consequence. Biaggi emphasized that the amendment would not entail any cost. Yet the measure was attached to a funding bill. The amendment could thus be construed simply as an expression of national policy, that is, a desired but not compelled objective. Assuming, though, that the measure was to have more than symbolic value, it was still unclear what its effect was to be. The phrase "special efforts" was nowhere defined. The amendment was phrased in terms of "rights," but it was unclear whether it was meant to confer a legal benefit, as a right does. The Biaggi amendment was intended to redress a deprivation, the lack of transportation for elderly and handicapped persons. By definition, if a right exists, it does so regardless of cost. Thus, if the "right" to use transportation was to be realized, presumably Congress would have to appropriate all the funds necessary to ensure this end. But Biaggi declared that his amendment did not require the expenditure of any additional monies or involve any increased costs. In so doing, he seemed to undercut the notion that the amendment was meant to secure a right, in the legal sense of the word.

It is perhaps all the more striking, given these apparent ambiguities and the lack of discussion surrounding its passage, that the Biaggi amendment later became the linchpin of the Department of Transportation's first set of regulations to address the needs of disabled and elderly individuals (see chapter 3). The DOT rulemakers chose to ignore the language referring to

33. Ibid., pp. 34180–81.

rights and instead concentrated on the requirement that "special efforts" should be taken to assure accessible transit, thus emphasizing the effective mobility approach. The House and Senate committees that had jurisdiction over mass transit matters did not challenge that interpretation and did not rely on the rights rhetoric in subsequent discussions of the Biaggi amendment.

Five Years of Disjointed Activity

In the years immediately following the passage of the Biaggi amendment, Congress continued to deal with the problems of providing transportation for disabled people in a haphazard, disjointed manner. Tenacious legislators pushed their preferences, either through authorization or appropriations bills, using low-visibility mechanisms, in ways that did not invite debate and sometimes as part of larger, unrelated measures. As was the case with prior enactments, the legislation was not part of an overarching conceptual framework, but represented responses to discrete problems. Adding to the confusion were jurisdictional conflicts among committees.

ATTACHING BILLS TO UNRELATED MEASURES

The central concern of those who crafted and discussed what would ultimately become the Federal-Aid Highway Act of 1973 was whether cities could finance a portion of urban mass transit projects from the Highway Trust Fund. But provisions relating to elderly and handicapped persons also became elements of the legislation—a part authorizing the subsidization of the elevators in the Washington, D.C., Metro system; an amendment authorizing grants and loans to private nonprofit organizations providing transportation services for the elderly and the handicapped; and a section requiring accessibility under the federal highway program.

Congress spent little time discussing the amendment authorizing grants and loans to nonprofit agencies. Introduced by Representative Bella Abzug, Democrat of New York, the aid was not meant to substitute for adapting the mass transit system for the needs of the elderly and the handicapped, but to assist, in the language of the bill, where "regular facilities were unavailable, insufficient, or inappropriate."[34] Among the projects were minibuses and dial-a-ride services.

Members of the Subcommittee on Public Buildings and Grounds of the

---

34. *Urban Mass Transportation,* Hearings before the Subcommittee on Housing of the House Committee on Banking and Currency, 92 Cong. 2 sess. (GPO, 1972), p. 59.

House Public Works Committee, particularly chairman Kenneth Gray, were the forces behind the Metro provision. Prompted by charges from disability groups that the Washington system was not being built in a way accessible to the handicapped, despite the 1970 legislation, the subcommittee held hearings at which Metro officials were criticized.[35] "The Congress of the United States stated in a mandate specifically on this specific issue that it directed Metro to design the system to be accessible to all the handicapped—not part of the handicapped, all of them," Gray declared. "The transit industry, as a whole, has resisted the idea of the wheelchair in a transit system." In the end, when Metro officials claimed that they could not build the elevators without additional funding, the subcommittee promised to "fully authorize in this system whatever is required."[36] The committee succeeded in attaching a $65 million authorization—the amount Metro officials claimed was necessary—to the highway bill of 1972. It survived, despite the opposition of the Department of Transportation, and was enacted as part of the Federal-Aid Highway Act of 1973.[37] The legislators were preoccupied with matters other than the problems of disabled people. Republican Senator Robert Dole of Kansas, who supported the authorization, noted nevertheless that he "fail[ed] to understand why at this point in the Metro construction process and in this piece of fundamentally unrelated legislation we are now addressing the needs of the handicapped."[38] Its passage demonstrates once again that committed legislators can find ways to press their preferences by attaching measures bearing only tangentially on the matter at hand.

Another feature of the legislation held that the secretary of transportation could not approve a capital assistance project "for construction or acquisition of new urban mass transportation facilities or equipment" unless he determined that the project provided "reasonable access" to elderly and handicapped persons or unless he found "in writing" that the responsible public body had taken "alternative actions" to ensure access. This language, part of the original bill, stirred no discussion or dispute in committee. Representatives of the disabled were not involved in the hearing pro-

35. Interview with Richard Heddinger of the National Paraplegia Foundation, September 23, 1982.

36. *Accommodations for Handicapped on Metro System,* Hearings before the Subcommittee on Public Buildings and Grounds of the House Committee on Public Works, 92 Cong. 2 sess. (GPO, 1972), pp. 45, 46, 92.

37. 87 Stat. 271.

38. *Congressional Record* (March 15, 1973), p. 8228.

cess. The wording seemed, by providing for "alternative actions," to back away from the spirit of the Biaggi amendment.

EXPANDING DEFINITIONS

A year later, in the context of amending the Federal-Aid Highway Act of 1973, Congress expanded the definition of "handicapped persons" in highway programs to include "semiambulatory" and "non-ambulatory wheelchair-bound" individuals and prohibited the secretary of transportation from approving any program that did not provide accessible transit. Senate Public Works committee chairman Jennings Randolph and Republican committee member Robert Stafford of Vermont, who were also respectively chairman and ranking minority member of the Subcommittee on the Handicapped, noted that representatives from disability groups had urged the strengthening of national policy. Senator Randolph claimed that accessible transit would not "impose an unacceptable demand on our transport system" and that the American people should willingly assume its cost to end discrimination against the elderly and handicapped.[39] The amendments' journey was uneventful and they became law in early 1975.[40]

USING THE APPROPRIATIONS PROCESS

Mario Biaggi added another element to the congressional concoction in 1974, this time through the appropriations process—though strictly construed, that process is to deal only with the level of funding for particular programs. Concerned that the DOT was not enforcing his 1970 amendment,[41] the Bronx congressman rose on the House floor to protest the department's alleged opposition to a San Francisco BART plan to make its bus system accessible to the handicapped and the DOT's apparent failure to approve a bus design that, he said, "could be mass produced for virtually the same cost" as the "Dial-A-Ride" system "and be fully accessible to the elderly and the handicapped as well as the general public."[42] Biaggi cited no studies to support his claims about cost, and none of his colleagues questioned them.

Determined to do away with "out and out discrimination," Biaggi proposed an amendment on the floor to the DOT appropriations bill for fiscal 1975, prohibiting the use of funds "for the purchase of passenger rail or

39. Ibid. (September 11, 1974), p. 30823.
40. 88 Stat. 1565.
41. Interview with Robert Blancato, aide to Mario Biaggi, November 1, 1982.
42. *Congressional Record* (June 19, 1974), p. 19852.

subway cars, for the purchase of motor buses or for the construction of related facilities unless such cars, buses and facilities are designed to meet the transportation needs of the elderly and the handicapped." Its content was vague; it did not, for example, define the standards by which it could be determined if the cars, buses, and facilities met the needs of the elderly and handicapped. Subcommittee chairman John McFall, Democrat of California, termed the amendment "absolutely essential" and ranking minority member Silvio Conte of Massachusetts praised it as being "very good."[43] Without further discussion, the amendment was accepted without a recorded vote and became part of the final appropriations legislation. Once again Mario Biaggi was able to influence policy, even though he was not a member of the committee charged with crafting the transportation legislation.

COMMITTEES IN CONFLICT

It is somewhat extraordinary that those committees with jurisdiction over mass transit—the committees on banking and currency—were not involved at all in any of these piecemeal efforts to address the problems of handicapped persons. In an orderly world, one might have expected that some means would have been devised to draw those committees into the process. If those committees were to confront the problem independently, one might have supposed that events would have followed a deliberative course, involving hearings, study, and debate. In fact, to dramatize its determination to preserve its autonomy, the House Banking and Currency Committee did create in 1973 a Subcommittee on Urban Mass Transportation. But it found itself in conflict with the Public Works Committee.

The two committees had different interests and approaches. As usual, when the House Banking and Currency Committee met in 1974 to consider mass transit-related matters, it was not fundamentally concerned with the mobility problems of disabled persons. Representatives of the disabled were not at all involved in the hearing process. To the extent that the committee was involved, its effort was geared toward increasing funding for specialized transit or providing financial relief for elderly and handicapped persons—mandating that such individuals not be charged more than half the usual fare during off-peak hours. That was the approach it took in legislation proposed in 1974.[44]

43. Ibid., p. 19851.
44. A bill proposed in 1974 by Democratic subcommittee chairman Joseph Minish of New Jersey included measures that would have raised the percentage of funding for elderly

But the perspective of the House Public Works Committee was quite different. Staking its claim, the House Public Works Committee declared itself to be in "the forefront" of efforts to aid handicapped persons.[45] This was with some justification, as the committee had promoted the Architectural Barriers Act of 1968 and the Washington Metro accessibility provisions. Its emphasis was on making transportation free of structural barriers. In 1974 the committee proposed that all public mass transportation facilities, equipment, and services receiving federal financial assistance be accessible to elderly and handicapped persons, including the nonambulatory wheelchair-bound and those with semiambulatory capabilities.[46] By making it clear that "facility" included buses and commuter trains, the committee went beyond its 1970 amendment excluding such vehicles from the accessibility requirements of the Washington Metro system.[47] Republican James Cleveland of New Hampshire, a minority member of the committee, criticized his colleagues for involving themselves in mass transit although they allegedly lacked substantive knowledge. But Representative Biaggi maintained in floor debate that "to make transit systems for the general public accessible to the handicapped is no more complicated than making public buildings accessible."[48]

Ultimately, the House Public Works Committee version did not become law. The banking and currency committees, especially the Senate Subcommittee on Housing and Urban Affairs, would not concede jurisdiction. They would not even meet with members of the House Public Works Committee to reach a compromise. In the end, and after the conferees of the banking committees consulted with the Ford administration, Congress enacted the measures originally sponsored by the banking and currency committees, providing for half-fares in nonpeak hours for elderly and handicapped individuals.[49]

The setback to the authority of the Public Works Committee was only temporary, however. Under the new House reorganization plan, effective

---

and handicapped services to 2 percent of the federal effort and would have mandated that elderly and handicapped persons traveling in off-peak hours not be charged more than half the usual fare. Although the committee did not report a bill including the former provision, it did endorse the latter one.

45. *Federal Mass Transportation Act of 1974*, H. Rept. 93-1256, 93 Cong. 2 sess. (GPO, 1974), p. 3.

46. *Congressional Record* (August 15, 1974), p. 28423.

47. *Federal Mass Transportation Act of 1974*, H. Rept. 93-1256, p. 3.

48. *Congressional Record* (August 15, 1974), p. 28414.

49. 88 Stat. 1565.

in January 1975, the Public Works Committee gained jurisdiction over urban mass transportation matters from Banking and Currency and over surface transit and civil aviation matters from Interstate and Foreign Commerce. It was renamed the Committee on Public Works and Transportation. The reorganization was significant, not merely because it shifted the balance of power. Vesting the committee with jurisdiction over mass transit meant that it would have to become more attentive to the transit operators who would look to it to further their policy objectives; as a consequence, the problems of the handicapped would be viewed against the backdrop of the needs of mass transit. Support for the concerns of the disabled within the committee might no longer be as automatic as it once seemed to be.

A More Deliberative Approach

By the mid-1970s Congress had passed a series of measures bearing on transportation for the handicapped in a rather helter-skelter fashion, with little discussion. At first, the Department of Transportation did not do very much in response to those legislative pronouncements (see chapter 3). But the very existence of those enactments—particularly the 1970 Biaggi amendment that spoke in terms of "rights"—spurred hitherto dormant interest groups to file legal suits based on the legislation. All this led the DOT to take steps to meet some of the needs of the disabled community.

WILLIAMS TAKES THE INITIATIVE

During this period, through the efforts of Senator Harrison A. Williams, Jr., Democrat of New Jersey, the Subcommittee on Housing and Urban Affairs of the Senate Committee on Banking, Housing, and Urban Affairs began to pay greater attention to the transportation problems of the disabled. Williams, a liberal Democrat, was a principal advocate of increased federal aid to public transportation and assumed a primary role in shepherding legislation assisting transit operators. By the end of the 1970s he rose to the chairmanship of the subcommittee. But Williams was not only a leader of a committee with jurisdiction over mass transit; he was also chairman of the Committee on Labor and Public Welfare and a member of its Subcommittee on the Handicapped, which had been created at his instigation in early 1972 to deal comprehensively with the problems of disabled individuals.[50] Williams was determined to use his Banking, Housing, and Urban Affairs committee assignment to find some appropriate, practical way to address the mobility problems of the handicapped that would also be consistent with his strongly felt obligation to support mass transit interests. The focus of those efforts was geared toward strengthening the "special efforts" requirements of the Biaggi amendment. The resulting Senate activity attests to the influence that a committed legislator can exercise.

Claiming that legislation was needed to end the Department of Transportation's "vacillation" between the equal accessibility and effective mobility approaches, Williams sponsored legislation in 1975 that would have required "effective immediately" that "any vehicle, building, station, or other structure for any new rapid rail system . . . and any other vehicle integrated with such a system" be accessible to elderly and handicapped persons. The secretary of transportation was directed to issue accessibility standards for "at-grade operations" (buses, for example) so that elderly and handicapped persons could effectively use the transit system.[51]

The department was at that time engaged in its first effort to issue regulations governing transportation for the elderly and the handicapped; the

50. In 1970, as chairman of the Senate Special Committee on Aging, Williams did not yet appreciate the linkage between the mass transit legislation being considered by the Senate and the mobility difficulties of the elderly and disabled. However, by the time the House held its hearings on urban mass transportation later that year, the National Council on Aging had educated him, and he endorsed the council's position in a letter to the House Subcommittee on Housing. In 1972, when Williams announced the creation of the Subcommittee on the Handicapped, he stated: "I have established a permanent subcommittee . . . because I want to make very clear that I believe that something must be done . . . now before more lives are wasted; more dreams shattered; more hopes destroyed. This is a commitment that I am making to the Congress and to the entire Nation. But most important, it is a commitment that I am making to the handicapped." *Congressional Record* (February 9, 1972), pp. 3321–22.

51. *Urban Mass Transportation–1975*, Hearings before the Subcommittee on Housing and Urban Affairs of the Senate Committee on Banking, Housing, and Urban Affairs, 94 Cong. 1 sess. (GPO, 1975), pp. 2, 4. (Hereafter *Mass Transit—1975 Hearings*.) Apart from requiring for the first time that vehicles be accessible, the bill adopted the approach taken in the Federal-Aid Highway Amendments of 1974 by forbidding the secretary from approving any program or project that did not comply with the standards and by expanding the definition of the population to be served to include both "nonambulatory wheelchair-bound" and "semiambulatory" individuals. Moreover, the bill set up local advisory committees and a national advisory council on accessible mass transportation, 50 percent of whose members were to be elderly and handicapped individuals. In addition, the bill included already existing provisions for aid to private nonprofit corporations. (S. 662, A Bill to Amend the Urban Mass Transportation Act of 1964.)

committee was obviously trying to prod the DOT to action. In its earliest preliminary form, these regulations seemed to lean toward effective mobility, giving local governments substantial leeway to devise their own programs. The bill itself did not mandate one approach over another. Indeed, Williams's own statements were ambiguous, seeming at once to call for a fully accessible system, while at the same time recognizing that "the costs of revamping an entire major existing rapid rail transit system would mean a huge financial undertaking which in cities like New York, would doubtless be impossible."[52]

Williams conducted hearings of the Subcommittee on Housing and Urban Affairs to examine the transit problems of the handicapped, at which a full range of viewpoints were expressed. Representatives of the handicapped, including the Paralyzed Veterans of America (PVA) and the President's Committee on Employment of the Handicapped, took note of the recent activism and victories of the disabled in court (see chapter 4). The spokesman for the PVA, John Lancaster, argued that all systems should be accessible to the elderly and handicapped as a matter of right, and that only legislation could compel the DOT to take immediate action. James Raggio, counsel for the Philadelphia Coalition for Equal Public Transportation Services, sought to cast doubt upon the DOT's willingness to devise and implement effective regulations by introducing into the record memoranda by key DOT officials that indicated the regulations were developed to protect the agency from political and legal attack, and that questioned whether full accessibility might not be abandoned after further study (see chapter 3).[53]

Earlier, UMTA administrator Frank Herringer had testified that the DOT supported the objectives of the proposed legislation, but he urged Congress not to take action before his department issued final regulations for elderly and handicapped persons. Moreover, he anticipated that within a "reasonable" period of time, a new low-floor bus—Transbus—which would meet the needs of the elderly, the handicapped, and the general public would be commercially available. For their part, representatives of transit systems and local governments emphasized that the alleged costliness of full accessibility made such an approach prohibitive.[54]

In the end, the Senate bill sailed easily through the chamber in mid-September 1975 by voice vote. The committee report did indeed consider costs, but they were set low. Referring to Transbus, the committee declared

52. *Mass Transit—1975 Hearings*, p. 2.
53. Ibid., pp. 13, 52, 54, 60.
54. Ibid., pp. 21, 171, 184.

that it expected the secretary of transportation "to take all appropriate actions necessary to ensure that accessible buses are made available for purchase."[55]

THE EDUCATION OF A HOUSE SUBCOMMITTEE

On the House side, Democratic Representative James J. Howard of New Jersey, chairman of the recently created Subcommittee on Surface Transportation of the reorganized Committee on Public Works and Transportation, introduced in February 1975 a bill that was very close to the Senate version. A year later, the subcommittee held hearings specifically focusing on the transportation problems of the elderly and the handicapped.[56] Those sessions began to shape Howard's approach. He ultimately concluded that the concerns of disabled persons should be weighed against the wide-ranging needs of the transit interests. His objective was to find a practical solution that was sensitive to the cost arguments of the transit operators: thus he adopted the effective mobility conception. The subcommittee's attention to the issue reflected the sensitivity of the parent committee to the needs of its new constituents—the transit operators—as it immersed itself in the transportation aspects of its work. The transit industry, through its representative organization, the American Public Transit Association, vigorously pressed its position that it should not be called on to assume the primary responsibility for providing transportation for the handicapped.

By the time of the hearings, the DOT had issued final regulations with respect to transportation for elderly and handicapped persons.[57] These regulations adopted an effective mobility approach, leaving the choice of the particular kind of service to local governments based on their needs. On another track, President Gerald Ford had signed Executive Order 11914, requiring that all federal programs be accessible to the handicapped and vesting the Department of Health, Education, and Welfare with the responsibility for coordinating the federal effort.

The hearings focused on those regulations, the costs of full accessibility,

---

55. *National Mass Transportation Assistance Act Amendments of 1975*, S. Rept. 94-365, 94 Cong. 1 sess. (GPO, 1975), pp. 1, 5.

56. *To Consider Amendments to the Urban Mass Transportation Act of 1964 to Provide Operating Assistance for Projects Located in Areas Other Than Urbanized Areas, to Provide for Mass Transportation Assistance to Meet the Needs of Elderly and Handicapped Persons, and for Other Purposes,* Hearings before the Subcommittee on Surface Transportation of the House Committee on Public Works and Transportation, 94 Cong. 2 sess. (GPO, 1976), p. 1. (Hereafter *UMTA Amendments Hearings.*)

57. 41 Fed. Reg. 18234 (1976).

and the technological feasibility of Transbus. UMTA administrator Robert Patricelli, who succeeded Frank Herringer, objected that the Senate and House bills were at odds with the newly issued UMTA regulations. The former assumed that full accessibility was the ultimate objective, whereas the regulations were geared, in his view, toward the "real goal, providing mass transportation which elderly and handicapped persons can effectively utilize." For UMTA, the appropriate approach was not one that focused on making systems fully accessible, but one that assured that local agencies were free to determine the mix of services (such as specialized door-to-door service or wheelchair-accessible fixed-route services) based on their particular circumstances, provided they satisfied certain "level of effort" guidelines. Representatives of state and local transit agencies used the hearing to argue vociferously that the costs of full accessibility were more than localities could bear. Leonard Ronis, general manager of the Greater Cleveland Transit Authority, commented that "there is no point in adapting 800 vehicles to take care of the potential use of 200 of those vehicles" and that "it would be cheaper to buy each . . .[handicapped individual] a special automobile with a lift" than to mandate full accessibility.[58]

Apart from the cost involved, transit officials questioned the feasibility of Transbus, which former UMTA administrator Herringer had indicated only a year earlier would soon be commercially available. Representatives of handicapped groups, sensing that the DOT was backing away from the Transbus program, blasted UMTA at the committee hearings, charging that the agency was bowing to pressure from General Motors. Vigorously contesting transit operators' statements about the feasibility of wheelchair lifts, Richard Heddinger of the National Paraplegia Foundation, and the leader of the fight to make the Washington Metro fully accessible, declared that the industry was not willing to make the necessary effort.[59]

For the subcommittee members, the bringing together of diverse interests had different effects. Bella Abzug, who believed that fully accessible transit was a right, was troubled by the testimony of the transit operators:

> Now, this cost question is a very serious one, and I do not belittle it. But if you are talking about integrating people into a society and making it possible

58. *UMTA Amendments Hearings,* pp. 196–203, 212, 383.

59. Ibid., pp. 228, 330. Heddinger dismissed "as absurd" the claim that wheelchair-lift-equipped buses decreased passenger capacity and called unfair the charge that such accessibility features increased the cost of transportation. Indeed, he alleged that transit operators used such costs as the basis for securing more funds than were actually needed.

for them to function . . . we are in 1976, and we are talking about trying to fulfill dreams of America for all people. . . .

Now, there are costs—social costs are enormous—and we either pay the price or our society goes down. And this is a small part of that debate.[60]

But for most others on the subcommittee, the hearings were an occasion to assimilate all viewpoints and to find, indeed grope for, a solution. Subcommittee chairman Howard, who was perhaps the key participant, explained in an exchange with Leonard Ronis of the Cleveland transit system:

All I am trying to do is bring out the problem that we do have in trying to provide as much freedom of mobility for all people in the country, no matter how handicapped they are—and also the practicalities or the inefficiency perhaps of requiring every city to have total accessibility. . . . We are pointing out that there are either problems, financial or otherwise, on the one hand, or not really meeting the needs of a great group of our people, on the other hand.[61]

In the end, the Ninety-fourth Congress adjourned without taking final action on either the House or the Senate bills. But the concerns raised in the hearings proved to be real ones. As the representatives of disability groups feared, UMTA decided in July 1976 (about a month after the hearing) to shelve Transbus.[62]

Forcing Technology and Considering Costs

In the latter part of the 1970s, the transit committees developed a growing concern with costs and with the feasibility of such technological solutions as Transbus. The transit industry increased its efforts to use those committees to alleviate administrative requirements that operators provide accessible transportation for disabled and elderly people.[63] At the same time, the disability groups lobbied hard to counter those efforts.

The decision to shelve Transbus disturbed Senator Williams, who thought that the low-floor vehicle would, over the long run, be the key to mainline accessibility. With Gerald Ford's defeat in November 1976 and the coming of a new administration and Congress, he saw a fresh oppor-

60. Ibid., pp. 215–16.

61. Ibid., p. 209.

62. Soon after, a coalition of elderly and handicapped groups filed court suits seeking to compel the DOT to pursue a full accessibility policy and to mandate Transbus (see chap. 3).

63. Interview with Lillian Liburdi, former associate administrator for policy and program development, UMTA, December 15, 1981.

tunity to send a message to the DOT. If the department would not proceed more vigorously, then legislation would be forthcoming.[64] Accordingly, Williams introduced a bill that sought in part to ensure that mass transportation was accessible to the elderly and handicapped. The existing requirement in section 16, that "special efforts" be made in the planning and design of mass transportation facilities and services, would be made more specific by adding a requirement that mobility be available for elderly and handicapped persons in any urbanized area seeking federal mass transportation assistance. This requirement would be satisfied if the applicant developed detailed plans for either a wheelchair-accessible regular fixed-route system within a reasonable time or a substitute service that provided "comparable coverage." In essence, it provided for the "effective mobility" option. Representative Howard followed suit a few months later.[65]

Williams's prodding worked. During this period, the new secretary of transportation, Brock Adams, reopened the Transbus matter and promised a timely decision. Meanwhile, the Senate Committee reported Williams's bill with its accessibility provision. A few days later, Secretary Adams promulgated the "Transbus mandate," which declared that after September 30, 1979, DOT money could be used to purchase only buses that met basic Transbus specifications. Until that time, the existing local option regulations would be applicable. In view of this major policy switch—a "landmark decision"—Senator Williams determined that those sections of the proposed legislation relating to transportation accessibility for the elderly and handicapped were no longer necessary.[66] Those provisions were in fact deleted, and the legislation that emerged from the first session of the Ninety-fifth Congress did not address the concerns of the handicapped population.

In early 1978 the Carter administration sent to Congress an ambitious surface transportation program, providing nearly $54 billion in federal aid for highways and mass transit over four years. The elderly and handi-

---

64. *Congressional Record* (June 23, 1977), p. 20532.

65. Both the Senate Subcommittee on Housing and Urban Affairs and the House Subcommittee on Surface Transportation held hearings with the familiar cast of participants and issues. *Mass Transportation Assistance to Meet the Needs of Elderly and Handicapped Persons*, Hearings before the Subcommittee on Surface Transportation of the House Committee on Public Works and Transportation, 95 Cong. 1 sess. (GPO, 1977); and *National Mass Transportation Assistance Act of 1977*, Hearings before the Subcommittee on Housing and Urban Affairs of the Senate Committee on Banking, Housing, and Urban Affairs, 95 Cong. 1 sess. (GPO, 1977).

66. *Congressional Record* (June 23, 1977), p. 20532.

capped sections were a relatively minor part. Among its provisions was one that revised the definition of "handicapped person" to include anyone "who is wheelchair bound or who has semiambulatory capabilities." The heated differences between transit industry and disability group representatives underscored the need to secure data about the costs of accessible rail transit. In section 321 of the legislation, Congress provided funds for transit operators to develop "detailed estimates" of the cost of refurbishing streetcar, subway, and commuter rail systems to make them "accessible to and usable by handicapped persons" and required the secretary to compile and report to Congress the results of those studies "together with his recommendation for such legislation as may be necessary to finance the improvements set forth in the cost estimates."[67]

Transbus figured in the legislative course, engaging the passions of both industry and disability groups. General Motors, which had poured millions of dollars into the research and manufacture of vehicles that did not meet the Transbus specifications, sought to change the DOT's policy course through the legislative process. To that end, Republican Representative Bud Shuster of Pennsylvania, the ranking minority member of the Subcommittee on Surface Transportation, wrote section 323 of the Surface Transportation Bill, requiring the secretary of transportation to reevaluate the Transbus program and report to Congress by January 1, 1979. That anticipated reassessment created such uncertainty that a consortium of three cities abandoned plans to purchase 530 Transbuses before the DOT deadline and caused other potential manufacturers to lose interest in building the vehicle.

Disability groups, for whom Transbus had become an important symbol, were mobilized to action and lobbied members of Congress. Once again, membership on the committee with jurisdiction over transit matters was not a condition for the exercise of policy influence. Mario Biaggi, who was not a member of the Public Works Committee, met with DOT officials to reach a compromise that would ensure that the Transbus program would not be impeded. In that effort he was joined by, among others, Claude Pepper, Democrat of Florida, chairman of the House Select Committee on Aging. As a result of extensive discussions, Secretary Adams agreed to revise the Transbus specifications, still requiring a low floor but permitting manufacturers to choose between a front door ramp or a lift—a compromise that secured the support of General Motors and Representative Shu-

67. 92 Stat. 2753.

ster. On the House floor, Biaggi then proposed to strike section 323 of the bill. By voice vote, that was done. Shuster, whose elderly mother was disabled, lamented:

> There are some of us who have been subjected to rather vituperative attacks because we felt that there might be some alternative to the very rigid require-ment for a ramp originally mandated by the Department of Transportation, and it is quite regrettable that there are those who saw fit to accuse those of us who felt there might be an alternative of not being interested in the best interests of the elderly and the handicapped.[68]

His fellow Pennsylvanian, Democratic Representative Robert Edgar, the second-highest ranking member of the subcommittee, remarked:

> This is an issue that many of us in Congress are nervous about. We have, on the one hand, the handicapped who are lobbying for full accessibility. On the other hand, we have real budgetary problems. And if you have a billion dollars to spend on modernization of transit, do you spend that billion dollars making the system accessible to the elderly and to the handicapped, or do you make other improvements to keep those systems running safely for the millions of people who rely on them now, while providing special services for the disabled plus accessible transbus service? . . . Congress has to face this issue.[69]

That matter of cost would, in fact, within the next few years dominate virtually all legislative discussions concerning transportation policy for disabled people. As the 1970s came to a close, much was still uncertain and unresolved. But before the decade ended, the effective mobility ap-proach would come into sharper focus as it clashed with the rights concept.

The Rights Approach and the Power of Symbolism

During the same period that a variety of legislators and transit commit-tees were attempting in some fashion to address the problems of disabled people from an effective mobility perspective, others in Congress, with quite a different orientation—a rights conception—were also pressing their claims. For the civil rights-oriented committees and staffs, the matter of transportation for the disabled was not a question of costs and benefits, as the transit committees had come to view it, but an issue of rights and principle. The concurrent existence of the two approaches only added to the confusion of the DOT, charged with implementing the legislative will.

Section 504 of the Rehabilitation Act of 1973 is the legislative basis of

---

68. *Congressional Record* (September 28, 1978), p. 32300.
69. Ibid., p. 32302.

the rights approach. It states that "no otherwise qualified individual in the United States, as defined in section 7(6) shall, solely by reason of his handicap be excluded from participation in, be denied the benefits of, or be subjected to discrimination under any program or activity receiving Federal assistance."[70] Although the statutory language says nothing about transportation policy per se, section 504 became the basis of the DOT's 1979 "full accessibility" regulations; more than that, those words became the foundation of a governmentwide regulatory scheme affecting the full range of handicapped policy. By the end of the 1970s, section 504 had become a lightning rod of both hope and dissatisfaction. It served as a rallying point for the handicapped in much the same way as *Brown* v. *Board of Education* had been for blacks a generation earlier. But for the institutions that would have to bear the costs of enforcement—such as schools and transportation systems—it became a symbol of excessive government regulation. Indeed, section 504 was an early target of Vice-President George Bush's regulatory task force charged with scrutinizing regulations and weeding out the unnecessary ones.

It might be supposed, given these intense but differing views, that section 504 was the object of much controversy before its enactment. That was hardly the case. It was a little-noticed part of the Rehabilitation Act of 1973. Virtually all of the conflict between the executive branch and the legislature centered upon the extent of federal support for rehabilitation programs, the expansion of existing services, the creation of new projects, and the restructuring of the administrative apparatus. If section 504 was so obscure, how did it become the linchpin of so ambitious a regulatory scheme? Much of the answer lies with the legislative process, the entrepreneurial activity of legislative staffs and bureaucrats, the use of such low-visibility mechanisms as conference committee reports to press policy preferences not envisioned in the legislation, and the nature of relations between Congress and the executive.

The Origins of Section 504

What would become section 504 was conceived in the office of Democratic Representative Charles Vanik of Ohio. The federal government had grappled with the problems of slavery, women's suffrage, and racism. The

---

70. 87 Stat. 355. The "otherwise qualified" individual was defined in section 7(6) as any person who "has a physical or mental disability which for such individual constitutes or results in a substantial handicap to employment and can . . . reasonably be expected to benefit in terms of employability from vocational rehabilitation services."

next step, Vanik believed, was to ensure civil rights for the handicapped. In the course of his travels, Vanik learned that wheelchair-bound persons were denied access to airplanes. From his disabled constituents, he received mail about employment discrimination, and on a case-by-case basis he sought to redress their grievances. Along with his staff, he became convinced, however, that a more efficient approach was necessary and was determined to see what could be done. James K. Pedley, a young legislative aide, shared Vanik's concern and devoted much time to finding a legislative solution. He believed the appropriate response was to amend the civil rights act to include handicapped persons.[71]

Vanik introduced such a measure on December 9, 1971, making it illegal to discriminate against any handicapped individual. Declaring that the "masses of the handicapped live and struggle among us, often shunted aside, hidden and ignored," at times in "snake pit mental institutions," and that "1 million handicapped children were excluded from school and . . . employers fear to hire the handicapped," he remarked that the "treatment and regard for the rights of the handicapped citizens in our country is one of America's shameful oversights." His measure would "insure equal educational and employment opportunities" for handicapped individuals.[72]

With respect to federally regulated transportation, the bill was to prohibit airlines, railroads, and buslines from denying access to handicapped persons. In promoting the measure, Vanik argued that it was needed to prevent carriers from requiring that wheelchair travelers be accompanied by attendants. It would make it illegal for buslines to plead lack of trained personnel as grounds for refusing patronage to the disabled. Invalidated would be air traffic regulations banning "persons who have malodorous conditions, gross disfigurement, or other unpleasant characteristics so unusual as to offend fellow passengers."[73] The legislation was intended, in Vanik's view, to be a nondiscrimination statute. At the time that it was introduced, he did not contemplate that the measure would one day be used to mandate bus lifts and subway retrofitting. "I could not even have imagined such a result," Vanik said years later.[74]

In the Senate, Hubert Humphrey, Democrat of Minnesota, sponsored the Vanik amendment. His interest deepened by his relationship with his own mentally retarded grandchild, Humphrey spoke eloquently of the need

71. Interview with James K. Pedley, January 13, 1982.
72. H.R. 12154; *Congressional Record* (December 9, 1971), pp. 45974–75.
73. *Congressional Record* (March 30, 1972), p. 11362.
74. Interview, February 10, 1983.

to ensure equal opportunities for those with physical and mental disabilities:

> No longer dare we live with the hypocrisy that the promise of America should have one major exception: Millions of children, youth, and adults with mental or physical handicaps. We must now firmly establish their right to share that promise, so well described by Thomas Wolfe: "To every man his chance; to every man, regardless of his birth, his shining golden opportunity—to every man the right to live, to work, to be himself, and to become whatever thing his manhood and his vision can combine to make him—this, seeker, is the promise of America."[75]

The measure was referred to the judiciary committees of each house, but it did not rank high in either committee's priorities. With little prospect that the measure would become part of an amended civil rights act through the judiciary committees, even though sixty members of the House and twenty members of the Senate had cosponsored it, Humphrey and Vanik sought another avenue to achieve their end. Although not a member of the newly constituted Subcommittee on the Handicapped of the Committee on Labor and Public Welfare, Humphrey succeeded in having the civil rights amendment incorporated in a comprehensive rehabilitation bill proposed by subcommittee chairman Jennings Randolph, Democrat of West Virginia.

The Randolph bill drew upon the hearings held a few months earlier by the Subcommittee on the Handicapped.[76] It is interesting to note that although a whole range of disability groups testified at those hearings, none advanced such a civil rights position; rather each was concerned with the effect of the legislation on various programs affecting its interests. The bill that emerged from the full committee, the Rehabilitation Act of 1972, retained the civil rights section, "Nondiscrimination Under Federal Grants." The committee report was hardly illuminating about its scope; it merely paraphrased the language of the section itself.[77] When the legislation reached the Senate floor, the nondiscrimination provision stirred no controversy. After sailing through the Senate, 70–0, the bill next went to a conference committee. The Vanik amendment survived conference deliberations and, as part of the Rehabilitation Act of 1972, unanimously approved by both houses, reached President Richard Nixon's desk for signing. But

75. *Congressional Record* (January 20, 1972), p. 525.

76. *Rehabilitation Act of 1972,* Hearings before the Subcommittee on the Handicapped of the Senate Committee on Labor and Public Welfare, 92 Cong. 2 sess. (GPO, 1972).

77. *Rehabilitation Act of 1972,* S. Rept. 92-1135 (GPO, 1972), pp. 77–78.

Nixon pocket-vetoed the $17 billion rehabilitation bill about a week before the presidential election. Citing "congressional fiscal irresponsibility," the president also claimed that the legislation would divert the program from its traditional vocational and medical objectives and that it would unnecessarily establish numerous committees and independent commissions. The memorandum of disapproval made no reference to the nondiscrimination section.[78]

Several months later, in early 1973, Congress challenged Nixon by enacting virtually the same bill, including the nondiscrimination provision. Both the House and the Senate held perfunctory hearings at which committee chairmen entered statements of their colleagues and various organizations reiterating support for the act.[79] Once again the nondiscrimination statute was largely ignored, with only John F. Nagle, chief of the Washington office of the National Federation of the Blind, referring to it.[80] Once more, and for the same reasons, the president vetoed the bill.[81] His action was upheld when the Senate failed by a margin of four votes to override his veto despite the protest of representatives of some thirty disability organizations who gathered in the Senate chambers on the day of the debate. President Nixon hailed the Senate vote as "a resounding victory for the American taxpayer."

Having been beaten, congressional leaders recognized the need to compromise. After consultation with the White House, subcommittee chairman Jennings Randolph introduced a considerably scaled-down version of the Rehabilitation Act; Representative John Brademas, Democrat of Indiana, similarly offered compromise legislation. Finally, the Rehabilitation Act of 1973 became law. Charles Vanik rose on the House floor to say that he was pleased that the compromise bill retained proposals to "protect the rights of handicapped people in employment, and in the issuance of federal grants."[82] As before, the nondiscrimination section was not debated. Mar-

78. President's Memorandum of Veto, October 27, 1972, reprinted in pertinent part in *Rehabilitation Act, 1973,* Hearings before the Subcommittee on the Handicapped of the Senate Committee on Labor and Public Welfare, 93 Cong. 1 sess. (GPO, 1973).

79. *Rehabilitation Act, 1973,* Hearings before the Subcommittee on the Handicapped of the Senate Committee on Labor and Public Welfare, 93 Cong. 1 sess. (GPO, 1973); and *Rehabilitation Act of 1973,* Hearings before the Select Subcommittee on Education of the House Committee on Education and Labor, 93 Cong. 1 sess. (GPO, 1973).

80. *Rehabilitation Act, 1973,* Senate Hearings, p. 282.

81. *Message from the President of the United States Returning without Approval the Bill (S. 7) Entitled the "Rehabilitation Act of 1972,"* S. Doc. 93-100, 93 Cong. 1 sess. (GPO, 1973).

82. *Congressional Record* (June 5, 1973), p. 18137.

tin LaVor, the senior minority legislative associate for the House Committee on Education and Labor, recounted:

> As the Conference on the 3rd bill concluded, a few items remained. The last of them was Section 504. Although members were tired, they all agreed there should be no discrimination against the handicapped. Because it seemed so simple and straightforward, Section 504 stayed in the final version and became law.[83]

Moving beyond the Law to Regulations

In the months following enactment of the Rehabilitation Act of 1973, both the Select Education Subcommittee of the House Education and Labor Committee and the Subcommittee on the Handicapped of the Senate Committee on Labor and Public Welfare monitored the executive agencies. Hearings were held to focus on the administration of rehabilitative services and to consider amendments to the 1973 act.[84] Section 504 was not on the formal agenda; indeed the proposed legislation did not seek to amend its language in any way. When the Subcommittee on Education reported its bill on the House floor, only Charles Vanik, who himself was not on the subcommittee, mentioned section 504. He noted that a number of cases involving education of handicapped children had been brought, and he urged Congress to assume the cost of implementing court orders pursuant to the civil rights section of the Rehabilitation Act. But at the same time, he was quite critical of what he perceived as the unresponsiveness of the Civil Service Commission, the Architectural and Transportation Barriers Compliance Board, and the Department of Health, Education, and Welfare. Declared Vanik, "Sections dealing with employment of disabled persons, architectural and transportation barriers to the physically handicapped, and nondiscrimination under Federal grants have not yet seen the full light of day."[85] He wrote in an article that

> the type of nondiscrimination provisions now in the law are not self-administering. The benefit of these provisions will not be gleaned automatically or even

83. Martin L. LaVor, "Commentary; Section 504; Past, Present, and Future," *Archives of Physical Medicine and Rehabilitation*, vol. 61 (June 1980), p. 283.

84. *Vocational Rehabilitation Services*, Hearings before the Select Subcommittee on Education of the House Committee on Education and Labor, 93 Cong. 1 sess. (GPO, 1973), pt. 2; and *Rehabilitation Act Amendments of 1974*, Hearings before the Subcommittee on the Handicapped of the Senate Committee on Labor and Public Welfare, 93 Cong. 2 sess. (GPO, 1974). (Hereafter *1974 Senate Hearings*.)

85. *Congressional Record* (May 21, 1974), p. 15743–74.

always, easily. . . . The handicapped and those interested in helping the hand-icapped will have to go out and demand their rights under the new law."[86]

It is perhaps noteworthy that Vanik, the author of the nondiscrimination statute, did not contemplate the issuance of regulations as an enforcement mechanism. On the House side, anyway, his interest in section 504 was atypical; of central concern were questions about the transfer of rehabili-tative services from one office to another. The extension and amendment of the Rehabilitation Act was hardly debated on the floor, and it sailed through the House by a vote of 400–1.

COMMITTEE STAFFERS AND AGENCY BUREAUCRATS FORM AN ALLIANCE

The deliberations of the Senate Labor and Public Welfare Committee went beyond the restructuring of rehabilitative services and included con-sideration of a number of other measures. During the course of its one day of hearings in June 1974, however, the committee did not examine the implementation of section 504. But this does not mean that the committee was oblivious to it. Indeed, the Senate subcommittee staff and HEW bu-reaucrats began discussions about section 504 in November 1973, two months after the enactment of the Rehabilitation Act. In a letter to HEW Secretary Caspar Weinberger, Senator Alan Cranston of California, joined by Jennings Randolph, Harrison Williams, Jacob Javits of New York, and ranking minority member Robert Stafford of Vermont, argued that the Of-fice for Civil Rights (OCR) was the most logical and qualified agency within HEW to oversee implementation of the nondiscrimination statute.[87] Although no effort was made during the June hearings to question HEW officials about section 504, committee staffers and OCR bureaucrats were active behind the scenes. Shortly after the hearings, the subcommittee, at the behest of Cranston, submitted to the department, for its response, a wide range of questions, including two sets on section 504. One asked whether HEW had been given governmentwide responsibility by the pres-ident to promulgate section 504 regulations. Questions were also asked about the timetable for preparing the section 504 regulations and about the staffing plans and funding needs of the OCR. Another dealt with HEW's commitment to use section 504 authority to promote the employment of handicapped individuals.[88]

86. Ibid. (May 28, 1974), p. 16579.
87. *1974 Senate Hearings*, p. 318. Even earlier, Senator Stafford had written Weinber-ger arguing that the OCR should oversee implementation of section 504. See ibid., p. 316.
88. Ibid., pp. 131, 132.

The subcommittee could not have been more delighted with the department's response. The agency, particularly the Office for Civil Rights, seized upon the opportunity to assume principal responsibility for the development and implementation of section 504 regulations. HEW stated that it "share[d] the view of the . . . subcommittee . . . that [it was] the appropriate Federal agency to assume government-wide responsibility" because of its "expertise, the programmatic responsibility, and the staff commitment."[89] To that end, the secretary sent to the Office of Management and Budget a proposed executive order in which the White House would recognize HEW's authority to formulate governmentwide substantive standards and to approve implementing regulations proposed by each federal agency involved. Although one of the subcommittee's questions viewed section 504 as a means of preventing employment discrimination—indeed, literally construed, the nondiscrimination section could be so constrictively read—the department saw its mandate extending beyond that to include the whole range of federally assisted programs:

Section 504 of the Rehabilitation Act of 1973, in language similar to two other civil rights statutes which this Department enforces, Section 601 of the Civil Rights Act of 1964 and Section 901 of the Education Amendments of 1972, enumerates a broad government policy that programs receiving Federal assistance shall be operated without discrimination on the basis of a condition of handicap. On the basis of the legislative history, this Department's Office of the General Counsel has concluded that this provision . . . requires enforcement with respect to all aspects of discrimination against handicapped individuals in federally-assisted programs—not just employment. To this end, this Department fully intends to treat Section 504 as civil rights legislation that is remedial in design and to construe the legislation broadly to effectuate its purposes, to correct and alleviate conditions adversely affecting handicapped individuals in federally-assisted programs.[90]

Although committee staffers and OCR bureaucrats had section 504 on their minds, the thrust of the Rehabilitation Act amendments that reached the floor of the Senate, following unanimous approval by the full committee, was with other matters. Only one part touched upon section 504, and that amended the definition of "handicapped individual" in a way that removed any doubt about the applicability of section 504 to matters other than employment. The change reinforced the original intention of Representative Vanik, who believed that the civil rights provision was needed to prevent discrimination against handicapped persons in all federally as-

89. Ibid., p. 215.
90. Ibid., p. 224.

sisted activities, including transportation, housing, and education. According to the new definition, a "handicapped individual" is any person who has "a physical or mental impairment which substantially limits one or more of such person's major life activities, . . . has a record of such an impairment, or . . . is regarded as having such an impairment."[91]

LEGISLATION BY REPORT AND AFTER THE FACT

Although section 504 was not altered in legislative language, the Senate subcommittee staff sought to affect its development and administration in subtle but important ways. It did so by creating legislative history—a year after passage of section 504—attributing to Congress an intent that had not been expressed at the time of enactment. The committee report was the avenue of expression. Although the legislative history is silent, the report declared that, at least in the employment area, "where applicable, Section 504 is intended to include a requirement of affirmative action as well as a prohibition against discrimination." The report noted that:

> Section [504] was patterned after, and is almost identical to, the anti-discrimination language of section 601 of the Civil Rights Act of 1964 . . . (relating to race, color, or national origin), and section 901 of the Education Amendments of 1972 . . . (relating to sex). The section therefore constitutes the establishment of a broad government policy that programs receiving Federal financial assistance shall be operated without discrimination on the basis of handicap.[92]

Title VI of the Civil Rights Act of 1964 and title IX of the Education Amendments of 1972 contain directives to promulgate regulations, a task that the OCR discharged. In contrast, the legislative history and language of section 504 say nothing about regulations and enforcement mechanisms. But by analogy to these other acts, the committee report asserted that although "Section 504 does not specifically require the issuance of regulations or expressly provide for enforcement procedures, . . . it is clearly mandatory in form, and such regulations and enforcement were intended by this Committee and by Congress." Having stated that such measures were contemplated, the report then claimed, without providing support:

> The language of section 504, in following the above-cited Acts, further envisions the implementation of a compliance program . . . including promulgation of regulations providing for investigation and review of recipients of

91. 88 Stat. 1617.
92. *Rehabilitation Act Amendments of 1974*, S. Rept. 93-1139, 93 Cong. 2 sess. (GPO, 1974), p. 24.

Federal financial assistance, attempts to bring non-complying recipients into voluntary compliance through informal efforts such as negotiation, and the imposition of sanctions against recipients who continue to discriminate against otherwise qualified handicapped persons on the basis of handicap. Such sanctions would include . . . the termination of Federal financial assistance to the recipient. . . . Implementation of section 504 would also include . . . pregrant review procedures and a requirement for assurances of compliance. . . . This . . . would ensure administrative due process . . . , provide for administrative consistency . . . as well as relative ease of implementation, and permit a judicial remedy through a private action.[93]

To assure uniform administration, the committee charged the secretary of the Department of Health, Education, and Welfare with coordinating the section 504 enforcement effort and regulations by the end of 1974.[94]

It is striking how congruent the views of the OCR and the subcommittee staff were with respect to the scope of section 504, the need for governmentwide regulations, and the enforcement role of HEW. Indeed, the committee report is very similar in language to the OCR's responses to subcommittee questions. Certainly, the legislative history of section 504 (or perhaps the lack of it) would not lead one to predict that both the agency and the legislature would share the same view about what the statute required. But that common perspective, however striking, is not surprising, given the interaction between subcommittee staff and OCR lawyers in the months following the passage of the Rehabilitation Act of 1973. In fact, the OCR staff, without the approval of the HEW secretary, suggested to their congressional counterparts ways to strengthen their role. The committee report was the vehicle for legitimating that vision. The committee, or perhaps more accurately its staff, could require what an agency was already willing to do but was reluctant to undertake without more pronounced legislative authority. The staffers knew, as did the OCR, that they were not only directing the agency to take affirmative action, but also were creating a legislative history supportive of their position, albeit after the fact. They understood that someday courts called on to resolve disputes about statutory interpretation would look to that history for guidance.

The ramifications of the committee report were significant. HEW was to create and monitor a governmentwide regulatory scheme. An array of federal agencies would be part of the effort. HEW's mandate was not limited to particular issues, but would include such policies as transportation, education, and housing. The nature of those regulations, the requirements of affirmative action, and the factors to be considered in issuing the regu-

93. Ibid., pp. 24–25.
94. Ibid., p. 25.

lations were not examined. Costs were not mentioned, perhaps because a problem, once defined in terms of absolute rights, must be resolved whatever the price. To ensure the enjoyment of a civil right, the report sought to provide injured parties with access to courts. Although the implications of all this were quite far-reaching, no one in Congress explored them. This may have been because section 504 was not changed in the legislation and therefore not subject to debate. Only after a careful reading of the committee report would questions about the section have been raised. It is evident that the senators who passed judgment on the Rehabilitation Act amendments were concerned not with section 504 but the visible structural issues before them.

Following Senate passage by voice vote, the Senate and House conference met. The House adopted the language of the Senate report regarding section 504; the conferees expected HEW regulations by the close of 1974, stating that "beyond this point would be most unfortunate since the Act . . . was created over one year ago."[95] In the end, the Senate accepted the conference report without debate and by voice vote. By a 334–0 margin, the House followed suit. President Gerald Ford objected to the shifts in the administration of rehabilitative services and vetoed the measure.[96] Because Congress was in recess, the president argued that he had pocket-vetoed the legislation and that the legislature could not override it. After the Congressional Research Service determined that the president's action was nothing more than a normal veto, the House overrode the veto by a 398–7 vote, and the Senate did so by a 90–1 margin.[97] But because of the legal uncertainty arising over the pocket veto issue, Congress enacted an identical bill, by a voice vote of both houses, so that the legislation could take effect immediately. Ford signed the bill into law, knowing that Congress would have overridden his veto.

Prodding the Regulatory Process

In the years following passage of the Rehabilitation Act Amendments of 1974, the Senate Subcommittee on the Handicapped and the House Subcommittee on Select Education monitored the course of section 504. Sec-

95. *Rehabilitation Act Amendments of 1974*, H. Rept. 93-1457, 93 Cong. 2 sess. (GPO, 1974), p. 28.
96. *Rehabilitation Act Amendments of 1974*, S. Rept. 93-1297, 93 Cong. 2 sess. (GPO, 1974), pp. 26–27.
97. *Congressional Record* (November 20, 1974), pp. 36621–22; and ibid. (November 21, 1974), p. 36882.

tion 504 became a visible issue; it was no longer merely the subject of posthearing written questions to the executive branch, but became a matter of discussion during the hearings themselves. The very existence of the nondiscrimination statute generated the birth of rights-oriented organizations that rallied in support of section 504. In addition, many established groups embraced the new law. Pressing their claims before Congress, they argued that the section was a civil rights statute in need of vigorous enforcement. During the course of Senate hearings in 1976, organizations such as the American Coalition of Citizens with Disabilities, the Paralyzed Veterans of America, and the National Center for Law and the Handicapped complained about the failure of HEW to issue section 504 regulations. John Lancaster of the PVA recommended that because of HEW inaction, the attorney general should be specifically given enforcement responsibilities. Reese Robrahn of the American Council of the Blind and the American Coalition of Citizens with Disabilities suggested that arbitration panels be created to resolve disputes arising under section 504.[98]

With increasing frequency, section 504 was seen as a means of promoting barrier-free transportation. Organizations representing the disabled were the first to recognize the value of the nondiscrimination statute in that regard; by 1976 they had filed many suits across the nation, charging in part that inaccessible transportation systems violated section 504. The groups themselves saw the utility of section 504 in transportation matters before the senators most supportive of their efforts did. In the 1976 Senate hearings, those legislators pressing the Department of Transportation did not raise the section as the basis of their argument, but seemed to rely on the Biaggi amendment to the 1970 Urban Mass Transportation Act.

Section 504 became more prominent as the key committees prodded HEW to promulgate its regulations. The Senate Subcommittee on the Handicapped noted in 1976 that although two-and-a-half years had passed since the 1974 act, the expected executive order and HEW regulations had still not surfaced.[99] In fact, President Ford did sign Executive Order 11914 later that year, requiring HEW to coordinate the governmentwide implementation of section 504, to set forth appropriate standards and guidelines to be used by other agencies in issuing their own regulations, and to estab-

---

98. *Rehabilitation of the Handicapped Programs, 1976*, Hearings before the Subcommittee on the Handicapped of the Senate Committee on Labor and Public Welfare, 94 Cong. 2 sess. (GPO, 1976), pt. 1, pp. 49, 496, 501, 503–05.

99. Ibid., pp. 1476–78.

lish enforcement mechanisms to ensure consistent application of the statute.[100] Meanwhile, the OCR, which had begun to prepare regulations
shortly after passage of the 1974 amendments, had circulated a first draft
within the department in April 1975.

A district court in Washington, D.C., spurred the process in response
to a suit, brought by the Institute for Public Interest Representation of
Georgetown University Law Center, by ruling that the secretary was required to promulgate regulations. As the basis of its decision, the court
stated that "reports from the Senate and the House on the 1974 Amendments to the Act indicate that Congress contemplated swift implementation
of section 504 through a comprehensive set of regulations."[101]

As those regulations covering HEW programs and activities bubbled to
the secretary's office, they stirred much controversy. Their universe was
all-encompassing, affecting school systems, hospitals, nursing homes, libraries, day care centers, institutions of higher learning, and home health
agencies.[102] The requirement that each facility be made accessible in every
respect was thought to involve great costs, running into the billions of
dollars. When the proposed regulations reached him, Secretary David Mathews would not sign them without congressional guidance. Just days before leaving office, he sent to Congress, along with the 185 pages of regulations, a letter that read in part:

> The Department has completed its work in preparing regulations to imple-
> ment Section 504 of the Rehabilitation Act. However, before these regulations
> go into effect, I believe it is in the public interest to lay them before the Con-
> gress. . . . The statute from which they derive is very brief, and there were no
> debates accompanying its passage. As a result, we have had some difficulty in
> reconstructing the intent of Congress. These regulations may, like those issued
> under Title IX of the Education Amendments of 1972, raise questions about
> whether the Federal Government is speaking with two voices. And I believe
> that the Executive and Legislative branches should work together so that it can-
> not be said that the Executive Branch has pursued policy beyond or in contra-
> diction to what Congress authorized. A way to prevent any such confusion is
> for the Department, where the intent of the statute is unclear, to lay its interpre-
> tation of the statute before the Congress so that it can provide whatever clarifi-
> cation is appropriate. . . .
>
> In our hearings, it also became obvious that the requirements under this
> statute could occasion expenditures by a number of institutions. Finally, there
> are no reliable estimates of what that cost might be. I should convey to you the

100. 41 Fed. Reg. 17871 (1976).
101. *Cherry* v. *Mathews*, 419 F. Supp. 922 (D.D.C. 1976); for an extended discussion
of *Cherry*, see chap. 4.
102. See the proposed rules, 41 Fed. Reg. 29548 (1976).

strong feeling of the people we heard from that the federal Government should pay for the costs attendant to its requirements, particularly if the Government intends for there to be comprehensive and immediate accessibility to all facilities. . . .

It is very important that the Congress acknowledge any regulation on a matter of this sensitivity as being consistent with the law. The experience with Title IX should be instructive to all of us and no one should want the 504 regulation to encounter the same difficulties. . . . There is, of course, precedent for Congressional review. . . . But . . . I would hope we would all learn from our previous experiences and improve upon the partnership that the two branches must have in matters such as this.[103]

When Joseph Califano assumed office in late January 1977, the regulations still had not been approved. After a fresh review of the regulations, and following demonstrations by disability groups throughout the land, Secretary Califano sent to Congress a revised set of rules dealing with HEW activities. Although rigorous, these regulations differed from the earlier ones in that they gave institutions more discretion by seeking program accessibility rather than structural changes. Thus not every schoolroom in an institution had to be accessible, but some rooms had to be so that handicapped students could attend the institution. Proclaiming that the regulations open "a new era of civil rights in America," the secretary added that "in light of the limited legislative history, I think it especially important that Congress evaluate the regulation, and the implementation process, to ensure that they conform to the will of Congress."[104]

During the three and one-half months between the time that Mathews asked Congress to evaluate the section 504 regulations and Califano signed them, the legislature did not provide any alternatives or further guidance about its legislative intent. Given that the House and Senate subcommittees had been exhorting HEW to promulgate regulations and were decidedly unhappy with the delay in promulgating them, it is not surprising that they did not inject themselves if it would have meant slowing the process still further. Califano, remembering the congressional reaction to his predecessor's letter, recounted:

The Committee chairmen involved—Jennings Randolph, Harrison Williams, and Claiborne Pell in the Senate, and John Brademas in the House—were irritated. They did not want the issue back in that form. It was more fun

103. *Implementation of Section 504, Rehabilitation Act of 1973*, Hearings before the Subcommittee on Select Education of the House Committee on Education and Labor, 95 Cong. 1 sess. (GPO, 1977), pp. 73–75.

104. Memo of HEW Secretary Joseph A. Califano, Jr., to Members of Congress, Subject: Regulation Prohibiting Discrimination Against Handicapped Americans, April 28, 1977.

to be Moses and deliver the commandments than to be the rabbis and priests who had to make them work.[105]

But congressional silence would make less tenable the claim in later years that the bureaucracy had run amok, that it had distorted its intent; more accurately, Congress was a not-so-silent partner to what some would later call the subversion of legislative history.

Ironing Out the Wrinkles

Once the regulations were issued, Congress began to look more closely at them. While this was occurring, the Office for Civil Rights was drafting section 504 guidelines for compliance by a range of agencies. Through hearings held in 1977 and 1978, the Senate and House subcommittees became aware of some of the concerns of the interests affected and sought to address them.[106] Many state and local institutions, especially educational ones, complained of the costs of making buildings barrier free. To help remedy this problem, Vermont Republican Representative James M. Jeffords proposed that some financial aid be given to those institutions.[107] By the time of the 1978 hearings, the breadth of the section 504 program became apparent. Once HEW issued its regulations in 1977, it began to devise guidelines every agency was to follow in preparing its own regulations. The American Public Transit Association (APTA), representing transit operators, objected that the Department of Transportation's notice of proposed rulemaking, issued pursuant to the HEW guidelines, would impose huge expenses on public transit. Interestingly, some of the disability groups vigorously opposed financial support to these institutions. Reese Robrahn of the American Coalition of Citizens with Disabilities commented that "section 504 is the Civil Rights Act. It is not an act which provides services. We think it is inappropriate and immoral to pay people

105. Joseph A. Califano, Jr., *Governing America: An Insider's Report from the White House and the Cabinet* (Simon and Schuster, 1981), p. 259.

106. See, for example, *Rehabilitation Extension Amendments of 1977*, Hearings before the Subcommittee on the Handicapped of the Senate Committee on Human Resources, 95 Cong. 1 sess. (GPO, 1977); *Implementation of Section 504, Rehabilitation Act of 1973*, Hearings before the Subcommittee on Select Education of House Committee on Education and Labor, 95 Cong. 1 sess. (GPO, 1977) (hereafter *Implementation Hearings*); *Rehabilitation Amendments of 1978*, Hearings before the Subcommittee on the Handicapped of the Senate Committee on Human Resources, 95 Cong. 2 sess. (GPO, 1978) (hereafter *1978 Senate Hearings*); and *Oversight Hearings on the Rehabilitation Act of 1973*, Hearings before the Subcommittee on Select Education of the House Committee on Education and Labor, 98 Cong. 2 sess. (GPO, 1978) (hereafter *Oversight Hearings*).

107. *Implementation Hearings*, p. 78.

or reward them for complying with the law to assure the rights of others."[108]

Representatives of the disabled argued that the expensive costs of litigation made it difficult to vindicate those rights. Section 504 was not covered by the Civil Rights Attorney's Fees Awards Act of 1976. As a result, many of the disabled could "neither afford an attorney, locate one able to represent them without a fee, nor seek an attorney's fee award from the courts." In supporting the call for an attorney's fee provision, David Tatel, a blind attorney and head of the OCR, asserted that HEW did not have the resources to do the "whole job" and that "one of the best ways to encourage litigation and make it possible for the indigent handicapped to seek redress in the courts, is to make provision for the award of attorneys' fees."[109] Both the House and Senate subcommittees were receptive; indeed the Senate report quoted approvingly from testimony by one disability group representative. The bills emerging from each body provided that a court may allow the prevailing party, other than the United States, a reasonable attorney's fee as part of the costs. In addition, the Senate formally extended the remedies, rights, and procedures of title VI of the Civil Rights Act of 1964 to section 504 cases, noting that the joint explanatory statement accompanying the conference report on the Rehabilitation Act Amendments of 1974 stressed the parallel relationship between the two laws.[110] In fact, the Senate amendment would simply have codified existing HEW practices.

Another concern was the scope of section 504. Answering a request from HEW General Counsel Peter Libassi, the Justice Department's Office of Legal Counsel concluded in an opinion that section 504 could not be invoked against the federal government itself, but applied only to state and local programs or activities receiving federal financial assistance.[111] In response, Congressman Jeffords proposed in 1978 an amendment extending the coverage of section 504 to include any function or activity of any federal department or agency and requiring that each department and agency promulgate regulations. Copies of any proposed regulations were to be submitted to appropriate authorizing congressional committees and could

108. *Oversight Hearings,* pp. 977, 1228.

109. *The Awarding of Attorneys' Fees in Federal Courts,* Hearings before the Subcommittee on Courts, Civil Liberties and the Administration of Justice of the House Committee on the Judiciary, 95 Cong. 1 and 2 sess. (GPO, 1978), pp. 118–22; and *Implementation Hearings,* pp. 265, 358.

110. *Rehabilitation, Comprehensive Services and Developmental Disabilities Amendments of 1978,* S. Rept. 95-890, 95 Cong. 2 sess. (GPO, 1978), pp. 18, 19.

111. Opinion of John M. Harmon, Assistant Attorney General, Office of Legal Counsel, to F. Peter Libassi, General Counsel, Department of HEW, September 23, 1977.

take effect no earlier than the thirtieth day after the regulation was sent to the committee,[112] indicative, perhaps, of a greater congressional willingness to assume responsibility for section 504 enforcement.

Another problem that surfaced had to do with the kinds of handicapped individuals protected by section 504. Read literally, the definition of "handicapped" as stated in the Rehabilitation Act of 1973 seemed to apply to alcoholics and drug addicts. The airline industry objected that, so construed, the Rehabilitation Act required recruitment and promotion of people in an active state of alcoholism or drug addiction.[113] President Carter—apparently in his only comment about the HEW regulations—agreed.[114] After considerable discussion in both houses, Congress adopted an amendment, stating that the term "handicapped individual" would not include any person who is an alcoholic or drug abuser if his condition "prevents such individual from performing the duties of the job in question or whose employment, by reason of such current alcohol or drug abuse, would constitute a direct threat to property or to the safety of others."[115] This less restrictive approach meant, for example, that a person suffering from alcoholism or drug addiction would be excluded from being a pilot, but could be a baggage handler if that condition did not interfere with work.

These amendments concerning section 504—providing for attorneys' fees, making it applicable to federal agencies, and narrowing the definition of handicapped individuals—were not controversial. They were part of a legislative package that dealt not only with rehabilitation service but also with developmental disabilities. In the end, Congress easily passed the Rehabilitation, Comprehensive Services and Developmental Disabilities Amendments of 1978.

Congress and the Conflicting Approaches

Meanwhile, HEW, acting according to the executive order, issued governmentwide section 504 guidelines that all other departments had to follow.[116] As a consequence, the DOT felt compelled to abandon the effective

112. Remarks of James Jeffords, *Congressional Record* (May 16, 1978), p. 13901; and 92 Stat. 2982.
113. *1978 Senate Hearings*, pp. 771–72.
114. Califano, *Governing America*, p. 261.
115. 92 Stat. 2985.
116. 43 Fed. Reg. 2132 (1978).

mobility approach and adopt the full accessibility conception (see chapter 3). It issued new regulations mandating potentially "extraordinarily expensive changes" in order to make each mode of transportation aided by federal money—bus, subway, streetcar, and commuter rail—accessible to handicapped persons, including those in wheelchairs.

The DOT's rights-oriented regulations changed the nature of congressional involvement. For most of the 1970s, legislative activity dealing with transportation policy for disabled persons had been largely the work of a few legislative entrepreneurs, who sought to prod the DOT to enforce the Biaggi amendment more vigorously. A generally uninvolved legislature left policymaking to the administrative process, which produced the 1976 "special efforts" regulations embodying the effective mobility approach. But when the DOT changed its policy to one of full accessibility, Congress had to contend with a concerted campaign by the transit industry to reverse the rights-based policy, which in some sense the legislature had set in motion. This in turn engaged the passions of the disability groups.

The leaders of the transit committees in Congress were not interested in confronting the handicapped issue, particularly in 1980, an election year; they were principally concerned with shepherding through increased authorizations for mass transit. The task of forcing consideration of the issue fell to legislative entrepreneurs—but this time their efforts were directed toward restraining administrative action, rather than promoting it.

Central issues were at stake: equity versus efficiency, rights or full accessibility versus effective mobility, federal control versus local autonomy. Into the mix came a Congressional Budget Office report critical of the full accessibility regulations. Another ingredient was a changing political mood—a shift from the rights ethos to a greater concern with cost by the end of the 1970s.

The Battle Begins

The reaction to the DOT regulations was swift. When interests are dissatisfied with the executive, they are apt to turn to the legislature or courts for redress. Transit groups were no exception as they sought relief through both the authorization and appropriations processes.

Although representatives of disability groups for the most part hailed the regulations as consistent with the spirit of section 504, transit operators, particularly in older cities such as New York and Chicago, condemned them as being excessively costly, unworkable, and unlikely to serve more than a minuscule percentage of the handicapped population. Mayor Edward Koch of New York City argued that the regulations would cost billions to implement and could lead to fiscal bankruptcy.[117] Officials of local government, through the American Public Transit Association, quickly moved to action, writing and lobbying key members of Congress in both the authorization committees and the appropriations committees.

Their message reached its target. In the hearings of the appropriations committees held in 1980, subcommittee members questioned DOT officials about the costs of regulations. The appropriations legislation enacted in 1979 specifically declared that "none of these funds shall be available to retrofit any existing fixed rail transit system to comply with the regulations issued pursuant to section 504 of the Rehabilitation Act of 1973." The House report accompanying the 1979 appropriations act expressed the committee's concern that "the regulations might require the expenditure of vast sums with only minimal benefits to handicapped persons." The committee noted that section 321 of the Surface Transportation Assistance Act requires "a study of this issue," and stated that pending completion of the study, it would recommend "language . . . prohibit[ing] the use of [federal] funds to retrofit any existing rail transit system." Congress agreed to bar such expenditures. Similarly, with respect to buses, the committee report called on the DOT to "evaluate the costs of benefits associated with equipping all regular bus routes with lifts . . . and ensure that any lifts which are currently being purchased with UMTA assistance are reliable, maintainable and operable."[118]

THE CBO REPORT

The reaction against the DOT regulations grew even more intense when in November 1979 the Congressional Budget Office released a report undertaken at the request of the Senate Budget Committee and the Surface Transportation Subcommittee of the House Public Works and Transportation Committee. The document offered an examination of three different policy options: (1) "the transit plan" embodied in the DOT regulations; (2) a "taxi plan" emphasizing door-to-door services; and (3) an "auto plan" facilitating the purchase by handicapped persons of specially equipped

117. See Gordon J. Fielding, "Transportation for the Handicapped: The Politics of Full Accessibility," *Transportation Quarterly*, vol. 36 (April 1982), p. 281; and Edward I. Koch, "The Mandate Millstone," *The Public Interest*, no. 61 (Fall 1980), p. 42.

118. 93 Stat. 1023, 1032; and *Department of Transportation and Related Agencies Appropriations Bill*, H. Rept. 96-272, 96 Cong. 1 sess. (GPO, 1979), p. 48.

cars. Although the CBO report made no recommendations, it was highly critical of the DOT regulations, concluding that "while the program would be very expensive—$6.8 billion over the next 30 years—relatively few handicapped persons would benefit from it." The report determined that the transit plan would serve 7 percent of severely disabled individuals, and that if patronage were to fall below the projected level, the cost per trip of serving handicapped passengers who did not then use transit would average $75 or more. By contrast, the other plans, according to the CBO, would serve more people at lower cost. Not confining itself to the merits of the particular plans, the report also included an analysis of section 504 and concluded that it was not at all clear whether, under the statute, full accessibility was required, as DOT and HEW claimed they were.[119]

Although the Department of Transportation vigorously disputed the CBO analysis,[120] the report from the highly regarded institution with ties to neither disability groups nor the transit industry had a damaging effect. The CBO report gave support to transit operators and local officials asking Congress to overturn the DOT regulations. In turn, members of Congress pointed to the study as justifying legislative efforts to modify the regulations.

LOCAL OPTION

Congress considered such a legislative solution in 1980. In the context of examining a comprehensive mass transit bill to aid older cities whose transportation systems were receiving an unduly low percentage of federal operating subsidies, the Senate debated whether to provide an alternative to DOT's full accessibility regulations. Democrat Edward Zorinsky, a former mayor of Omaha—a city that had devoted resources to specialized transit—originally proposed a simple local option. Local governments would have to use 5 percent of their federal mass transit money for transportation for elderly and handicapped individuals, but they were free to spend those funds as they saw fit. Citing both the CBO study and his own experience in Omaha, Zorinsky argued that a local option exemption was needed to counteract the "inflexible" rules of the Department of Transportation.[121]

Although it was clear that there was support within the chamber for

119. Congressional Budget Office, *Urban Transportation for Handicapped Persons: Alternative Federal Approaches* (GPO, 1979), pp. xi, xiv, xvi.

120. DOT, "Comments on Transportation for Handicapped Persons," June 9, 1980.

121. *Congressional Record* (June 25, 1980), p. 16696.

local option—senators had heard from transit operators and local governments in their states—some, such as Alan Cranston and, most significantly, Harrison Williams, now the chairman of the Senate Subcommittee on Banking, Housing, and Urban Affairs, opposed the proposal in its purest form. They argued that local option without some performance standards could adversely affect the target population. "Local option," Cranston commented, "has resulted in a variety of systems which range from no service at all to discriminatory service that provides a level of service which is far inferior to that available to the general public."[122] Williams and Cranston, working principally with Zorinsky and his Democratic colleague from Nebraska, James Exon, negotiated a compromise. Under its terms, transit operators could provide alternative service, subject to the DOT secretary's approval, if the program allocated at least 5 percent of its federal funds to transportation for handicapped persons and if it offered service no less beneficial than the DOT rules required. Moreover, the program was to meet certain service criteria.[123]

The amendment—known as the Zorinsky amendment—passed by a voice vote. Williams, who was "willing to stay with the [DOT] regulation," observed that "because so many communities have found difficulty in meeting the absolute demands of regulation, we have been in some turmoil here in Congress how to handle this." While "previous Congresses . . . [have] struggled to balance the many difficult policy and economic questions," Williams commented, "there has been everything but positive and demonstrable progress to solve these difficult issues." He hoped the amendment would "bring an end to the controversy and launch a new era of effective public transportation for our transportation disadvantaged."[124]

THE HOUSE JOINS THE DEBATE

In the House of Representatives, the Subcommittee on Surface Transportation was also drawn into the matter, almost against its will. Not long before hearings on the Surface Transportation Act began in March 1980,

122. Ibid., p. 16700.
123. For example, local programs had to provide transportation services throughout the recipient's normal service area; there were to be no waiting lists or prior registration or approval of handicapped persons wishing to use the system; there were to be no restrictions as to trip purpose; and there were to be reasonable minimum waiting periods. In addition, a city with a population of 50,000 to 750,000 would have to have at least 50 percent of its new buses fully accessible unless the secretary determined that a different percentage would be satisfactory. Where the population exceeded 750,000, 100 percent would have to be fully accessible unless the secretary concluded that a lesser percentage would be appropriate. Ibid., p. 16695.
124. Ibid., pp. 16697–98.

the Subcommittee on Oversight and Review, another offspring of the House Committee on Public Works and Transportation, released a report on UMTA's technology development and procurement programs, subtitled "Do We Know What We're Trying to Do?"[125] Spurred by the apparent collapse in 1979 of the Transbus program, the Subcommittee on Oversight and Review held hearings to study UMTA's technology development and program practices. In its report, the subcommittee found that recent legislation had resulted in "undeniable confusion about the concepts of accessibility and mobility and . . . rights," and it called on Congress to clarify its intent with respect to the Rehabilitation Act of 1973 and other legislation providing for the needs of the elderly and the handicapped. Although a subcommittee majority concluded that Congress needed more data about the costs and benefits of the full accessibility and mobility options, nine minority members—citing the CBO report—argued that further study was unnecessary.[126] They declared that full accessibility should be abandoned.

> With respect to the issue of rights versus economics, we find it difficult to accept the argument that the rights of the handicapped require both fully accessible mainline service, regardless of the small proportion of handicapped served and regardless of cost, plus alternative service for those who are still unable to avail themselves of mainline service. If the demand is for mobility, we agree; if it is for a symbol, we take exception. In so doing, we also point out that the financial burdens imposed on communities required to provide full accessible mainline service could well exhaust resources otherwise available for alternative service.[127]

That view, championed by Republican Representative James Cleveland of New Hampshire, the ranking minority member of the Subcommittee on Oversight and Review, found support in the Subcommittee on Surface Transportation, of which he was also a member. Cleveland (who hailed from a state without a subway system) introduced an amendment that would allow local governments to choose between fully accessible transportation as required by DOT regulations and a plan of their own devising—a local option. If a community should decide to develop its own service, it would have to meet certain minimum criteria.[128] The proposed

---

125. *Urban Mass Transportation Administration's Technology Development and Equipment Procurement Programs (Bus and Rail Rolling Stock) "Do We Know What We're Trying to Do?"* H. Comm. Print 96-34, 96 Cong. 2 sess. (GPO, 1980).

126. Ibid., pp. 21, 23.

127. Ibid., p. 24.

128. Fares, service area, and hours of service would have to be the same as for the regular transit system; no more than twenty-four hours' notice could be required of the hand-

amendment required the secretary of transportation to consult with the Architectural and Transportation Barriers Compliance Board before approving any plan.[129] It further provided a partial cutoff of federal funds for noncompliance. Where full accessibility was cost effective—as in the case of new rail systems and extensions of existing rail systems—it was to be mandated. At least 3 percent of the federal funds for operating costs had to be used for the alternate service (subject to a decision, made at the secretarial level, to reduce the amount under some circumstances). Commented Cleveland, "The emphasis is on making every effort to meet the actual needs of the disabled, not an abstract and unrealizable theory."[130]

A bipartisan majority, by a vote of 29–6, adopted the Cleveland amendment, which subcommittee chairman James Howard hailed as "a courageous effort to provide a more reasonable approach to the problem of local transportation for the handicapped."[131] In fact, Howard would have preferred not to deal with the issue, believing that it would complicate passage of proposed legislation whose objective was to increase aid to older cities. For that reason the original bill did not address the matter of transportation for the handicapped, but Cleveland's determination meant that the issue would have to be considered.

The measure was approved without hearings or testimony of representatives from the disabled community. Viewing the proposed legislation as an ominous retreat from the full accessibility conception, such disability groups as the Paralyzed Veterans of America and the American Coalition

icapped rider; no undue burden could be imposed if preregistration was found necessary; no restrictions on trip purpose could be imposed, except that priority could be given trips to meet a medical need; and handicapped riders could be accompanied by an able-bodied companion of their choice where feasible.

129. The Architectural and Transportation Barriers Compliance Board, established in 1973 as a mechanism to enforce the Architectural Barriers Act of 1968, consists of twenty-two members—eleven from federal agencies and eleven appointed by the president from the public. It is charged with setting minimum guidelines and requirements for standards issued pursuant to the Architectural Barriers Act. Based on those minimum guidelines, four federal agencies—the Department of Defense, General Services Administration, Department of Housing and Urban Development, and the United States Postal Service—are to prescribe standards for the design, construction, and alteration of certain federal and federally assisted buildings "to insure, whenever possible, that physically handicapped persons will have ready access to, and use of, such buildings." (42 U.S.C. sec. 4152–4154a.) During the waning days of the Carter administration, the board sought to issue wide-ranging requirements that would have covered, among other things, transportation requirements—but that effort was short-lived. Indeed, during the early years of the Reagan presidency, the administration proposed zero funding. The board has not had an impact on DOT regulations or policy.

130. *Congressional Record* (November 21, 1980), p. 30544.

131. Ibid. (December 2, 1980), p. 31549.

of Citizens with Disabilities engaged in an energetic lobbying campaign to prevent the measure's passage. Howard recounted that "many, many members of this body voiced their concerns to me and to the distinguished chairman of the full committee about the Cleveland amendment and the controversy which a very articulate and aggressive group of handicapped persons generated." Howard explained that in light of that intense opposition, the committee "entered into the most lengthy negotiating process which I have seen during my tenure in the House."[132]

Clyde Woodle, a committee staffer with an engineering background, met in the basement of one of the House office buildings with representatives from the American Public Transit Association, the Paralyzed Veterans of America, the American Coalition of Citizens with Disabilities, the Department of Transportation, the Congressional Budget Office, and the Committee on Education and Labor.[133] The meetings were often emotionally charged, with groups such as the Paralyzed Veterans of America arguing vigorously against any retreat from the DOT's full accessibility regulations. In essence, the committee staff was conducting a negotiated rulemaking proceeding with all the interested parties present in the same room.

Concerned that disability groups might bitterly and publicly oppose any deviation from the full accessibility regulations and mindful of the possible consequences at the ballot box, Howard decided not to propose a compromise until after the November 1980 election. The compromise, advanced by Howard's staff, retained some of the basic features of the Cleveland amendment, but delineated in far greater detail the criteria governing acceptable alternative service.[134] The secretary had to approve each plan, in consultation with the Architectural and Transportation Barriers Compliance Board and the local handicapped community. Finally, new rail stations would have to be fully accessible to the disabled.[135]

In Howard's view, the proposed criteria provided local governments

132. Ibid.

133. Interview with Clyde Woodle, December 14, 1985.

134. In addition to the more general criteria for fares, service, and hours, it required, for example, that the requested transportation had to be provided in a time period less than twenty-four hours after receipt of such request during the first two years after the date of program approval by the secretary, less than eight hours after receipt of such request during the following two years, and less than six hours thereafter; and to the extent operationally practicable, trip time and transfer frequency were to be reasonably comparable to that on the public transit system.

135. *Congressional Record* (December 2, 1980), p. 31549.

with great flexibility; they could, for example, develop a program that did not include the purchase of any accessible buses. Representative Cleveland reacted strongly, however, charging that the compromise was "phony." Congress, he said, should not write unworkable regulations. The Howard criteria, Cleveland claimed, did not define what constitutes "comparable" service or "effective" transportation and would lead to endless court suits. He charged that DOT "birdbrains" crafted the Howard amendment so that "they could be back in business after it passed." In a bitter attack on the "vocal types and their allies in DOT ever eager to coerce their vision of compassion down our throats," he charged that his "amendment . . . [and] motives . . . have been distorted and misrepresented practically beyond recognition. . . . And for whom? The original, vocal absolutist groups whose claim to our natural sympathies distorts the simple fact that it is just a bunch of lobbyists, using the age-old tactic of keeping its purported constituency stirred up grabbing headlines, and not so incidentally keeping its financial support coming in." In conclusion, Cleveland offered this view of the origins and reasons for the controversy:

> The Congress deserves its share of the blame. We passed out an amendment to the Vocational Rehabilitation Act with no hearings, no committee discussion, nothing until it got to the floor. The Congress wrote into statute an attractive-sounding, compassionate, fair-minded, right-thinking statement of good intentions with no earthly idea of the consequences. Then the fanatics at DOT got hold of it and we wound up with a costly, inefficient and disruptive set of regulations to impose requirements which the Congress never intended, much less specified.[136]

If Cleveland believed the Howard amendment was too onerous, others supported it even though they feared it weakened the full accessibility objective. Illinois Democrat Paul Simon, who chaired the House subcommittee with jurisdiction over section 504 and most issues relating to the handicapped population, supported the Howard amendment although "without enthusiasm" because he believed it came much closer to maintaining the basic rights assured by section 504 than any other proposal likely to be adopted by the House.[137] Similarly, Mario Biaggi, who in 1970 had sponsored what became section 16 of the Urban Mass Transportation Act, stated quite revealingly:

> We must be realists in this legislation. It is apparent that the absolute adherence to full fixed-route accessibility cannot be achieved by a number of localities in

136. Ibid. (November 21, 1980), p. 30545; and ibid. (December 2, 1980), p. 31570.
137. Ibid. (December 2, 1980), p. 31570.

this Nation, most significantly, my own home city of New York. We cannot be blind to studies which have been undertaken which show that the participation by the handicapped in transportation services may in fact be higher under a paratransit type of program.[138]

Such was the division within the House that the Cleveland amendment came within two votes of passage (181–183).[139] Given the closeness of the vote, Howard recognized that his own amendment was not assured passage. Concerned that a failure to reach some agreement could doom the whole mass transit bill, he sought to reach some accommodation with Cleveland. A compromise was adopted on December 4, 1980, by voice vote. The political sensitivities of legislators concerned about being perceived as antidisabled was obviously acute. A motion to record the vote failed for lack of support.

Producing a list of forty-eight groups representing the elderly and handicapped who he said supported the local option approach, Howard stated:

> I think that [it] is very, very significant that some of the Washington-based people who are looking at language, redtape and bureaucracy feel that they have the only right to speak for the handicapped. Yet . . . the handicapped people who are the locals across this country, they are the people who have to live with it and . . . who have seen that in their own communities, despite all of the flowery words about so-called total accessibility, the handicapped cannot go anyplace.[140]

The PVA later questioned the accuracy of Howard's statement. In fact, his claim was not based on reactions from communities and organizations that had reviewed his proposed compromise. Rather, it stemmed from a list compiled by APTA and submitted to the DOT rulemaking docket in opposition to the 1979 full accessibility regulations. Howard implied that a group opposed to the DOT rules would have endorsed his alternative.

In the end, for reasons not having to do with the provisions for transportation for handicapped and elderly individuals, Congress failed to enact the mass transit bill. A Senate Republican filibuster in the waning hours of the Ninety-sixth Congress prevented the bill—which dealt principally with the vast array of mass transit programs—from reaching a final vote. The Republicans blocked consideration, arguing, in part, that the incoming Reagan administration should have the chance to assess mass transit programs before new legislation was enacted.

138. Ibid., p. 31577.
139. Ibid.
140. Ibid. (December 4, 1980), p. 32165.

USING THE APPROPRIATIONS PROCESS AGAIN

Attempts in 1980 to neutralize the DOT regulations also focused on the appropriations process. The chairman of the House appropriations transportation subcommittee, Robert Duncan, Democrat of Oregon, who had become convinced of the costliness of the DOT rules, succeeded, as he had the year before, in inserting language in the appropriations bill prohibiting funds from being used to retrofit any existing rail transit system to comply with DOT regulations. But, by a vote of 24–8, the committee rejected his proposal to prevent UMTA from compelling local authorities to buy buses equipped with wheelchair lifts. A Republican representative from Massachusetts, Silvio Conte, the ranking minority subcommittee member, remarked that the measure was defeated because of the apparently widely shared view that the Appropriations Committee should defer to the Howard subcommittee, which had devoted considerable effort to resolving the problem. "An appropriations bill," Conte declared, "was not the place to consider this matter. There was no formal hearing, giving the handicapped the opportunity to come in and testify and give their point of view." Nevertheless, Texas Democrat Charles W. Stenholm proposed virtually the same amendment on the House floor. Arguing that the DOT regulations were unworkable, he claimed that in Abilene, Texas, the largest city in his district, the wheelchair-bound user of an accessible bus would have to ride in the street itself to get to the bus stop.[141] In the end, the Stenholm amendment, by the close vote of 190–217, met the same fate, and for apparently the same reasons, as the Duncan proposal.

In the Senate, the bill that the appropriations transportation subcommittee reported did include a provision prohibiting the use of funds for programs that compelled local operators to buy wheelchair lifts for buses. Such a restriction was counter to the Zorinsky amendment to the mass transit bill, which had already passed the Senate. So as not to undo that compromise and to avoid conflicting mandates that would complicate resolution of the basic problems, Kansas Republican Robert Dole proposed on the Senate floor an amendment to the appropriations bill to make it conform to the Zorinsky measure. The Dole initiative would have carved out two exceptions to the prohibition against the use of federal funds to compel the purchase of wheelchair lifts: first, where the local program was consistent with the terms of the Zorinsky amendment, and second, where

141. Ibid. (July 31, 1980), pp. 20785, 20791–92.

a transit authority chose to purchase lift-equipped buses. The amendment passed by voice vote. Ultimately, Senate and House conferees struck both the amendment and the original language prohibiting the use of funds to compel the purchase of bus lifts. But the final appropriations legislation did retain the restriction passed by the House against using money for retrofitting of rail systems.[142]

COURT RULINGS

Although Congress was unable to resolve some of the basic problems enveloping transportation for handicapped persons, the judiciary relieved it of some of the pressure to do so. First, the Supreme Court took the steam out of section 504 when it held that the statute was a nondiscrimination measure and that the sparse legislative history did not mandate "expensive" affirmative action. Then in 1981 an opinion of the U.S. Court of Appeals for the D.C. Circuit, applying the Supreme Court's ruling to the 1979 DOT regulations, ruled that section 504 did not require the full accessibility approach.[143] Soon thereafter, in July 1981, Secretary of Transportation Drew Lewis rescinded the 1979 full accessibility regulations and replaced them with interim rules. Those regulations, much like the 1976 special efforts–local option regulations, called for a far less intrusive federal role. To receive funds, local governments simply had to "self-certify" that they were undertaking "special efforts."[144] The change in policy reflected a shift in the political environment. The country had elected Ronald Reagan as president, who brought with him a Republican Senate. The growing conservative mood and the emphasis on costs would frustrate those legislators who were sympathetic to the rights conception.

Rights Entrepreneurs in a Cost-Conscious Period

Six months after the interim rules took effect, spurred by complaints from disability groups that those interim regulations were not serving their needs, Senators Alan Cranston, Paul Sarbanes of Maryland, Donald Riegle of Michigan, and Christopher Dodd of Connecticut asked the comptroller general to conduct a study of the experience at the local level. They

142. 94 Stat. 1689.
143. *Southeastern Community College* v. *Davis,* 442 U.S. 397 (1979); and *American Public Transit Association* v. *Lewis,* 655 F.2d 1281 (D.C. Cir. 1981). See discussion in chap. 4.
144. 46 Fed. Reg. 37490 (1981).

were moved to action when the results showed that, pursuant to those interim regulations, only thirty of eighty-three systems surveyed intended to
have 50 percent or more of their buses lift-equipped and that nineteen systems that had planned to purchase such vehicles canceled their orders once
the interim regulations were issued.[145] Along with Riegle, who was the
ranking minority member of the Senate Banking, Housing, and Urban Affairs Committee, Cranston proposed that the secretary of transportation be
required to establish, within ninety days of enactment of the legislation,
minimum criteria for providing handicapped and elderly persons with
transportation services that were comparable to those afforded the general
public and to design procedures so that the secretary could monitor and
ensure compliance with those criteria.[146] The regulations were also to include provisions for guaranteeing that organizations representing handicapped and elderly groups were fully consulted in devising and implementing programs to implement those criteria. Another part of the
proposal would have authorized, but not required, the secretary of transportation to set aside for handicapped and elderly transit purposes 3.5 percent of "transit capital infrastructure" program funding.

Cranston, who had long fought for fully accessible transit, appreciated
the mood of the Republican-controlled Senate when he stated "I recognize
that it is not . . . feasible to gain approval of legislation that would provide
a full guarantee of eventual accessibility."[147] He emphasized that he was
not proposing a costly measure or one that required an immediate return to
the controversial tough standards that were in place before July 1981. Certainly, the measure was modest, compared with earlier legislation that
would have defined the factors that the secretary would have to take into
account in devising regulations. The DOT had made it clear to Cranston's
and Riegle's staffs that they would vigorously oppose such detailed proposals.

What is perhaps most striking is that the Cranston initiative was proposed in the waning days of a lame-duck Congress as an amendment to a
complicated and intensely discussed mass transit bill that focused on raising the gasoline tax to provide funds for restoring the transportation infrastructure. Transportation for the elderly and the disabled was not an issue
that concerned the legislators: as a result of the court decision and the

145. General Accounting Office, *Status of Special Efforts to Meet Transportation Needs
of the Elderly and the Handicapped* (GAO, 1982).
146. *Congressional Record*, daily edition (December 14, 1982), p. S14740.
147. Ibid.

interim regulations, the transit lobby had shifted its attention to other matters. In the end, the Cranston amendment sailed through without debate and became part of the final legislation.[148] Such was the outcome, probably because the measure seemed rather innocuous and because the weary legislators, eager to adjourn for Christmas, wanted to resolve the larger mass transit questions. Once again, a few tenacious legislators achieved their purposes by attaching their proposals, largely free from congressional scrutiny, as tangential amendments to the legislation at hand.

The Problems of Policy Formulation

Congress could hardly have made the task more difficult for agency administrators seeking to implement its will. For all the activity in the legislative process, there was a singular lack of direction, a seeming inability to issue unambiguous directives to the executive branch. Commenting on the failure to choose between the effective mobility and equal accessibility approaches, one DOT official stated: "We were never sure what those people on the Hill wanted; and even now, after all this time, we're still not quite certain." I have described how Congress contributed to that end; it remains for me to explain why. What is it about the language of legislation or the institutions and processes of Congress that can account for this result? And what implications can be drawn about the workings of the legislative process, the meaning of congressional responsibility, and the role of Congress in the federal system?

In part, vacillation was a consequence of the imprecise way in which Congress defined the problem needing attention. Section 504 of the Rehabilitation Act of 1973 was framed in the language of prohibition: no otherwise qualified individual was to be discriminated against solely by reason of his or her handicap. Section 16(a) of the Urban Mass Transportation Assistance Act of 1970—the Biaggi amendment—declared that elderly and handicapped individuals, as a matter of national policy, had the same "right" to use mass transit facilities and services as other persons and that "special efforts" were to be made to achieve that end. Neither act mandated that anything specifically be done; they lacked programmatic direction. It was unclear whether section 504 was simply a nondiscrimination

148. 96 Stat. 2097. The provision authorizing the secretary to set aside 3.5 percent of transit capital infrastructure funding was deleted.

statute or whether it required such affirmative steps as the retrofitting of rail systems. Similarly, the Biaggi amendment did not define what constituted "special efforts." Although written in terms of a "right," it was uncertain whether the Biaggi amendment meant to confer a legal benefit, as a right does, or whether it was simply a statement of national policy, that is, a desired but not compelled objective (a view taken by those sympathetic to transit interests). Failing to differentiate between the particular needs of the elderly and the handicapped also complicated the task of administrators seeking to devise effective policy. There was a fundamental conceptual weakness, a failure to define unambiguously "full accessibility" or "effective mobility," much less choose between them.

Some aspects of the legislative process itself contributed to the difficulties in defining the problem. That process provides points of opportunity for legislators determined to push through measures, often largely free from close congressional scrutiny. Neither section 504 of the Rehabilitation Act of 1973 nor section 16(a) of the Urban Mass Transportation Assistance Act of 1970, for example, was the subject of hearings. Section 16(a) was an amendment tacked on to a mass transit bill on the House floor. The legislative process permits measures only tangentially related to the proposed legislation at hand to be appended to it. If the congressional focus is on the central issues in question, then those seemingly peripheral matters are likely to receive far less attention than if they were introduced separately and for consideration on their own terms.

The chances of passage are increased to the extent that these measures are framed in a noncontroversial way. Both section 504 and the Biaggi amendment had programmatic consequences with costs attached; but the statutory language, crafted in terms of rights, obscured those costs. The symbolic power of rights is inexorable;[149] to deny a "right" in the service of a worthwhile objective is seemingly more drastic than to object to a program because the costs outweigh the benefits. The latter course, at least, does not necessarily reject the validity of the basic purpose, and it leaves room for compromise, for some alternative means to reach the end. The denial of a right seems to reject the value of the underlying grievance.

149. On the power of symbols, see Murray Edelman, *The Symbolic Uses of Politics* (University of Illinois Press, 1964); Edelman, *Politics as Symbolic Action: Mass Arousal and Quiescence* (Academic Press, 1971); Stuart A. Scheingold, *The Politics of Rights: Lawyers, Public Policy, and Political Change* (Yale University Press, 1974); and Timothy J. Conlan and Steven L. Abrams, "Federal Intergovernmental Regulation: Symbolic Politics in the New Congress," *Intergovernmental Perspective*, vol. 7 (Summer 1981), pp. 19–26.

Thus, even though the transit committees were sensitive to concerns about costs and eventually supported the effective mobility approach, they were also reluctant to confront the trade-offs between that view and the rights-oriented conception embodied in section 504. Were it not for the efforts of one member of the minority, James Cleveland, the House might not have even addressed the issue—and even then it did so without explicitly amending section 504 and without the benefit of hearings, but rather through the consideration of various amendments to a largely unrelated piece of legislation.

Committee fragmentation added to the policy confusion. It is difficult to know the legislative will when Congress is divided into so many committees with differing orientations. The rights-oriented committees worked independently of the transit-oriented committees. Appropriations committees entered the policy fray as well. The absence of any effective consultative or coordinating mechanisms made it less likely that Congress would compare the merits of the rights and transit approaches and send to the executive a clear statement about what the direction of policy should be.

Amidst this confusion about problem definition, section 504 had spawned an ambitious regulatory scheme within five years of its passage. Section 504 did not mandate that course. The absence of congressional hearings and debate made it impossible to divine legislative intent. The regulatory scheme that evolved in later years was not, therefore, the only conceivable consequence; for example, section 504 could have been fleshed out through judicial enforcement on a case-by-case basis.

If the legislative language itself provides little guidance, then other explanations must be sought to account for outcomes. Once again, examination of the institutional arrangements and processes can provide some clues. Among the targets of inquiry are the workings of committees and of staffs; the interaction between staff and committee, staff and bureaucracy, committee and bureaucracy, committees and the whole chamber, and one house with the other; and the role of such external influences as interest groups.

The lack of obvious direction in the language provided opportunities for at least some of these institutional elements to press for their preferences. With respect to section 504, the relevant committees, particularly their staffs, played crucial roles.[150] Influenced by the Civil Rights Act of 1964

150. For other examples of the efforts of staffs to produce legislative histories to further their policy ends, see Bruce A. Ackerman and William T. Hassler, *Clean Coal/Dirty Air* (Yale University Press, 1981), pp. 57–58; Malbin, *Unelected Representatives;* and R. Shep

and the Education Amendments of 1972, they favored an approach that would entitle the disabled to rights and would invoke the full force of the federal government to secure them. By means of a committee report written a year after passage of section 504, they were able to require the issuance of regulations, asserting that Congress intended such action when it enacted the legislation. They were able to do so without amending section 504 itself. Making policy through a committee report rather than through legislation can be effective precisely because it is less visible. Constituencies hold members of Congress accountable for their votes on particular pieces of legislation; therefore legislators may be more mindful of the text of the bills before them than of seemingly obscure committee reports upon which few will judge them. Presumably, given their considerable workload, even committee members may be more likely to give attention to pending bills than to committee reports. Parts of committee reports may be examined in relation to aspects of the proposed legislation. Where the committee report does not specifically deal with the legislation, its pronouncements may go largely unnoticed in Congress as a whole, though its ramifications may be all-important. Such was the case with section 504, at least for a number of years after its passage.

A sympathetic bureaucracy can foster committee plans. The committee staffs recognized that if section 504 were to be vigorously enforced, the cooperation of the bureaucracy would be most helpful. They found the Office for Civil Rights of the Department of Health, Education, and Welfare to be more than a willing partner. Having had experience in civil rights regulation, the OCR was eager to become involved in the section 504 effort.

It is striking that in this account of legislative definition groups representing the disabled play such a negligible role. Although individuals were involved, for the most part organizational activity began *after* the passage of legislation, particularly section 504. Indeed, the American Coalition for Citizens with Disabilities, for one, did not come into being until 1974; another group, Disabled in Action, was born in 1972. The rights orientation of section 504 provided the impetus for the creation of new groups and the building of a coalition among diverse interests. But the role of these organizations was limited essentially to protecting gains already se-

Melnick, "The Politics of Partnership," *Public Administration Review,* vol. 45 (November 1985), pp. 653–60.

cured, and generally they turned to the courts for reinforcement. A district court bolstered the work of the congressional committees and of the OCR when it mandated the promulgation of regulations. The committee report of 1974, which engaged in dubious retrospective legislative history, provided litigants with a powerful anchor, as will be shown in chapter 4. Indeed, the report was written with an eye toward the judiciary, on the assumption that someday the courts might be called upon to resolve disputes about the statute's meaning. The court based its opinion in part upon that historical account and thus sanctified the report's assertion that regulations were intended.

The section 504 effort proceeded without congressional opposition up to the late 1970s in part because those who were to bear the costs of enforcement did not seek relief until then. This is not surprising, because it was not clear which institutions would be affected and in what manner until the regulatory effort was well under way. The regulatory program that section 504 spawned followed a tortuous path. President Gerald Ford signed an executive order vesting HEW with authority to coordinate government-wide activity. Next, HEW issued regulations covering its own programs; then it set forth guidelines that other departments and agencies were to follow. And then those departments and agencies promulgated regulations pursuant to the guidelines. It was not until 1978—five years after the passage of the Rehabilitation Act—that the Department of Transportation and the transit industry, for example, became involved in the section 504 regulatory maze. Until that time, they were largely unaware of the effects of the legislation on their operations. The transit industry then turned for assistance, not to the rights-oriented committees that championed section 504, but to transit-oriented committees.

In assessing the story of section 504, it is tempting to view it simply as illustrative of the wide discretion sometimes enjoyed by congressional staffs and bureaucracies. To be sure, the way in which the regulatory program developed may lessen the confidence of those who believe in an open congressional process. But if Congress were dissatisfied, it could have intervened. HEW Secretary Mathews asked for guidance but received none. A combination of congressional support for section 504, the perceived costs of opposing the disability lobby and the key congressional committee leaders, and indifference may have contributed to that apparent unwillingness to respond to the secretary's request. In the 1978 amendments, Congress passed legislation that furthered the section 504 effort by extending coverage to the federal agencies and providing for attorneys' fees. In view of all this, those in the disabled community who maintain that Congress supported the section 504 program can make a credible claim.

In a larger sense, this account raises doubts about the congressional role. In the view of some, Congress aggregates and reconciles narrow group or individual interests; for others, it is engaged in a process of deliberation and discussion, and it fashions programs consistent with those decisions.[151] By either standard, Congress did not fare well. It did not pursue much of the key legislative activity in a deliberative way. Nor did it devise effective means to make trade-offs between the equal accessibility and effective mobility approaches. Congress could not forge a coherent policy, in part because each chamber lacked some workable mechanism to coordinate the work of its committees. In the typical case, Congress is best prepared to make policy in conjunction with the presidency when the executive takes the lead in initiating legislation—especially if the subject matter is complex. Unlike the executive, Congress, by reason of its organization, structures, and resources, is generally not equipped to perform the functions of leadership and integration. Those "missing capabilities" tend to hinder coherent, comprehensive policymaking.[152] Moreover, the role of the committee staffs raises doubts about committee control of the legislative process. The failure of Congress to respond to executive requests for clarification of the meaning of section 504 raises questions about the responsiveness of one branch to the other and the responsibility of each in the federal system. These concerns will be addressed later.

151. Arthur Maass, *Congress and the Common Good* (Basic Books, 1983), pp. 3–5.
152. Sundquist, *Decline and Resurgence of Congress,* pp. 417–39. On executive capacity, see Paul C. Light, *The President's Agenda* (Johns Hopkins University Press, 1982).

CHAPTER THREE

The Administrative Process

THE congressional failure to set a coherent policy course, to choose between the effective mobility and full accessibility approaches, doubtless exacerbated the difficulties for the administrative process charged with implementing the legislative will. But that does not explain why or how the administrative process chose particular policy responses.

In fact, within a period of only a few years, the Department of Transportation changed policy three times, wavering between the two sharply differing concepts. Defined in terms of the effective mobility approach, the DOT's task would be to assure transportation for the disabled by any cost-effective means that would bring them to their destination. The matter could be addressed through separate paratransit services and such demand-responsive systems as dial-a-ride taxis. The full accessibility approach is premised on the view that the disabled should be able to use the same facilities—buses, subways, railroads—as the rest of the population. Programmatically, it would entail such steps as the retrofitting of inaccessible subways, the installation of ramps and wheelchair lifts on buses, and the development of new technologies. The rights-oriented full accessibility regulations sparked much controversy and opposition from the forceful transit community; indeed, that the DOT would have adopted such a course is surprising, given those strenuous objections from its transit constituency. Nor would one have expected the department to shift policy so quickly; bureaucracies are thought to be slow to change direction, supported as they are by experts whose professional norms give consistency and predictability to their actions.

What follows will seek to explain the reasons for the sharp twists and turns of policy responses, the back-and-forth change from effective mobility, to full accessibility, and then once more to effective mobility. Consideration of the administrative process raises several issues: the factors affecting decisionmaking; more specifically, the impact of rulemaking on outcomes; and presidential control of policymaking. This study also lends itself to an examination of the problems administrators face in trying to mandate technological change.

First, with respect to the factors affecting decisionmaking, a variety of explanations are possible. The leadership of the particular bureaucracy might have an important effect. From this perspective, much would depend upon the ability of executives or other agency officials to institutionalize a distinctive competence and infuse it with value, or to develop purposes, provide a system of communication, and use incentives to secure the essential contribution of effort and resources.[1] Another view maintains that a key determinant is the character of the bureaucracy itself. That is, organizational dynamics—such as standard operating procedures—driven by their own internal logic, largely govern outcomes.[2] Decisions and policies are also fundamentally affected by the agency's mission—a "distinctive and valued set of behaviors," a shared feeling among organization personnel about the nature, feasibility, and importance of the organization's tasks.[3] To develop this feeling of mission, bureaucracies must cultivate an organizational ethos, an attitude about the value of the tasks and the work of the organization. It is that mission and ethos which help shape outcomes. Still another but related perspective is that the personnel within an agency, guided by their personal and career objectives, behave in ways that further those aspirations. To the extent that a profession is dominant within an agency, its norms, values, and conceptual approach will shape how problems are defined and addressed. In some circumstances, outcomes may be the product of conflict between different professions with clashing perspectives.[4]

Another explanation stresses that the power structure of an organization can determine outcomes. Policy results from bargaining; and the ability of an actor to affect decisions depends on such factors as formal position in

1. Philip Selznick, *Leadership in Administration* (Harper and Row, 1957), pp. 17, 42–56; Chester I. Barnard, *The Functions of the Executive* (Harvard University Press, 1956), pp. 72, 215–34; and Francis E. Rourke, *Bureaucracy, Politics, and Public Policy,* 2d ed. (Little, Brown, 1976).

2. See, for example, Richard M. Cyert and James G. March, *A Behavioral Theory of the Firm* (Prentice-Hall, 1963); and James G. March and Herbert A. Simon, *Organizations* (Wiley, 1958).

3. James Q. Wilson, *The Investigators: Managing FBI and Narcotics Agents* (Basic Books, 1978), p. 14; and Selznick, *Leadership in Administration,* pp. 17, 52–56.

4. See Robert A. Katzmann, *Regulatory Bureaucracy: The Federal Trade Commission and Antitrust Policy* (MIT Press, 1981).

the hierarchy, role in upper-level policymaking, access to information necessary to identify options, control over resources required to implement decisions, and personal capacity to persuade others.[5] A premium is placed on entrepreneurial skills.

Yet another view focuses on external factors and constraints as determinants of bureaucratic outcomes. Thought central to understanding administrative action are such forces as courts, legislatures, interest groups, and other bureaucracies, particularly those charged either with coordinating the activities of government agencies or enforcing cross-cutting requirements.[6]

My discussion of the administrative process will show that no single approach can explain the administrative course over time, that its twists and turns are the product of the interplay of various factors, and that the primacy of one or another may depend on particular circumstances and shifting constraints.[7] To advance this view, this chapter examines the factors affecting the decisions of the DOT, the bureaucracy charged with devising regulations providing for the mobility needs of disabled persons.

Second, consideration of the administrative dimension can further understanding of rulemaking, the process by which the DOT formulated and then promulgated policy.[8] The Administrative Procedure Act, which

5. Graham T. Allison, *Essence of Decision: Explaining the Cuban Missile Crisis* (Little, Brown, 1971); and Richard E. Neustadt, *Presidential Power: The Politics of Leadership from FDR to Carter* (Wiley, 1980).

6. Donald L. Horowitz, *The Courts and Social Policy* (Brookings, 1977); Morris P. Fiorina, *Congress—Keystone of the Washington Establishment* (Yale University Press, 1977); Richard A. Posner, "Theories of Economic Regulation," *Bell Journal of Economics and Management Science,* vol. 5 (Autumn 1974), p. 353; George Stigler, "The Theory of Economic Regulation," *Bell Journal of Economics and Management Science,* vol. 2 (Spring 1971), p. 3; Christopher C. DeMuth, "A Strong Beginning on Reform," *Regulation,* vol. 6 (January–February 1982), pp. 15–18; Harold Seidman and Robert Gilmour, *Politics, Position and Power,* 4th ed. (Oxford University Press, 1986), pp. 219–45; and Report of the Advisory Commission on Intergovernmental Relations, *Regulatory Federalism: Policy, Process, Impact and Reform* (ACIR, 1984), pp. 7–10.

7. See Robert A. Katzmann, "Judicial Intervention and Organization Theory: Changing Bureaucratic Behavior and Policy," Note, 89 *Yale Law Journal* 513–37 (1980). My perspective obviously owes much to the work of James Q. Wilson.

8. On rulemaking, see A. Lee Fritschler, *Smoking and Politics: Policymaking and the Federal Bureaucracy,* 3d ed. (Prentice-Hall, 1983); Robert A. Kagan, *Regulatory Justice: Implementing a Wage-Price Freeze* (Russell Sage Foundation, 1978); John E. Chubb, *Interest Groups and the Bureaucracy: The Politics of Energy* (Stanford University Press, 1983), pp. 137–47; and Lawrence D. Brown and Bernard J. Frieden, "Rulemaking by Improvisation: Guidelines and Goals in the Model Cities Program," *Policy Sciences,* vol. 7 (December 1976), pp. 455–88.

Detailed accounts of the administrative process include R. Shep Melnick, *Regulation*

established the basic framework of administrative law governing agency action, recognized that bureaucracies differ and that different procedures should be applied consistent with the nature of the problem at hand.[9] Thus it provided for a variety of proceedings, commonly known as formal adjudication, formal rulemaking, informal rulemaking, and informal adjudication. DOT regulations were issued pursuant to procedures for informal or "notice and comment" rulemaking. This form requires publication of a notice of proposed rulemaking (essentially a draft), opportunity for public participation through the submission of written comments, and publication of a final rule and accompanying statement of authority and purpose not less than thirty days before its effective date. These requirements were the procedural minimum, below which an agency could not descend; later, courts imposed other procedures that went beyond the requirements of the act, ostensibly in an effort to guarantee fairness and rationality.[10]

---

and the Courts: The Case of the Clean Air Act (Brookings, 1983); Martha M. Shapiro, *The Supreme Court and Administrative Agencies* (Free Press, 1968); and Jerry Mashaw, *Bureaucratic Justice: Managing Social Security Disability* (Yale University Press, 1984). On administrative law and decisionmaking theory, see Colin S. Diver, "Policymaking Paradigms in Administrative Law," 95 *Harvard Law Review* 393 (1981); Robert Rabin, *Perspectives on the Administrative Process* (Little, Brown, 1979); and Peter H. Schuck, "Organization Theory and the Teaching of Administrative Law," 33 *Journal of Legal Education* 13 (1983).

9. 5 U.S.C., secs. 501–706 (1976 and Supp. V1981). The Attorney General's Committee on Administrative Procedure had called for such flexibility. See Attorney General's Committee on Administrative Procedure, *Final Report on Administrative Procedure in Government Agencies*, S. Doc. 77-8, 77 Cong. 1 sess. (Government Printing Office, 1941). For a historical review of the Administrative Procedure Act, see Paul R. Verkuil, "The Emerging Concept of Administrative Procedure," 78 *Columbia Law Review* 258, 261–79 (1978).

10. On the judiciary and rulemaking, see J. Skelly Wright, "The Courts and the Rulemaking Process: The Limits of Judicial Review," 59 *Cornell Law Review* 374 (1974); Stephen Breyer, "Vermont Yankee and the Courts' Role in the Nuclear Energy Controversy," 91 *Harvard Law Review* 1833 (1978); Richard B. Stewart, "Vermont Yankee and the Evolution of Administrative Procedure," 91 *Harvard Law Review* 1805 (1978); Antonin Scalia, "Vermont Yankee: The APA, the D.C. Circuit and the Supreme Court," *Supreme Court Review* 345 (1978); and Paul R. Verkuil, "Judicial Review of Informal Rulemaking," 60 *Virginia Law Review* 185 (1974).

On informal rulemaking, see James DeLong, "Informal Rulemaking and the Integration of Law and Policy," 65 *Virginia Law Review* 257 (1979); Carl Auerbach, "Informal Rule Making: A Proposed Relationship Between Administrative Procedures and Judicial Review," 72 *Northwestern University Law Review* 15 (1977); William F. Pedersen, Jr., "Formal Records and Informal Rulemaking," 85 *Yale Law Journal* 38 (1975); and Administrative Conference of the United States, "Procedures in Addition to Notice and the Opportunity for Comment in Informal Rulemaking (Recommendation No. 76-3)," I.C.F.R. sec. 305.76-3 (1978).

On rulemaking generally, see David Shapiro, "The Choice of Rulemaking or Adjudication in the Development of Administrative Policy," 78 *Harvard Law Review* 921 (1965); and Glen O. Robinson, "The Making of Administrative Policy: Another Look at Rulemaking

For present purposes, an effort will be made to understand the effect of these rulemaking processes on policy—procedures that were used for both the effective mobility and full accessibility approaches. On the surface, at least, one might expect the process to facilitate rational and informed decisions for at least three reasons—because of the way information is collected, the nature of the participants, and the professional virtues of those vested with decisionmaking authority. That is, data would be secured from a variety of sources through the notice and comment procedures; all interested parties would have a chance to participate; and those charged with reaching judgments based on a review of the information would be technically skilled experts. Whether this vision reflects reality will also be examined.

Third, examination of the administrative process raises still another issue, that of presidential control over agency behavior.[11] Although the DOT was a primary actor in developing the transportation regulations, the Department of Health, Education, and Welfare claimed a role in accord with its responsibilities for coordinating the section 504 effort. Units within the White House also sought to affect DOT actions. All this brings to the fore questions about the role of the president in setting policy, his impact on the departments under his formal authority, and the relationship between the departments themselves.

Finally, this study also allows an exploration of the role of administrators as technology forcers. The DOT believed that it could ultimately resolve the problem of providing integrated, accessible transit by mandating the design of a bus that would accommodate both handicapped and non-handicapped riders. The outcome illustrates the consequences of frequent changes in government policies and the reluctance of industry to alter its behavior, especially in an uncertain environment.

The Historical Context

It was not until the 1950s that the executive branch of the federal government began to pay any attention to the problem of making buildings accessible to the disabled. Not surprisingly, therefore, the effort to provide

and Adjudication and Administrative Procedure Reform," 118 *University of Pennsylvania Law Review* 485 (1975).

11. See Richard P. Nathan, *The Administrative Presidency* (Wiley, 1984); Harold Bruff, "Presidential Power and Administrative Rulemaking," 88 *Yale Law Journal* 451 (1979); and "Symposium: Presidential Intervention in Administrative Rulemaking," 56 *Tulane Law Review* 811 (1982).

barrier-free transportation did not engage decisionmakers until about a decade later.[12] To understand that involvement, it is useful to review briefly earlier administrative attempts to address the problem of architectural barriers before describing the first halting efforts to deal with transportation.

The Focus on Buildings

An event filled with both irony and poignance triggered the federal effort to address the mobility problems of the handicapped. The date was May 23, 1957, the place was the auditorium of the Department of Labor in Washington, D.C., and the occasion was the presentation of the "Handicapped American of the Year" award by the President's Committee on Employment of the Handicapped.[13] Created soon after World War II, from which 1,800 Americans returned as paraplegics, the president's committee has sought public support for a sustained program to encourage the hiring of physically handicapped workers. Operating under the aegis of the Department of Labor, the committee consists of both public and private members and works closely with governmental agencies, disability groups, professional organizations, state bodies, unions, and industry.[14] In recognition of outstanding achievement, the president's committee annually singles out one individual for special commendation.

In 1957 that award went to Hugo Deffner of Oklahoma City because of his work to make his community aware of the daily difficulties of the wheelchair-bound. In presenting the honor, President Dwight D. Eisenhower remarked: "He [Deffner] has . . . tried to make every building in the United States accessible to one who possibly cannot climb stairs. I hope that he is having every success in that effort."[15] The meeting between

12. To be sure, there were some programs with transportation components that dated back to the 1940s, such as the 1944 amendment to the Social Security Act, providing transportation assistance to the elderly, blind, and disabled. But they were of little impact and did not involve making transit systems or vehicles accessible.

13. *Accessibility of Public Buildings to the Physically Handicapped,* Hearing before the Subcommittee on Public Buildings and Grounds of the Senate Committee on Public Works, 90 Cong. 1 sess. (GPO, 1967), p. 8. (Hereafter *Accessibility Hearings.*)

14. The notion of drawing upon the advice of those outside the government was at first an afterthought. In a letter to Secretary of Labor Lewis B. Schwellenbach, authorizing a "National Employ the Physically Handicapped Week," President Truman penned the following postscript: "You may want to call upon officials and leading citizens outside the Federal Government for all possible assistance in this program." Letter from President Harry S. Truman to Secretary of Labor Lewis B. Schwellenbach, August 27, 1947. As a consequence, the President's Committee on Employment of the Handicapped was established.

15. Quoted in *Accessibility Hearings,* p. 8.

honoree and chief executive was very nearly ill fated, for moments before, Deffner was sitting in his wheelchair on the sidewalk, unable to enter the inaccessible Departmental Auditorium. Two Marines had to lift him bodily up the steps so that he could make his way into the building and receive the award. Harold Russell, chairman of the President's Committee on Employment of the Handicapped, recounted that this episode so disturbed the committee that its Advisory Council considered the problem of architectural barriers in a White House meeting later that year.[16]

The Advisory Council of the president's committee concluded that physical barriers posed an architectural problem and that professional experts should be approached to aid in its resolution.[17] Thus in May 1959 the committee approached the American Standards Association (now known as the American National Standards Institute), a nonprofit corporation and federation of some 1,000 company members and 180 national organizations, to coordinate the development of voluntary standards of building design.[18] The final product, issued in 1961, was devised through a consensus process and was intended to cover only public buildings, but did not include mass transportation systems.[19]

Throughout the 1960s, the president's committee, the Vocational Rehabilitation Administration, and such organizations as the Easter Seal Society, the Paralyzed Veterans of America, the Disabled American Veterans, the American Institute of Architects, the AFL-CIO, the National Associa-

16. Subsequently, an ad hoc group was created, consisting of representatives from the Vocational Rehabilitation Administration, the Department of Labor, and the administrator of Veterans Affairs. It secured the cooperation of the Veterans Administration, which drafted a guide covering facilities needed by the ambulatory handicapped for entrance to and basic accommodations within public buildings. The Department of Labor distributed the guide to state employment security agencies.

17. This account draws heavily on interviews with Bernard Posner and Edmund Leonard, executive director and program director, respectively, of the President's Committee on Employment of the Handicapped, December 8, 1981.

18. As a result of a conference called by the American Standards Association, the president's committee and the National Society for Crippled Children and Adults sponsored a project (financed by the society and a small grant from the Office of Vocational Rehabilitation) to establish minimum criteria to be used by architects, designers, and engineers in building public facilities. To do the work, the American Standards Association created a special sectional committee, represented by seventy-five professional and trade associations, societies, and federal government agencies.

19. ANSI A 11711 (1961). In 1980 the American National Standards Institute approved a revised standard, ANSI A 117.1-1980; see "How and Why the 1980 ANSI Standard for Accessibility Was Developed" (National Easter Seal Society, April 1980). While the ANSI standards are not binding upon governmental agencies or the private sector, the former does apply them.

tion of the Physically Handicapped, the Associated General Contractors, and the National Rehabilitation Association spearheaded efforts exhorting federal agencies and state governments to adopt the ANSI standards. By 1968 more than thirty-one states had passed architectural barriers acts that quoted the ANSI standard in total or in part or used it to set forth additional or substitute provisions; today every state has such a law.

Parallel to, but independent of, these activities at the state level was the increasing involvement of the Vocational Rehabilitation Administration. Its director, Mary Switzer, and her assistant, Kathaleen Arneson, concluded that if the federal government were to play an active role in encouraging a barrier-free environment, then it should study the problem comprehensively.[20] To that end, the Vocational Rehabilitation Administration drafted legislation, as part of President Lyndon B. Johnson's 1965 program, to establish a "National Commission on Architectural Barriers to Rehabilitation of the Handicapped." The measure received widespread support and became part of the Vocational Rehabilitation Act Amendments of 1965, major legislation that changed the vocational rehabilitation program. The national commission was established within the Department of Health, Education, and Welfare and was charged with assessing the extent of the problem, defining the role of public and other nonprofit agencies, and preparing "plans and proposals . . . to achieve the goal of ready access to and full use of facilities in buildings of all types by the handicapped."[21]

The commission report, issued in May 1968, made several recommendations designed to ensure that new buildings constructed with federal support would be accessible to the handicapped. It urged the passage of legislation, including a measure that would vest HEW with the authority to establish and enforce governmentwide policies to achieve at least minimum standards of accessibility in public buildings. Significantly, the commission found that the lack of usable transportation "is the most serious problem encountered by the aged and handicapped," noting that there were

20. Interview with Kathaleen Arneson, November 5, 1981.
21. 79 Stat. 1282, 1289. The HEW secretary or his designee was to chair the group and to appoint representatives of the general public and of private and professional organizations able to contribute to the solution of architectural barriers. HEW Secretary John W. Gardner appointed Leon Chatelain, Jr., an architect, as chairman. Chatelain headed the American Standards Association group, whose work led to the 1961 ANSI specifications. Kathaleen Arneson served as the commission's executive director. The commission held nine two-day hearings across the country, met with experts, contracted with the National League of Cities for a survey of state and local programs and with the American Institute of Architects for a study of the attitude of architects, and arranged for a national public opinion poll.

"no federal, state, or local requirements for accessible public transit." But the commission made no recommendations pertaining to transportation because it was not asked to do so.[22]

The report itself was released after the Senate had enacted the Bartlett-sponsored architectural barriers legislation (see chapter 2). But the commission staff did cooperate with the Senate Public Works Committee, and its chairman, architect Leon Chatelain, Jr., testified at the hearings. Perhaps the most important effect of the report was that it educated bureaucrats about the problem of architectural barriers and catalogued the efforts made by various departments to deal with those obstacles.

The First Halting Steps toward Accessible Transit

The problem of overcoming architectural barriers was not on the agenda of most agencies; it is not surprising, therefore, that the matter of accessible transportation was of even lesser importance. To the extent that interest existed in providing transportation, it was scattered across a few agencies and, throughout the 1960s, went little beyond discussion and the commissioning of studies. How then did providing mass transportation for disabled people become the object of government concern, particularly by the Department of Transportation? The answer is relatively simple. Whatever the DOT did in the late 1960s and early 1970s was due to political executives who were interested in the problem and to policy generalists who had a broad view of the department's mission. In that period, those government officials did not define the problem precisely, nor did they frame it in terms of either effective mobility or full accessibility. They merely recognized that a problem existed and deserved further attention.

The limited nature of those early efforts can perhaps best be explained by understanding the DOT's immediate priority: improving the transit infrastructure throughout the nation. That mission guided department professionals: planners, engineers, and analysts. For them, the problems of mobility were best dealt with by such social services agencies as the Rehabilitation Services Administration of the Social and Rehabilitation Service of HEW, which provided the staff for the national commission. However, in 1968 the Office of Economics and Systems Analysis of the DOT did commission an Abt Associates study examining the transportation

22. *National Commission on Architectural Barriers to Rehabilitation of the Handicapped,* H. Doc. 90-324, 90 Cong. 2 sess. (GPO, 1968), pp. 12, 13.

needs of the handicapped.[23] Apart from determining that travel barriers existed, the report was not a blueprint for action and had no programmatic consequences. Another study in that year dealing with ways to make non-rail transit accessible emanated from the Department of Housing and Urban Development, which until 1968 shared mass transit responsibilities with the DOT.[24]

The DOT took some halting steps at the direction of Secretary John Volpe, a moderate Republican governor from Massachusetts, who was appointed by Richard Nixon following the 1968 election. Not long after assuming office, he met with representatives of such groups as the Easter Seal Society. The President's Committee on Employment of the Handicapped, the Social and Rehabilitation Service of HEW, and Mrs. Erwin Griswold (the wife of the solicitor general and a person long interested in the problems of disability) encouraged the department's involvement. Volpe, a builder by profession, was sympathetic to the view that the needs of the physically disabled should be taken into account in planning and designing transit systems. He directed the Office of the Assistant Secretary for Environment and Urban Systems to look into the matter. It was that office, consisting of political appointees and broad-ranged bureaucrats, that came to maintain the greatest interest in the problems of the disabled. Staff members Ira Laster and Martin Convisser, who were actively involved in the issue throughout the 1970s, looked into it and determined that the DOT should do more. Both men had wide experience beyond transportation.[25] Convisser entered the federal civil service in 1956 and worked in the Department of Defense and the Bureau of the Budget before joining the Office of the Secretary of Transportation as deputy director of the Office of Planning and Program Review in 1967. Laster had been employed by social service agencies before coming to the DOT.

Congress bolstered their efforts when it enacted the Biaggi amendment, declaring that elderly and handicapped persons have the same right to use transit systems as other persons. To be sure, many in the department felt that the amendment was little more than an expression of sentiment whose spirit could be satisfied simply by studying the problem. But the legislation

23. Abt Associates, *Transportation Needs of the Handicapped* (Cambridge, Mass.: Abt Associates, 1969).

24. Under the terms of a presidential reorganization plan, HUD's mass transit duties were transferred in 1968 to the Department of Transportation and lodged in the Urban Mass Transportation Administration. 33 Fed. Reg. 6965 (1968).

25. Interviews with Martin Convisser, December 8, 1982, and Ira Laster, October 20, 1981.

did spur those in the Office of Environment and Urban Systems who wanted the department to take a more active role. A series of meetings coordinated by the office was held in 1971 and 1972, bringing together representatives of the various divisions within the DOT. Ultimately, these sessions were short on results because the Office of Environment and Urban Systems could not induce the operating bureaus to do very much.

The Urban Mass Transportation Administration (UMTA)—that part of DOT charged with devising and operating a wide range of transit programs, and staffed by transit planners, engineers, and analysts—believed that the problems of the handicapped were essentially a social service concern. Reinforcing the professional inclinations of the transit planners were the transit manufacturers and state and local transit agencies—all of which wanted more money and technical support for their allegedly underfunded and sometimes decaying systems. Illustrative of UMTA's lack of enthusiasm for activities to aid handicapped persons was UMTA administrator Carlos Villareal's opposition to demonstration grants for an inclinator, a device which its proponents argued could make subway transportation accessible to the disabled.

To be sure, there would always be a handful of people in UMTA who believed that more should be done for the elderly and the handicapped and pressed the agency to allocate resources to research and development.[26] Pointing to the Biaggi amendment as evidence of the public's growing concern with the problems of the elderly and the handicapped, UMTA's project manager, Patricia Cass, secured funding in 1972 to study the urban mass transit market for the transportation disadvantaged.[27] For the most part, however, the character of the interaction between UMTA and the program-planning offices in the DOT became familiar and predictable, with the latter pressing for increased efforts to provide transportation for elderly and handicapped persons and the former resisting such entreaties.

Although UMTA was reluctant to devote much attention specifically to the problems of the handicapped and elderly, a by-product of some of its efforts was beneficial to the transportation disadvantaged. For example, in the early 1970s, in an attempt to increase bus ridership, UMTA began a major program to encourage the design of a new generation of low-floor

26. Interviews with UMTA analysts Douglas Gurin and Patricia Simpich, February 17 and March 18, 1982, and Patricia Cass, March 18, 1982.

27. U.S. Department of Transportation, Urban Transportation Advisory Commission, *The Handicapped and Elderly Market for Urban Mass Transit,* prepared by UMTA and Transportation Systems Center (1973).

vehicles, which would also have been accessible to disabled people. Moreover, shortly after passage of the Biaggi amendment, UMTA issued guidelines to applicants for capital grants stating in part that they must make "every reasonable effort" to ensure that the elderly and the handicapped could use mass transportation effectively.[28] Project proposals were to describe any plans to aid these groups, the costs of special equipment or facilities, and probable ridership. These instructions did not require that any specific steps be taken or provide any criteria by which "reasonable efforts" would be judged. Grantees, as a consequence, did not have a clear sense of what was expected of them.[29] For its part, UMTA tended to pay little attention to its own instructions about the elderly and the handicapped, and applicants were not concerned that their grants were contingent upon doing more for the transportation disadvantaged. One UMTA official commented, "Admittedly, we did as little as possible, always emphasizing that we were studying the matter. Once you start to do something, there are always those who complain that you're not doing enough. Sometimes it's easier to do less rather than more, to deny having responsibility."

Round One: Effective Mobility Regulations

In order to deflect external threats, government agencies can be induced to pursue actions not dictated by their preferred agenda. Agency officials are ever mindful of Congress, particularly those committees, legislators, and staffs upon whom they depend for funding and legislative support—and of the need to satisfy their expectations.[30] Similarly, they are cognizant of litigation designed to compel them to pursue particular courses of action. Thus, in an effort to prevent legislatures or courts from imposing policies that it deems unacceptable, an agency might take anticipatory steps in the hope of satisfying those external forces. As a consequence of that exercise, an organization determines its position: in this case, the result was a set of regulations issued by UMTA in 1976 that embodied the effective mobility approach to transportation for disabled people.

28. UMTA, "Application Instructions for Capital Grant Projects," May 10, 1974, app. 3.
29. General Accounting Office, *Mass Transit* (GAO, 1977), p. 29.
30. Herbert Kaufman, *The Administrative Behavior of Federal Bureau Chiefs* (Brookings, 1981), pp. 47–57.

The DOT Begins to Act

As the early 1970s went by, some of the attorneys and policy planners who observed the congressional scene realized that the DOT and UMTA would have to assume a more active role in providing assistance to handicapped persons.[31] Congress enacted a series of transportation measures, such as the Federal-Aid Highway Act of 1973 and the 1974 amendments to that act, that reaffirmed the Biaggi amendment's intent to make transportation available to the elderly and the handicapped. More generally, the legislature passed section 504 of the Rehabilitation Act of 1973 prohibiting discrimination against handicapped persons in any program receiving federal aid or assistance. By themselves, the statutes did not appear to require immediate action. The haphazard way in which the measures were enacted, and the fact that they were not the product of much deliberation and were not high priorities of the committees to which the DOT reported, suggested that little was called for in response. But when disability groups, basing their actions on the various pieces of legislation, brought legal suits to compel UMTA to provide accessible transit, DOT officials recognized that something had to be done.

Both those who were sympathetic to the concerns of the disabled, and others who sought to avoid a legislatively or judicially enforced solution, determined that the DOT should take some initiative. Bruce Barkley, director of program development in UMTA, drafted a memorandum urging that steps be taken.[32] The center of attention soon shifted to the UMTA legal staff. Chief Counsel Sallyanne Payton assumed responsibility for devising policy. A former White House staffer, Payton was reportedly on Richard Nixon's "court track." John Ehrlichman, for whom she worked, recounted that Nixon proposed that she be moved to a lawyer's job in one of the agencies until he could appoint her to a Court of Appeals vacancy. The chief counsel's position at UMTA was thus to be a stepping-stone to a judicial career.[33] By reason of her intellect and force of personality, Payton established the confidence of UMTA administrator Frank Herringer.

31. Interview with Bruce Barkley, former director of program development, UMTA, December 3, 1981.

32. *Rehabilitation of the Handicapped Programs, 1976,* Hearings before the Subcommittee on the Handicapped of the Senate Committee on Labor and Public Welfare, 94 Cong. 2 sess. (GPO, 1976), pt. 1, pp. 617–19.

33. John Ehrlichman, *Witness to Power: The Nixon Years* (Simon and Schuster, 1968), p. 239. In fact, after serving with distinction at UMTA, Payton resigned in 1976 to become a professor of law at the University of Michigan.

That the legal staff should direct efforts leading to a transportation policy for the handicapped and the elderly might seem surprising. After all, the matter is one involving complex technical questions that might seem more appropriately the bailiwick of experts. But the legal staff's dominance becomes more understandable once one appreciates that the purpose of the enterprise was not simply to devise a substantive response that addressed the needs of handicapped persons. Just as important an objective (if not more so) was to craft a policy that would immunize UMTA from lawsuits brought by affected groups. Indeed, in a memorandum to an UMTA official that led some disability organizations to question the depth of her commitment, Payton stated that the "regulations were developed for litigation and political reasons, and say what they must in order to satisfy those concerns."[34] Contributing to the relative ease with which Payton proceeded was the reluctance of the transit specialists to become involved in areas they thought should be the concern of social service agencies, rather than the DOT. In sum, the need to satisfy legal standards, combined with the transit planners' relative lack of interest, provided the lawyers with an opportunity to play the role of policy entrepreneur.

Having assumed the lead, Payton had to determine how best to proceed. For example, UMTA could have issued guidelines for state and local agencies. But in the end, Payton decided that the most sensible course was through regulations. UMTA was entering virgin territory and the regulatory process seemed to offer special advantages. Structured in accordance with the spirit of the Administrative Procedure Act, the rulemaking process offered an orderly way to make decisions. UMTA would issue an advanced notice of proposed rulemaking—essentially a rough draft of regulations. Then, after having received comments from the public, UMTA would set forth a notice of proposed rulemaking, presumably a more sophisticated version of the regulations. Following another round of public hearings and written comments, the agency would then publish final regulations. The rulemaking process thus appeared to be the very model of rationality: information would be secured, tentative judgments would be reached, a wide range of parties would be consulted, and refinements would be made, leading to a final decision. Apart from the hope that the process would produce informed substantive policy, it seemed well suited to insulate the agency from legal attack. The judicial standards were clear; as long as UMTA did

34. *Urban Mass Transportation—1975*, Hearings before the Subcommittee on Housing and Urban Affairs of the Senate Committee on Banking, Housing, and Urban Affairs, 94 Cong. 1 sess. (GPO, 1975), p. 52.

not proceed in an "arbitrary or capricious" way, the judiciary presumably would sustain the agency's judgments regardless of its views about the merits of the policy itself.

Having selected the rulemaking route, UMTA soon formally bound itself to issuing regulations. Disabled in Action of Baltimore, a disability group, filed a class action suit in federal court against a number of parties, including the secretary of the Department of Transportation, seeking to enjoin the purchase of 205 buses that were allegedly inaccessible to the plaintiffs. As part of the out-of-court settlement, the DOT agreed to "propose rules and regulations within one (1) year governing the planning and design of mass transportation facilities and services to assure the availability to elderly and handicapped persons of mass transportation which they can effectively utilize."[35] Payton recounted that the settlement was useful for bureaucratic reasons; she could tell her UMTA colleagues who were reluctant to become involved in handicapped policy that her hands were tied, that legally she had no choice but to comply with the terms of the agreement. With the chief counsel at the center, a task force was created drawing upon staff in UMTA's offices of transit assistance, research, planning, and policy.

The Legislative Basis

Typically, legislation is the basis of a rulemaking proceeding; an agency seeks guidance from specific statutes so that its regulations are consistent with congressional intent. UMTA based its rulemaking efforts primarily upon section 16(a) of the Urban Mass Transportation Act of 1964 as amended (the Biaggi amendment), which stated that elderly and handicapped persons have the same right as other persons to utilize mass transit and further directed that "special efforts" be made in the planning and design of services and facilities to ensure that those groups can effectively use them. Another legislative prong was section 165(b) of the Federal-Aid Highway Act of 1973, as amended, which extended the mandate of section 16 to mass transportation projects funded under the federal aid highway program. The third statute was section 504 of the Rehabilitation Act of 1973, banning discrimination against persons because of their handicap in any program receiving federal aid or assistance. Of all of these, the trans-

35. Memorandum of Understanding, *Disabled in Action of Baltimore* v. *Hughes,* Civil Action No. HM-74-1069 (October 30, 1974). In exchange for the agreements reached, the plaintiffs sought voluntary dismissal of their suit.

portation legislation—the Biaggi amendment and its logical extension, section 165(b) of the Federal-Aid Highway Act of 1973—were the primary support for the rulemaking effort. In 1974, when the process began, section 504 had been on the books for only a year and seemed little more than a nondiscrimination measure.

Establishing the legislative authority is but a first step. Of obvious importance is ascertaining the meaning of the statutes so that the regulations will be consonant with their intent. The Biaggi amendment was imprecise and thus raised questions for the UMTA staff. Because the Biaggi amendment used the term "right," did that signify that it meant to confer a legal right? The measure directed that "special efforts" be taken, but the amount of activity that would be required was not specified.

Payton determined that the regulation should be crafted in the context of UMTA's total mission—providing mass transit. The regulations were to take into account real situations and to be sensitive to differences among communities across the nation. As a matter of law, they were to be devised so that a federal court would uphold them.

The Rulemaking Process

Guided by these purposes, the UMTA task force set about its work, which would culminate nearly two years later in the issuance of final rules.[36] The staff quickly determined that it had scant information about those who would be affected by its actions—the elderly and the handicapped, operators of mass transportation systems, and manufacturers of mass transit equipment. Payton decided to devise a rough proposal and then to hold a series of meetings with those groups to discern their perspectives. UMTA's program office provided much of the technical assistance. Because UMTA did not have any experience in rulemaking in this area, it looked to proceedings in other regulatory matters to determine what could be gleaned in fashioning the structure and substance of the proposed draft rule. Reviewing a draft, UMTA administrator Herringer sought to ensure that the regulations would not constrain the agency's latitude. He expressed concern that language approving full accessibility could lock the agency "into a position that may be politically inevitable, but may not make any sense from a transportation effectiveness or cost benefit standpoint. At some future date it may be recognized that alterna-

36. UMTA attorney Michael S. Bates guided me through the various phases of that rulemaking process; interview, December 12, 1981.

tive service is a preferable way of handling the transportation needs of the elderly and the handicapped."[37]

In November 1974 UMTA issued a notice inviting interested parties to review and comment upon the draft at three informal hearings held later that month at DOT headquarters in Washington, D.C. Representatives of the concerned groups—the elderly and handicapped, the transit operators, and the manufacturers—all appeared. The spokesmen for the elderly and handicapped, drawn mostly from their groups' national offices, objected that the draft did not recognize that they are important members of the general public. While recognizing the value of such special services as taxis and vans, they rejected the concept of a totally separate transportation system for the elderly and the handicapped. Such segregation, they maintained, would obviate efforts directed toward full accessibility.[38] Representatives of the transit operators—the American Public Transit Association—emphasized that regulations should take account of the needs of localities and should vest communities with flexibility in meeting their obligations. (APTA later submitted a completely redrafted regulation.) The manufacturers who participated in the hearings called for performance standards rather than design specifications as a means of encouraging creativity and flexibility in producing equipment adapted to the needs of elderly and handicapped persons.

As a result of those meetings, UMTA made substantial changes and in February 1975 published a revised version of the proposed rules (notice of proposed rulemaking) in the Federal Register.[39] The proposed regulations dealt primarily with the service and hardware aspects of public transportation. They required local transportation planners and officials to identify the requirements of elderly and handicapped persons and develop specific plans and programs to meet those requirements, and they made the approval of grants for capital assistance conditional on the creation and implementation of such plans and programs. In an effort to be responsive to the transit community, UMTA restated a number of the requirements as performance rather than design standards.

These proposed rules were, of course, subject to public comment. In addition, UMTA held six public hearings across the nation, reflecting its view that the regulations should take into account local conditions and its determination not to impose a uniform federal standard. The sessions,

37. *Urban Mass Transportation—1975*, Hearings, pp. 30–51.
38. 40 Fed. Reg. 8316 (1975).
39. Ibid. at 8315–16.

which were informal, revealed the diversity of perspectives. Some positions were predictable. Manufacturers tended to emphasize that regulations should leave enough time for the technological development needed to make equipment accessible. Transit operators generally agreed that policy should concentrate on specialized transportation services and should be sensitive to the concerns of individual localities; some objected that the regulations provided no criteria to determine whether they had satisfied the "special efforts" requirement. Perhaps most striking were differences between the elderly and handicapped communities and among disabled persons themselves. For the most part, the elderly, while recognizing the ultimate objective of integrating all people in public transit, stressed the value of door-to-door paratransit services. But others argued in support of ensuring that physical barriers were removed so that disabled individuals could use mainline transit. Such was particularly the view of Vietnam War veterans, who objected to what they perceived to be "segregated" paratransit systems. Borrowing from the civil rights struggle of the 1960s, they believed that they were entitled to use the same transportation systems as the rest of the population.

Apart from the statements at the hearings, UMTA received 324 comments for this docket. UMTA staff reviewed the comments and made changes based on them. Preoccupied with other duties, Chief Counsel Payton and the task force did not finish their work until a year later, when UMTA issued its final regulations on April 30, 1976.[40]

Final Regulations

The final regulations, effective July 1, 1976, remained true to the basic policy philosophical tenets that guided the UMTA staff from the outset: the problems of elderly and handicapped persons would be viewed in the context of the overall concerns of transportation policy, and the federal government would not impose a solution on state and local authorities. Rather, it would afford them freedom to devise programs that took into account their individual circumstances. UMTA noted that comments about the proposed regulations revealed

> substantial disagreement over the best type of service for wheelchair users—accessible fixed route service, with or without accessible feeder service, de-

40. 41 Fed. Reg. 18234 (1976).

mand-responsive van or small-bus service, subscription service, subsidized shared ride taxi service, or some combination of these or other services. Given present knowledge, we cannot say that one of these services, or even one combination is best for all communities. In fact, it is likely that site-specific planning and tailoring of appropriate services will always be necessary. We say this with full appreciation of the psychological and rehabilitation advantages of integrating wheel chair users into regular as opposed to specialized transit service.[41]

Taking into account the concerns of the transit operators who sought guidance about what would satisfy the "special efforts" requirement, UMTA provided three concrete examples: (1) a program for wheelchair users and semiambulatory handicapped persons that expended an average amount equal to a minimum of 5 percent of the operating funds the local authority received from UMTA (known as "section 5"); (2) purchase of only wheelchair-accessible new fixed-route equipment until one-half of the fleet was accessible, or, in the alternative, provision of a substitute service providing comparable coverage and service areas; and (3) a system assuring every wheelchair user or semiambulatory person ten round trips per week at fares comparable to those charged on standard transit buses for trips of similar length, within the service area of the public transportation authority.[42] These examples were meant only to be illustrative of the level of activity that would satisfy the "special efforts" requirement. They appeared for the first time as an appendix to a final regulation and thus were not subject to the standard comment procedures involving interested parties. Nor were they developed in a rigorous fashion; by one account they were conceived in the course of a special gathering involving UMTA officials and some friends working for the American Public Transit Association.[43] Despite this, these three "special efforts" examples became, however inadvertently, the focus for state and local governments seeking to comply with the regulations.

The regulations further stated that the administrator would approve grant proposals only if the local planning process showed satisfactory "special efforts," if the transportation improvement program authorities were required to submit annually contained projects designed to benefit

41. Ibid. at 18236.
42. Ibid. at 18234.
43. Interviews with Sallyanne Payton, December 10, 1981, and Lillian Liburdi, UMTA associate administrator for policy and program development during the Carter years, December 15, 1981.

elderly and handicapped persons, and if reasonable progress had been demonstrated in implementing previously programmed projects. At the urging of elderly and handicapped groups, the planning process at the local level was also required to involve them.[44] The regulations also covered fixed facilities, buses, and rapid and light rail vehicles. Among the requirements was one mandating bus manufacturers to offer a wheelchair accessibility option consisting of a level-change mechanism (for example, a lift or ramp). That provision was not meant to compel retrofitting of existing buses.[45]

Round Two: Bureaucratic Imperialism

Policymaking at the federal level is fragmented, both among and within the branches; outcomes are thus the product of many participants, with differing, even competing, perspectives. If there are differences of opinion within a bureaucracy, the minority faction in that agency may form an alliance, tacit or explicit, with those who share their views in another agency. In this case, those in UMTA who believed that the special efforts regulations were inadequate found support from HEW lawyers, whose civil rights orientation led them to attempt to impose a full accessibility standard on the DOT.

HEW's role was formally authorized, just two days before UMTA published its final regulations, when President Gerald R. Ford, in the midst of an election campaign, issued Executive Order 11914, vesting the secretary of HEW with the responsibility for coordinating the implementation of section 504 of the Rehabilitation Act of 1973 by all federal departments and agencies.[46] The secretary was ordered to establish standards for determining who were handicapped individuals and guidelines for ascertaining discriminatory practices within the meaning of section 504. Agencies were to issue rules, regulations, and directives consistent with the standards and procedures set by the HEW secretary. They were to cooperate with HEW, furnishing such reports and information as the secretary deemed necessary. The HEW head was authorized to adopt rules and regulations and issue orders that he thought necessary to discharge his duties.

44. 41 Fed. Reg. 18235–26 (1976).
45. Ibid. at 18238.
46. Reprinted in 43 Fed. Reg. 2139 (1978).

The OCR Takes the Initiative

HEW's Office for Civil Rights (OCR) and the staff of the Subcommittee on the Handicapped of the Senate Committee on Labor and Public Welfare had been the impetus behind the presidential action. Section 504, as was discussed in chapter 2, said nothing about the issuance of regulations. But a conference committee report accompanying the Rehabilitation Act Amendments of 1974—legislation that did not change the words of section 504 in any respect—had declared that Congress intended that regulations be promulgated pursuant to section 504 and had charged the secretary of HEW with coordinating the enforcement effort. The committee expected HEW to issue regulations by the end of 1974.

For its part, the OCR viewed section 504 as a means of securing rights for handicapped persons.[47] The OCR already had among its responsibilities the task of enforcing title VI of the Civil Rights Act of 1964 and title IX of the Education Amendments of 1972, which was modeled after title VI.[48] Section 504 was also patterned after the provision in the Civil Rights Act of 1964. Thus the OCR concluded that section 504 should fall within its domain and that it should devise regulations, just as it had under title VI and was in the process of doing under title IX. It should be noted, however, that these acts, unlike section 504, specifically mandated the issuance of regulations.

Within two months of the passage of the Rehabilitation Act of 1973, HEW bureaucrats and staff members of the Senate Subcommittee on the Handicapped had met to discuss the agency's role in enforcing the statute. It was the OCR, unbeknownst to HEW Secretary Caspar Weinberger, that had initiated those talks and proposed language that found its way into the 1974 committee report. Moreover, even before the report was issued, the OCR—consistent with its conversations with the subcommittee staff—had drafted an executive order vesting HEW with lead responsibilities. The report in effect ratified a role for HEW that the OCR had hoped to assume. Weinberger transmitted the proposed executive order to the Office of Man-

47. Interview with John Wodatch, head of the section 504 unit, September 9, 1982, and discussion with Martin Gerry, former director, Office for Civil Rights, March 15, 1985, at conference in Grailville, Ohio.

48. Title VI prohibits discrimination on racial grounds, and title IX prohibits discrimination on the basis of sex. On OCR enforcement of these laws, see Jeremy Rabkin, "Office for Civil Rights," in James Q. Wilson, ed., *The Politics of Regulation* (Basic Books, 1980), pp. 304–53.

agement and Budget for its review. The order wove its way through the OMB bureaucracy for Ford's signature. By the time Ford approved the document, the OCR had already circulated a draft of the regulations that were to be issued to carry out the executive order. So determined was the OCR to maintain an active presence that it sought an eightfold increase in its staff (from 12 to 105).

The OCR's unit on special programs assumed responsibility for section 504 enforcement. John Wodatch, a young attorney, directed a staff ranging at any one time from eight to ten lawyers—not many, given the task of formulating section 504 regulations and coordinating policy government-wide. Not surprisingly, given the OCR's involvement with title VI, a rights ethos governed the unit. Staff attorneys believed that disabled persons, like blacks and other minorities, had been deprived of their rights and had suffered discrimination and segregation. They believed government should take whatever steps necessary to remedy wrongs. They embraced an expansive interpretation of section 504, arguing that it required affirmative action in all areas involving federal assistance, not just employment. Having defined the problem in terms of rights, they saw funding constraints as irrelevant: rights are absolute and cannot be compromised by fiscal considerations.

The OCR first set about drafting regulations pertaining to programs that received HEW aid or assistance. A federal district court decision requiring the HEW secretary to promulgate regulations added impetus to the OCR's efforts.[49] The OCR's approach reflected its rights orientation and was all-inclusive, affecting about 16,000 school systems, 7,000 hospitals, 6,700 nursing homes and home health agencies, 2,600 institutions of higher education, and hundreds of libraries and day care centers.[50] The cost of simply making every room in each of these institutions accessible to the handicapped was estimated to be in the billions of dollars.

The proposed regulations eventually reached the HEW secretary—now David Mathews—for his decision. Mathews was sufficiently disturbed by their scope that he refused to sign them without congressional guidance. Three days before leaving office, Mathews sent to Congress, along with the 185-page text of regulations, a letter seeking legislative assistance (see chapter 2). His message was an invitation to Congress to review the pro-

49. *Cherry* v. *Mathews*, 419 F. Supp 922 (D.D.C. 1976). See chap. 4.
50. 42 Fed. Reg. 31647 (1977).

posed regulations and to offer advice as to whether they satisfied legislative intent. The secretary clearly believed that the OCR's work exceeded the meaning of section 504; constrained by his own bureaucracy, and by a judicial decision that ordered the issuance of regulations, he looked to Congress for a way out of his predicament. But, as was noted earlier, Congress did not respond to his entreaties for direction.

Mathews left office in January 1977 without signing the regulations, and the matter of section 504 became the responsibility of his successor, Joseph A. Califano. The new secretary had never heard of section 504; his sense of civil rights, formed by his experience in the Kennedy and Johnson administrations, had focused on race. But from the moment that Califano glanced at section 504, he felt that the country was on the verge of another, albeit different, civil rights revolution. Determined not "to start from the dead-of-night posture in which the Congress had acted," he thought it essential to assess the regulations carefully.[51] For that purpose, he appointed an intradepartmental task force whose work was guided by Daniel Marcus, a Washington lawyer. It was clear that Califano, who was well familiar with bureaucratic life, sought to control the decisionmaking process; it was he who would make the fundamental policy decisions, and not the OCR.

The disability organizations reacted promptly and bitterly to Califano's decision to reexamine the proposed regulations. Dismayed about the delay, they staged demonstrations across the nation; they occupied Califano's office, singing "We Want 504" to the melody of "We Shall Overcome." "Their representatives, and the bureaucrats in OCR," Califano would later write, "pressed me just to sign the regulations, without thinking about what it would cost or even reviewing them." Although sympathetic to their concerns, the HEW secretary recounted that:

> Those most interested, the handicapped, were, like all special interest groups, rather one-dimensional in their views. It's hard enough to deal with interest groups in black, and even gray, hats, but it's nothing like dealing with those in white hats with an unqualified ticket to equality and opportunity issued by the Congress. Relief was long overdue. Basically, we had hidden the handicapped, put them out of sight in separate schools and homes. But there were other worthy demands on the resources of the institutions that would be affected by the regulations. This was particularly true for hard-pressed universities, urban schools and libraries, and city transit systems. Preoccupied with meeting

51. Joseph A. Califano, Jr., *Governing America: An Insider's Report from the White House and the Cabinet* (Simon and Schuster, 1981), pp. 258, 259.

often urgent needs, these institutions and transit systems had not focused on the impact of the regulations that dealt with handicapped persons.[52]

Califano signed a new version of the regulations on April 28, 1977, a few days ahead of his announced deadline. In light of the cost factor, the regulations focused on program accessibility rather than structural changes: for example, not every classroom had to be accessible, although some had to be so that handicapped persons could use them.

Three weeks after signing HEW's regulations, Califano wrote to DOT Secretary Brock Adams and other cabinet secretaries, indicating that his department planned to move as quickly as possible to coordinate implementation of section 504 by all federal agencies extending financial assistance to any program or activity.[53] Not long thereafter, HEW set forth a proposed rule covering enforcement procedures, standards for determining which persons are handicapped, and guidelines for ascertaining discriminatory practices.[54] Following the model of HEW's own regulations, the OCR devised a proposed rule designed to ensure that handicapped persons could be part of the mainstream.

Given the OCR's rights perspective, the cost of implementing the rule was irrelevant; but the fact that it did not have to pay the bill probably meant that the office was even less concerned about the financial consequences of its directive. With respect to "program accessibility"—that part most relevant to the Department of Transportation—the proposed rules declared that a recipient operate each program or activity so that "when viewed in its entirety, [it] is readily accessible to and usable by handicapped persons." The preamble explained that "program accessibility" did not require that existing facilities be completely barrier free. Where structural changes were necessary to make programs or activities in existing facilities accessible, they were to be made "as soon as practicable, but in no event later than three years after the effective date of the regulation." New facilities were to be readily accessible to handicapped persons, and alterations to existing facilities were "to the maximum extent feasible" to be designed and constructed so that the disabled could use them.[55]

---

52. Ibid., p. 259.

53. Letter from HEW Secretary Joseph A. Califano, Jr., to DOT Secretary Brock Adams, May 20, 1977.

54. 42 Fed. Reg. 32264 (1977). On section 504 enforcement and education policy, see Richard K. Scotch, *From Good Will to Civil Rights: Transforming Federal Disability Policy* (Temple University Press, 1985).

55. 42 Fed. Reg. 32268 (1977).

The DOT Reacts

The DOT, through UMTA, had already issued regulations pertaining to elderly and handicapped persons. The UMTA regulations, based on the effective mobility concept, were more flexible, geared more toward providing state and local governments with discretion than HEW's approach, which sought to ensure the integration of handicapped individuals into society. One might have thought, in view of these sharply differing perspectives, that the DOT would have clashed with HEW. The DOT might have contested HEW's authority to issue guidelines governing its activities; after all, both were cabinet-level departments and presumably coequal. Moreover, the DOT might have objected that it had already addressed the problem of providing transportation for handicapped persons and that HEW's efforts were therefore superfluous. On the merits, the DOT could have disagreed with HEW's approach.

To a large extent, however, the DOT accepted the HEW role. Much of the explanation lies in the change in DOT leadership that took place once the Carter administration assumed office in 1977. The new DOT secretary, Brock Adams, a liberal Democrat from Washington, had risen quite high in the House of Representatives. At the time that he left Congress, he was chairman of the influential Budget Committee. He was sympathetic to the problems of disabled persons and to the view that government should do all that it could to ensure that the handicapped could enter the mainstream. Thus HEW's rights-oriented full accessibility approach was compatible with his own. The secretary was also mindful of some of the disability groups' determination to secure their objectives through such political activity as demonstrations. Adams further believed that advances in research and development were key to improving transportation services and that government could create technology-forcing devices to spur industry to action. DOT regulations could specify design or performance standards and impose deadlines manufacturers and operators would have to meet. Indeed, Adams revived the Transbus project—which the previous administration had canceled—convinced that it was technically feasible, if only the DOT and industry had the will to make it work.

Thus Adams did not challenge HEW's authority to set the standards guiding DOT regulations. In fact, a memorandum prepared by the DOT's Office of General Counsel had concluded that the president, in an effort to discharge the mandate to faithfully execute the laws, could order a department to coordinate the activities of other agencies. But apart from the legality of the presidential executive order, Adams and his staff recognized that the HEW role furthered their own policy interests. To those within the operating agencies, such as UMTA, who favored the effective mobility approach, the secretary could claim that his hands were tied, that he had no choice but to comply with HEW. Adams's inclinations were reinforced by the views of staff members within the policy unit—the Office of the Assistant Secretary for Environment, Safety and Consumer Affairs—some of whom had long been interested in the problems of providing transportation for elderly and disabled persons. Martin Convisser, who was by now acting assistant secretary, was called upon to negotiate with HEW.[56]

In the summer of 1977 Convisser submitted the DOT's comments on the 504 guidelines to HEW Deputy General Counsel Daniel Marcus. The DOT was in "general agreement" with the proposed guidelines, but was particularly concerned about the requirement that all existing facilities funded by the DOT, then or in the past, be made accessible within three years. That requirement, Convisser wrote, "would be physically impossible given a complex and diverse transportation system that included urban buses, commuting and intercity train systems, and even aircraft and aviation terminals and would pose an unreasonable immediate financial cost that would be difficult for the Federal government and local grantee agencies to meet."[57] UMTA estimated the cost would be in the billions and over a three-year period would greatly exceed the budgeted federal resources, as well as the matching local resources required under the DOT's grant program. The DOT sought a change in the three-year deadline for the retrofitting of existing facilities and an extension of the sixty-day time limit in which each agency was to develop proposed regulations pursuant to HEW guidelines.

The department further urged HEW to state explicitly that the intent of its effort was to provide "guidance" to agencies and not to create substantive, judicially enforceable rights (other than perhaps to compel an agency to adopt regulations under section 504 if it failed to do so). Otherwise, the DOT reasoned, agency actions taken after the HEW guidelines became effective, but before the adoption of agency regulations, would have to conform to the more general HEW requirements, rather than the more detailed agency regulations. The risk was that in this interim period courts

56. Interview with Convisser, December 8, 1982.

57. Letter and accompanying comments from Martin Convisser, acting assistant secretary for environment, safety and consumer affairs, DOT, to Daniel Marcus, deputy general counsel, HEW, July 25, 1977.

would promulgate inconsistent or unintended interpretations of the HEW guidelines, setting perhaps irreversible precedents. "Courts rather than agencies would have the ability to control how Section 504 would relate to various government programs."[58]

To clarify these points, Convisser and some DOT colleagues discussed their concerns with Marcus and OCR attorney Anne Beckman. As a result of that meeting, the DOT and HEW reached agreement on several points. "Program accessibility" did not obligate a recipient to make each of its existing facilities or every part of a facility accessible. At the same time, however, each mode—for example, buses, subways, light rail—when viewed in its entirety, would have to be accessible. The DOT's position— consistent with HEW's full accessibility approach—was thus at odds with that of transit operators, who proposed that the word "program," for purposes of program accessibility, be interpreted to mean the entire transportation system of a certain geographic area, as opposed to particular modes of transit in that locality. The operators favored the existing "special efforts" regulations, which did not mandate that each manner of transit be accessible.

The DOT convinced HEW to make clear in its final guidelines that it did not preclude in all circumstances the provision of specialized services as a substitute for, or supplement to, totally accessible services. Nor would it require door-to-door transportation service. HEW further agreed to modify the three-year deadline if the particular mode of transit (for instance, a subway system) could be made accessible only "through extraordinarily expensive structural changes to, or replacement of, existing facilities and if other accessible modes of transportation . . . [were] accessible."[59] The DOT could extend the time period, but only for a reasonable and definite interval, as set forth in its regulations.

With respect to bus transit, in 1977 Secretary Adams had already issued a mandate requiring that all buses acquired with UMTA assistance and ordered after September 30, 1979, meet low-floor specifications that presumably would ensure wheelchair access (see pages 139–40). Still unanswered was what HEW policy would be in the meantime—during the period between issuance of the final guidelines in January 1978 and the date the specifications for the low-floor vehicle were to become effective. In

58. "DOT's Comments on the DHEW's Notice of Proposed Rulemaking Embodying Procedures To Be Followed by Each Federal Department and Agency in Issuing Its Own Section 504 Regulations," July 25, 1977.

59. 43 Fed. Reg. 2132, 2139 (1978).

December 1977 UMTA administrator Richard Page learned that Secretary Califano was leaning toward mandating wheelchair lifts on all interim buses. He promptly directed an urgent memo to Secretary Adams:

> FLASH!!
>
> Secretary Califano tentatively decided yesterday to require wheelchair lifts on all new buses. The effective date is not clear, but once he makes that decision public we would probably be obligated to require such lifts beginning with grants early in 1978.
>
> This will increase the cost of each advance design bus by about 10% (ten thousand dollars) and will, consequently, reduce the total number of buses we can purchase in FY 78 by about 10%.
>
> I recommend you call Secretary Califano and suggest that he either drop this requirement or make it effective September 30, 1979, the same date as your Transbus mandate.[60]

Ultimately, HEW allowed the DOT to defer the deadline for requiring all new buses to be accessible until October 1, 1979, as Page recommended.

HEW extended the 60-day deadline for agencies to publish proposed rules pursuant to the guidelines. The DOT had asked for 120 days, but was given 90. HEW did reject the DOT's recommendation that the guidelines explicitly state that they did not create judicially enforceable rights, declaring that "whether any legally enforceable rights are created by this regulation is a matter for courts to decide."[61] The OCR, of course, would not have been unhappy if the courts viewed the guidelines as creating such rights.

All things considered, Califano was receptive to the DOT's concerns. His willingness to accommodate them was based not only on the strength of the argument but the perception that the DOT was genuinely willing to fulfill its obligations under section 504. After all, Adams accepted the full accessibility approach. On January 13, 1978, HEW issued its final guidelines implementing Executive Order 11914.

Round Three: Full Accessibility Regulations

When the prevailing organizational ethos is at odds with a proposed policy, change is made more difficult. The dominant forces in and surrounding the DOT—the transit planners and operators—had only reluc-

60. Memo from Richard Page to Secretary Adams, December 14, 1977; interview with Richard Page, May 12, 1983.

61. 43 Fed. Reg. 2133 (1978).

tantly accepted the effective mobility regulations. Thus they could be expected to vehemently oppose the more stringent full accessibility approach, arguing that it was costly and impractical and diverted energies away from the DOT's real mission. The task for the political executives and policy generalists who anticipated such a reaction was clear, though difficult: to overcome that opposition and to impose a new direction. What was called for was nothing less than the exercise of consummate bureaucratic skills.

Changing the Rules

Almost immediately after HEW issued its guidelines, the DOT reviewed its existing "special efforts" regulations and determined that they did not fulfill HEW's 504 requirements.[62] Martin Convisser quickly moved to begin the DOT's rulemaking process. Because the regulations were to be departmentwide, encompassing buses, subways, airports, railroads, highways, and paratransit, Convisser's task was formidable. He believed it imperative that he act decisively to control the process, to build up enough momentum so as to make it less likely that divisions resistant to the 504 guidelines would prevail. Although the principal decisionmakers for the 1976 effective mobility effort were in the operating bureaus, the locus of authority for the new round of regulations was at the top—at the secretarial level and in the policy and general counsel offices. Together with colleagues Ira Laster and Leslie Baldwin, Convisser drafted regulations, consulting at various points with offices that had jurisdiction over the particular modes of transit.[63] Convisser was the consummate entrepreneur; "He played the bureaucracy the way Isaac Stern bows the violin," commented one key participant. Not surprisingly, in view of his policy bent, Convisser approached the problem analytically. He was convinced that providing equal or full accessibility was a matter of technology and that wheelchair lifts and low-floor ramps on buses could be perfected. Mindful of the fiscal concerns of operators, Convisser felt that a timetable should be devised so that local governments could meet the accessibility requirements consistent with their other obligations. After drafting the proposed regulations, Convisser and Laster had Cynthia Straker, a lawyer in the General Counsel's Office, review them to make sure that they would withstand any legal test.

62. HEW instructed the DOT to assess its existing regulations. Ibid. at 2134.
63. Interview with Leslie Baldwin, October 20, 1981.

The DOT issued the proposed regulations on June 8, 1978, several weeks past the HEW deadline. The DOT proposal applied the HEW guidelines to the federal mass transportation program and declared that in addition to implementing section 504 the proposed regulations were designed to execute section 16(a) of the Urban Mass Transportation Act and section 16(b) of the Federal-Aid Highway Act of 1973, as amended.[64] All new fixed facilities were required to be accessible, that is, usable to those who could not climb steps. With respect to bus systems, program accessibility was to be achieved "as soon as practicable but no later than 3 years after the effective date of the regulation"; where "extraordinarily expensive changes" were involved, bus systems could have up to six years to make their systems accessible to wheelchair users. Basically, accessibility would be attained when one-half of the peak-hour service was provided by buses that could accommodate wheelchair users. Moreover, the DOT proposal sought comment about the feasibility of requiring new buses to be accessible to wheelchair users by October 1, 1979.

The proposed regulation mandated existing rapid rail, commuter rail, and light rail systems to become 100 percent accessible. The DOT determined that the great bulk of the cost of implementing the regulation related to the retrofitting of those rail facilities—an estimated $1.6 billion (in 1977 dollars) of the total $1.8 billion. In view of the strain on resources that retrofitting might demand, the DOT set forth three options for the compliance period for altering mass transit stations—twelve years, twenty years, and thirty years—and requested comments on the appropriate deadline. Noting that HEW guidelines required that existing rail facilities be made accessible over time, the DOT nevertheless invited comments on alternative approaches that could provide substantially similar benefits at less cost.[65]

Public Comments

The notice of proposed rulemaking invited public comment for a ninety-day period, which was later extended forty-four more days until October 20, 1978.[66] In view of the complexity of the issues, in the autumn of 1978 the department held public hearings in New York, Denver, the San Fran-

64. 43 Fed. Reg. 25020 (1978). It also stated that the 1976 regulation would remain in effect until the DOT had completed its rulemaking.
65. Ibid. at 25017.
66. Ibid. at 31444.

cisco-Oakland area, Chicago, and Washington, D.C. About 220 persons and groups expressed their views at the hearings, and some 650 individuals and organizations supplied written comments for the docket. Among the participants were representatives of local and state governments, transit operators, disability groups, and many private individuals.

TRANSIT OPERATORS

Perhaps the most systematic and vigorous challenge to the proposed rules was waged by transit operators through the American Public Transit Association. APTA, whose membership included the major transit systems across the nation, objected to the 100 percent accessibility requirement on the grounds of money, feasibility, benefits, and alternative preferences. APTA estimated that capital costs to implement the proposed mainline accessibility regulations would be from $3 billion to $5 billion in 1978 dollars—or more than double the DOT figure.[67] Over 90 percent of this amount, they claimed, involved retrofitting light, commuter, and heavy rail vehicles and reconstructing stations. They further anticipated that the increased annual operating cost would be more than $300 million, or more than four times the amount assumed by the DOT. APTA argued that federal, state, and local resources for public transit were insufficient to bear such costs—especially in the largest urban areas, where some 95 percent of capital spending would be concentrated.

With regard to feasibility, APTA observed that although the proposed regulations were hardware-intensive, much of the new technology did not yet exist—for instance, retrofit-lifts for light and commuter rail cars. Wheelchair lifts for buses, it maintained, would greatly slow bus service, were of unproven safety and reliability, and posed a danger should it be necessary to evacuate passengers in an emergency.

APTA also argued that the magnitude of the benefits to the handicapped population and the general public was not large enough to justify the full accessibility approach. The organization claimed that over 80 percent of all handicapped persons already used public transit, and that only 3 percent were current nonusers who both could and would use accessible fixed-route transit. The remainder, APTA asserted, would still face critical mobility barriers even after all bus and rail systems became physically accessible: these people would still be unable to get to and from transit stops, to

---

67. Testimony of James J. McDonough, chairman of APTA, in U.S. Department of Transportation, "Public Hearing on Notice of Proposed Rulemaking, Discrimination against the Handicapped," Washington, D.C., September 19, 1978, p. 5.

wait out of doors, to travel alone or in crowds, or to ride while standing. Far more rational, in its view, was the effective mobility approach, as embodied in the 1976 "special efforts" regulations. APTA claimed that specialized transportation, aided by the work of private operators and social service agencies, would better meet the needs of handicapped individuals. Although local officials generally opposed the full accessibility approach, many recognized that the DOT would not accept the effective mobility position. Thus some sought to advance a compromise as an alternative to 100 percent accessibility. In New York City, pointing to the expense of retrofitting its old and vast subway system, officials proposed the "key station" concept: only those stations thought most central to the transportation system would have to be retrofitted.

THE DISABLED COMMUNITY

Groups representing disabled persons did not have as coherent a strategy as did the transit operators. Some, while supportive of the full accessibility ideal, also hoped that specialized door-to-door transit services would not be cut. But most of the organizations supported the HEW-DOT equal accessibility approach. Chief among them were the Paralyzed Veterans of America (PVA), which drew upon the recent Vietnam War veterans for support, and the American Coalition of Citizens with Disabilities (ACCD).[68] Both the PVA and the ACCD were very much influenced by the civil rights struggle; disabled Vietnam veterans who returned home from an unpopular war viewed themselves as suffering the same kind of discrimination and ostracism that minorities had endured and sought to overcome. Having responded to their country's call to service, they now demanded that the nation assure that they not be shunted aside. For wheelchair-bound veterans, fully accessible transportation was a right to which they were entitled; the right to use the same buses and subways as everyone else was, by definition, fundamental.

68. Interviews with Arlene Battis, attorney, Paralyzed Veterans of America, December 5, 1984, and Reese Robrahn, ACCD executive director, May 26, 1982. The ACCD is a nationwide umbrella association of more than eighty national, state, and local organizations of almost every category of disabled people, including the American Council of the Blind, Coalition for Barrier Free Living, various state offices of Disabled in Action, National Association of the Deaf, National Association of the Physically Handicapped, National Paraplegia Foundation, Paralyzed Veterans of America, National Association for Retarded Citizens, United Cerebral Palsy Associations, and Association for Children with Learning Disabilities. Professional member groups of ACCD include the Association for Exceptional

The ACCD, which was created in the aftermath of section 504 of the Rehabilitation Act of 1973, took as its charge the enhancement of the human and civil rights of disabled people; disabled consumers themselves ran the organization. It is questionable whether the ACCD could have been born without the rights premise. If government defined federal policy toward the disabled as a matter of claims involving the allocation of finite resources, then presumably each of the many groups within the ACCD would have competed with the others to secure funds for its own constituency.[69] But because the government defined the issue in terms of rights, questions of cost became irrelevant: each group could champion the demands of others without financial sacrifice. The many groups within the ACCD could thus support the full accessibility conception regardless of the fiscal impact. The ACCD and the PVA backed the DOT's approach, but argued for quicker implementation: the alternative deadlines of twelve, twenty, and thirty years for making subway transit fully accessible were unacceptable to those groups. Moreover, the organizations sought to ensure that consumer groups would have a significant role in the planning and implementation of programs at the local level.

THE WHITE HOUSE

A third notable actor was the Executive Office of the President, or perhaps more precisely the Regulatory Analysis and Review Group (RARG) and the Council on Wage and Price Stability (COWPS). These two offices were created as a response to the growing perception that the governmental apparatus had become swollen and often ineffective. Many across the political spectrum had concluded by the 1970s that something had to be done to control the far-flung activities of the many agencies and departments, to provide an effective mechanism to make trade-offs among competing policies, and to inhibit the issuance of unnecessary regulation.[70]

President Jimmy Carter created RARG, an interagency body consisting of seventeen representatives from major executive branch agencies, including the Council of Economic Advisers, as a means of providing a more

---

Children, Council of State Administrators of Vocational Rehabilitation, National Easter Seal Society for Crippled Children, and National Rehabilitation Association.

69. On the distinction between claims and rights, see James Q. Wilson, "Responses," *Harvard Educational Review,* vol. 52 (April 1982), pp. 415–18.

70. See, for example, American Bar Association, Commission on Law and Economy, *Federal Regulation: Roads to Reform* (ABA, 1979).

coherent policymaking machinery.[71] COWPS, a unit within the Executive Office of the President, was to supply the economic staff assistance for the regulatory review group. RARG was to identify a select number of proposed major rules of the executive branch—defined as those that would have an impact on the economy of $100 million or more or that would lead to a major increase in cost or prices—and submit its views on them during the public comment period. In fact, the review group's impact on agency behavior was often quite limited because it could not prevent a department from pursuing a particular rule or policy course. Its hope was that an agency would be influenced by its peers to make changes.

With respect to the section 504 regulations, the likelihood that RARG could speak authoritatively as the White House voice was diminished by the role President Ford had assigned HEW in coordinating agency rulemaking. HEW's duty was not limited to providing comments; it had to approve each agency's proposed regulations before the final ones were issued. The role of both HEW and RARG raised an important question about presidential control: which spoke for the chief executive? The answer was never explicitly determined, as RARG did not go beyond its responsibility for reviewing the proposed DOT regulations and submitting comments to the record.

Less than two weeks after the DOT issued its proposed regulations, the executive committee of RARG, upon the recommendation of the COWPS staff, voted to review the section 504 regulations.[72] Four aspects of the DOT proceedings concerned the group. First, in its view the costs appeared quite substantial relative to the number of potential beneficiaries and the number of trips those people were likely to make.

The second issue was the cost effectiveness of the DOT's plan—whether the transit network could be changed in a less costly fashion than the DOT required and still produce the added mobility. In its initial draft, COWPS staff noted that DOT data showed that essentially similar benefits could be obtained at substantially lower cost if accessible buses could be used instead of accessible subways. Two other options—special services for handicapped persons and taxis—were judged more expensive than the DOT's proposal, both in per trip cost and total cost.

A third concern had to do with what COWPS perceived to be a possible

71. 43 Fed. Reg. 12668 (1978).

72. "Regulatory Analysis Review Group Revised Schedule: DOT Nondiscrimination on the Basis of Handicap," in letter from Barry P. Bosworth, director of COWPS, to DOT Secretary Brock Adams, July 19, 1978.

conflict between two objectives that it believed the DOT was called on to fulfill. Mainstreaming—assuring that federally assisted programs and activities be provided in an integrated setting—would require elevators in subways and the retrofitting of vehicles. Equal access, COWPS claimed, meant equal mobility and could be satisfied by a specialized bus or taxi service, coupled with accessible transit buses; it did not require full accessibility, the retrofitting of buses and subways. If funding was limited and resources were scarce, then, the COWPS staff argued, a choice had to be made between the objectives of mainstreaming and equal access.

A final concern related to the DOT's interpretation of the HEW guidelines and section 504 itself. Noting the cost of retrofitting subways, RARG questioned whether section 504 and the guidelines required full accessibility.

In preparing its report, the COWPS staff consulted, among others, DOT officials, disability groups, and APTA (which provided information challenging the proposed regulations). A draft of the comments was circulated among RARG member agencies. As a result of these exchanges, the COWPS staff modified some of its earlier comments. In the final draft, RARG did not address the legal issue of whether the DOT was bound to pursue the full accessibility approach. HEW Deputy General Counsel Daniel Marcus stated categorically that the section 504 guidelines did not permit the DOT to totally exempt existing subway systems. Moreover, although RARG persisted in its judgment that substituting an extended bus system for subway retrofit would result in substantially lower total costs (but also in less convenient services), it modified its earlier assessment that the benefits of the former would essentially be the same as the latter; ultimately it concluded that the DOT had not gathered sufficient evidence of benefits to support adoption of any alternative.[73] In the end, the DOT rejected RARG's positions.

Crafting the Final Regulations

Throughout most of the proposed rulemaking process, the Office of Assistant Secretary for Environment, Safety and Consumer Affairs was the key bureau, and its acting head, Martin Convisser, the central player. But

73. Report of the Regulatory Analysis Review Group, submitted by the Council on Wage and Price Stability, "Department of Transportation's Proposed Regulations on Nondiscrimination on the Basis of Handicap," October 20, 1978; and letter from Deputy General Counsel Daniel Marcus to Thomas D. Hopkins, assistant director for government operations and research, Council on Wage and Price Stability, October 20, 1978.

a departmental reorganization altered that arrangement. The office was abolished and essentially became a division, with Convisser as director, in the Office of the Assistant Secretary for Policy and International Affairs. That division—the Office of Environment and Safety—continued to have important responsibilities, but its influence was diminished.

In part, the explanation for that reduced role lies with the fact that the assistant secretary for policy and international affairs, Chester Davenport, did not enjoy particularly close relations with Secretary Brock Adams. Moreover, a restructuring of the DOT's rulemaking process shifted power to the general counsel, who was effectively charged with overseeing regulatory analysis and review.[74] General Counsel Linda Kamm, who had worked with Adams on Capitol Hill, had the secretary's confidence. A vigorous advocate, she shared her chief's view that every effort should be made so that disabled persons could enter the mainstream. Hers was most assuredly a rights perspective. It was no accident, she later commented, that Martin Luther King and other civil rights activists concentrated their early efforts on integrating the bus system—equal access to transportation was not simply a right in itself, but a means to the enjoyment of other total rights.[75]

The DOT, she believed, should move swiftly to implement the HEW guidelines. Aware of the resistance of the transit-oriented bureaus to the equal accessibility approach, Kamm determined, as did Convisser before her, that it was imperative to control the agenda in order to set the terms under which the debate would take place. She did this through "options papers." She and a small unit in the general counsel's office, led by Assistant General Counsel Neil Eisner and Robert Ashby, as well as Richard Clark, a legal officer on detail from the Coast Guard, developed a series of questions on particular issues, sought responses from the operating bureaus and other divisions, and held a series of meetings with the relevant officials.[76] Kamm moderated such sessions and, together with Adams, made decisions about which policy options to pursue. Having made these choices, the general counsel's regulatory unit, aided by Michael Bates of UMTA, wrote the regulations. The "options paper" process was thus a means to reinforce the policy approach already chosen, gather information, manage conflict within the DOT, make authoritative choices, and set

74. 43 Fed. Reg. 9582 (1978).

75. Interview with Linda Kamm, September 28, 1982.

76. Interviews with Neil Eisner, January 13, 1982, and Robert Ashby, January 11 and 12, 1983, and October 15, 1984.

deadlines to assure that regulations would issue within a reasonable period of time. It was a top-down approach to policymaking, with the operating bureaus playing a clearly subsidiary role.

The options papers, which were based on the premise that each transit mode must be accessible "when viewed in its entirety," addressed nine major issues, such as when the DOT should require new full-sized buses to be accessible; what the DOT should mandate in accessibility for fixed-route bus systems; what would be required of seven inaccessible subway systems, six existing light rail systems, and the commuter rail systems; the extent to which the DOT should require paratransit even if an area's fixed-route bus and rail systems met its obligations; and what should be expected with respect to the interim service that would be needed until fixed-route systems were made accessible.[77]

The general counsel presented options for each issue to guide the discussion and ultimately the final rules. For example, in assessing what to do about subways, the DOT considered whether to require full accessibility within a fixed period (twelve, twenty, or thirty years); whether to mandate that all stations be accessible to persons who do not need elevators within a specified number of years; whether to limit accessibility to "key" stations or to a specified percentage of stations within a given period of years; and whether to allow localities to have some discretion in meeting standards for accessibility.

These options were the battleground for discussion among the various offices. Convisser's unit fought for 100 percent accessibility (although it was willing to accept 60 percent if the key station concept were accepted); the general counsel argued for key stations; and UMTA and the Office of the Assistant Secretary of Program and Budget contended that if the key station approach were adopted, it should apply to a low figure (perhaps 40 percent). For each issue and concomitant options, bureaus were assigned "tasks," that is, asked to supply technical support. Thus UMTA, for example, was called upon to provide information about the feasibility of bus lifts after March 1979.[78]

A briefing book, which included a background paper on the issues and

77. DOT, Office of General Counsel, "Outline of Options Paper for Mass Transportation Portion of Final Section 504 Regulations," November 29, 1978.

78. Interview with Margaret Ayres, former chief counsel of UMTA, February 9, 1982. Because the feasibility of wheelchair lifts had already been shown, the response addressed the question of whether a suitable and satisfactory product could, or would, be available. See memo of George J. Pastor, UMTA associate administrator for technology, development and deployment to UMTA Chief Counsel Margaret M. Ayres, November 15, 1978.

options for implementing section 504, as well as general summaries of the docket comments, was submitted to Secretary Adams. Once the key policy decisions were made—generally ratifying the general counsel's full accessibility preferences—the regulatory unit within the general counsel's office began to write the final rules. Each of the operating divisions was then asked to prepare detailed summaries of the docket comments, stating the views expressed and indicating the number of those who held particular positions. The process of reviewing the docket took longer than expected, and many of the regulations were written before all the comments had been assessed. One of the general counsel staffers asserted that the DOT could afford to give less attention to those regulations essentially involving statements of predetermined policy. Data about the costs of accessibility generated by APTA and the various offices within the DOT were thought unreliable. Those writing the regulations in the general counsel's office argued that they sought to be reasonable, while remaining faithful to the underlying philosophical premise that disabled individuals have the right to enter the mainstream of society. The process of justifying the policy decisions in the preamble of the regulations, responding to the commenters who urged a different course, had the salutary effect of forcing the decisionmakers to think hard about their directives—though critics claimed that Adams and Kamm had their minds made up even before reviewing the docket summaries.

Apart from crafting regulations that would be clear to the transit authorities charged with implementing them, the general counsel's office engaged in preventive lawyering to assure that the final product would survive judicial review—in much the same way that Sallyanne Payton had sought to immunize the 1976 "special efforts" regulations from attack. The regulations would be sustained so long as they were not conceived in an arbitrary or capricious manner (or at least not so perceived by the judiciary), regardless of the court's view of their substantive merits. To protect the department from procedural attacks from disability groups who might object to a softening of the 100 percent full accessibility requirements, Ashby and Eisner included in the preamble to the final regulations a letter from HEW Secretary Califano to Secretary Adams approving the regulations as consistent with his responsibilities under the section 504 executive order.[79] In fact, Adams, in accordance with the HEW guidelines, had submitted the DOT's proposed final regulations for review. Over a period of five weeks

79. 44 Fed. Reg. 31468 (1979).

representatives of the two departments examined the regulations, ultimately reaching agreement on them.

On May 31, 1979, nearly a year after the issuance of the proposed rules, the DOT issued its final rule. The department noted its support for the HEW guidelines requiring that all modes of transportation be accessible. It specifically rejected the definition that suggested that "program accessibility" would be achieved even if every mode was not accessible so long as the components of an area's overall transportation system, taken together, offered mobility.[80]

With respect to transit buses, the rule required that all new buses for which bids were accepted after the effective date of the regulation—July 2, 1979—had to be wheelchair accessible. Thus the DOT was effectively mandating the introduction of the wheelchair lift—the only technology then existing to make bus transportation accessible to wheelchair-bound persons. Rewriting the confused language of the proposed rule, the DOT stated that "program accessibility" would be attained when at least one-half of buses were wheelchair accessible; during off-peak hours, a recipient would have to deploy all of its available accessible buses before it could place inaccessible buses in service. To ease the expenses borne by local operators, the DOT extended the outer time limit for program accessibility from six to ten years.[81]

In addition to promulgating the requirements for mainline bus transit, DOT sought to respond to those who argued that its approach was costly, benefited only a small population, and was dependent upon technologically deficient equipment. The DOT concluded that the costs were likely to be lower than commenters suggested, contending that some of the differences were based on ill-founded assumptions about such matters as the presumed slowing of service, increased costs for garages, greater insurance costs, and the need for additional personnel and training.[82] The DOT found that the absence of data comparing mainline versus special services (in terms of such variables as trip time, waiting time, trip purpose, restrictions, and hours of service) made it difficult to determine whether paratransit was indeed comparable to fully accessible services.

As to the population served, the DOT alluded to a survey that indicated that some 1.5 million people for whom bus steps are a barrier live within a half-mile of a bus stop. The DOT asserted, moreover, that the average

80. Ibid. at 31442, 31448.
81. Ibid. at 31455.
82. Ibid. at 31456.

populations of mobility-handicapped people would increase as the average age of the population rose. Finally, the DOT claimed that the use of bus service by disabled people would increase once they became aware of the existence of accessible vehicles.

With regard to the feasibility of lifts, the DOT rejected the view that they would greatly slow bus service, that they posed dangers in an emergency evacuation situation, and that they did not work properly. Any problems could be remedied with experience. The DOT believed that a lift requirement would create a much stronger demand for lift equipment, which in turn would encourage companies with high engineering skills and production capacity to enter the market and to sell equipment at competitive prices.[83] As for the expense of the lifts, the DOT noted that it was not mandating that current buses be retrofitted with lifts; almost all cities would achieve program accessibility within ten years through the normal bus cycle, by gradually replacing old buses with new accessible vehicles.

Although transit operators were for the most part steadfastly opposed to making existing rapid and commuter rail systems accessible, the final rule retained that objective. All stations were to be accessible to handicapped individuals who could use steps (for example, hearing-impaired or mobile blind people). But, recognizing the high cost and difficulty of retrofitting existing facilities so that wheelchair-bound persons could have access to them, the DOT adopted the key station concept set forth by New York City.[84] The DOT estimated that the application of the key station formula would make accessible a nationwide average of about 40 percent of rapid rail stations, perhaps as high as 60 percent in some cities. In essence, the figure reached was a compromise: agency officials rejected New York City's proposed 10 percent as too low and Convisser's proposed 60 percent as too high. The final percentage was close to that supported by Morton Downey, assistant secretary for program and budget. As part of the compromise, the regulations mandated connector bus service between inaccessible and accessible stations. From the perspective of transit operators, who believed that even total "full accessibility" would benefit only a small

83. Ibid. at 31457.

84. A key subway station was one that satisfied any of the following criteria: passenger boardings exceeded average station boardings by at least 15 percent; the station was a transfer point on a rail line or between rail lines, a major interchange point with other transportation modes, or served major activity centers (employment or government centers, institutions of higher learning, hospitals, health care centers); the station was an "end" station, unless an end station was close to another accessible station; or the station was a "special trip generator" for sizable numbers of handicapped persons. Ibid. at 31478.

fraction of disabled people, the compromise percentage seemed too high; for the disability rights groups, the DOT decision was a retreat from a stricter standard.

With respect to the time period for obtaining full accessibility for facilities, the DOT decided upon the thirty-year deadline, rather than the twelve- or twenty-year option. However, one-third of all key stations had to be made accessible within the first twelve years. While it understood the view of handicapped people who had "already waited a long time for the removal of transportation barriers," the DOT believed that it had to "take care to mandate only what can be accomplished practically by recipients and by the Department." The DOT calculated that over the thirty-year compliance period, the cost of achieving program accessibility would be about $1 billion.[85] Transit agencies could seek a waiver of the program accessibility requirement if, after consultation with the handicapped community and a public hearing, the operator could show to the secretary that it could provide alternate service "substantially as good as or better than" the service that would have been provided by making the system accessible. Service "as good as or better" was defined generally in terms of the equivalency of the service area, fares, hours, wait and travel frequency, lack of restriction on trip purpose, and general availability. The waiver provisions were tightly drawn so as to discourage transit operators from seeking ways to circumvent the goals of accessible transit.

Further, the rule generally required that rapid rail vehicles purchased after July 2, 1979, would have to be accessible, and, that on a system basis, one vehicle per train would have to be accessible within three years of the effective date of the regulation. Up to five years would be allowed if extraordinary costs were involved.

The rule called for accessibility in commuter rail transit within three years, but permitted extensions (thirty years for facilities and ten for vehicles) for "extraordinarily expensive structural changes." As to light rail (trolley and streetcars), the DOT imposed the same time limit, except that for costly structural alterations it allowed twenty years for facilities and for vehicles.

From the third year of the effective date of the regulations—July 2, 1982—the department mandated "interim accessible service." That service involved the expenditure of an amount equal to 2 percent of the area's section 5 and section 18 funds (urban and rural formula grants, respec-

85. Ibid. at 31459.

tively). Operators were to use their best efforts to coordinate all available special transportation services in the community, and were to develop their plans in cooperation with an advisory group of local representatives of handicapped persons. Finally, the DOT stated that the regulations were not intended to discourage door-to-door paratransit services or programs that helped handicapped travelers directly through user subsidies or other methods.[86]

Round Four: Negative Reactions

Not surprisingly, a regulation that promised substantial costs evoked a sharp reaction from those who would bear some of the financial consequences, directly or indirectly. Almost immediately after publication of its final rule, the DOT found itself on the defensive. A critical report by the Congressional Budget Office questioned the whole enterprise, concluding that the full accessibility approach would be very expensive (an estimated $6.8 billion over thirty years) and few disabled persons would benefit from it.[87] In an effort to stave off a hostile legislative reaction, Convisser and his staff responded with a short document challenging the Congressional Budget Office's predictions of the latent demand for transit facilities by the handicapped and the cost estimates of making existing transit systems accessible.[88] The brief for the DOT position also defended the merits of the section 504 rule itself, contending that a "special services" approach (vans, paratransit vehicles) would be more expensive over the long term than pursuing the full accessibility conception. Special services, so the argument went, would involve considerably more continuing operating costs than full accessibility. Further, federal grants for operating costs could not exceed 50 percent, while grants for capital expenditures could cover 80 percent of costs. The DOT claimed, moreover, that a special services approach would require a significant enforcement effort to ensure that required standards were achieved on a continuing basis, thus increasing federal intrusiveness at the local level. The ACCD weighed in on the side of full accessibility, arguing that the costs for fixed-rate transit were over-

86. Ibid. at 31443, 31460.
87. Congressional Budget Office, *Urban Transportation for Handicapped Persons: Alternative Federal Approaches* (GPO, 1979).
88. DOT, "Comments on Transportation for Handicapped Persons," June 9, 1980.

estimated, while those for specialized services were underestimated.[89] Further, it contended that local option did not work.

The Transit Community Resists

A few months after the publication of the final rule, APTA was engaged in a strategy to nullify and overturn the regulations. Transit officials sought to persuade Brock Adams's successor, Neil Goldschmidt, to reevaluate the section 504 effort. A former mayor of Portland, Oregon, Goldschmidt had experience with mass transit and was well known to the transportation network. Significantly, the day after his appointment as secretary, but before his confirmation hearings, Goldschmidt wrote to Patricia Roberts Harris, Califano's successor as HEW secretary:

> It is my intention to undertake a comprehensive review of the Section 504 matters in early September, when I return to Washington for the confirmation hearings. It is furthermore my intention to develop a strategy which will respond to the interests of the handicapped, but which, in doing so, will also be reasonable and flexible with respect to the needs of transit operators and manufacturers. . . .[90]

Goldschmidt asked that HEW delay any actions on section 504 until he and Secretary Harris had an opportunity to discuss and review the situation. DOT officials involved in the section 504 proceedings later explained to Goldschmidt that the department had, in fact, already completed its rulemaking activities, and that, realistically, little could be done at that point without risking a major controversy. In an attempt to sidestep the issue gracefully, Goldschmidt wrote that he was of "the view that the regulations issued this past summer by the Department of Transportation are well within the Department's authority and should remain in effect until we consider whether further legislative or rulemaking action should be pursued."[91] New to a job encompassing a broad range of complex, pressing issues, Goldschmidt thus ultimately chose not to expend the time and political resources needed to change a policy that had only recently been put in place, after considerable effort, by the very people whose support

89. Dennis Cannon and Frances Rainbow, *Full Mobility: Counting the Costs of the Alternatives* (Washington, D.C.: American Coalition of Citizens with Disabilities, 1980). Cannon, one of the foremost experts on transportation for the disabled, later joined the staff of the Architectural and Transportation Barriers Compliance Board.

90. Letter from Neil Goldschmidt to Patricia Roberts Harris, August 16, 1979.

91. Letter from Goldschmidt to Harris, September 25, 1979.

he would need, at least during the early part of his tenure. He would not have been able to do so without incurring the wrath of those disability organizations for whom section 504 had become an important symbol. Any effort to undo all that—without judicial sanction—was likely to be difficult, as the beneficiaries fought for understandable reasons to preserve what they claimed as theirs by right, absolutely and for all time.

APTA did not limit its efforts to the DOT. It promoted the abortive attempt in 1980 to enact legislation (the Cleveland and Howard amendments) that would have given state and local governments discretion in meeting the transportation needs of the elderly and the handicapped (see chapter 2). APTA also championed the successful attempts in the appropriations process to prohibit the expenditure of UMTA funds for the retrofitting of buses and subways. In the courts, it mounted a challenge to the 504 regulations, arguing in part that the legislative history of the Rehabilitation Act of 1973 and Supreme Court opinions did not support the full accessibility mandate.

Affected localities found ways to register their displeasure with the DOT rules. In New York City, whose transit system is the most extensive in the country, the board of directors of the Metropolitan Transit Authority (MTA) voted not to comply with the federal regulations.[92] The MTA concluded that compliance would be too costly—$1.5 billion at the outset—while the annual federal aid to be forfeited would have been only $435 million. Although MTA eventually reversed its decision—choosing to seek a formal waiver of compliance with the rail portion rather than forgo federal support—APTA unanimously supported its initial refusal and urged other cities to follow suit.[93]

The U.S. Court of Appeals for the D.C. Circuit sounded the death knell for the regulations when it sustained APTA's legal challenge to the DOT's interpretation of section 504.[94] The court remanded the regulations to the DOT secretary to determine whether other statutory authorities on which the department had also relied in promulgating the rule—including sections 3, 5, and 16 of the Urban Mass Transportation Act and section 165(b) of the Federal-Aid Highway Act of 1973—provided a proper basis for the

92. *New York Times*, September 20, 1980.

93. Letter from Richard Ravitch, MTA chairman, to Neil Goldschmidt, DOT secretary, December 31, 1980, reprinted in Metropolitan Transit Authority, "Draft Section 504 Transition Plan for Handicapped Accessibility" (September 1980); and *New York Times*, October 19, 1980.

94. *APTA* v. *Lewis*, 655 F.2d 1272 (D.C. Cir. 1981).

regulatory requirements in the absence of authorization by section 504. In fact, the DOT had no intention of using the other statutes to support the full accessibility mandate. By the time the court reached its judgment, the Reagan administration had held the reins of government for four months. Early in its tenure, the DOT, under the direction of the new secretary, Drew Lewis, began to review the accessibility requirements. The Presidential Task Force on Regulatory Relief, headed by Vice-President George Bush, also identified the section 504 regulations as one of the federal government's costly requirements meriting review. The task force was one of the Reagan administration's means of implementing a policy that sought to reduce the regulatory burden on local governments and other affected parties. As a consequence of these reassessments, the department had already determined, by the time the appellate court ruled, that it should change policy. The DOT concluded that while recipients of federal aid for mass transit were obligated to ensure that provisions were made for handicapped persons, the major responsibility for deciding how that transportation should be provided should be returned to local communities. In essence, the department wanted to return to the "special efforts" formulation of the 1976 regulations. The decision of the U.S. Court of Appeals for the D.C. Circuit afforded such an opportunity.

The Reagan Administration Loosens the Regulatory Rein

In the summer of 1981 the DOT issued an interim final rule amending its section 504 regulations. In view of the court's opinion, the amendment deleted the sections requiring full accessibility in mass transportation. The DOT decided to require recipients of federal assistance to simply self-certify that "special efforts" to provide transportation for handicapped persons were being made in their service area. The examples of the level of activity that would satisfy the special efforts requirement were taken from the appendix to the 1976 regulations (see page 97). The one change was that a recipient could meet its obligation if it spent 3.5 percent of its section 5 funds on programs for the handicapped, rather than the 5 percent required under the 1976 regulations. The interim rule took effect immediately.[95]

95. 46 Fed. Reg. 37489, 37493 (1981). Under the Administrative Procedure Act, publication of a rule must normally take place thirty days before the rule's effective date. However, exceptions are permissible in the case of "a substantive rule which . . . relieves a restriction and as otherwise provided by the agency for good cause found and published with the rule." (5 U.S.C. 553[d][3])

The rule was intended to remain in force only until the department published a new permanent regulation. The DOT announced on July 20, 1981, that it would invite comments on what it should do before publishing a notice of proposed rulemaking. It identified two alternatives, although declaring its receptiveness to others. The first would be to make the interim provision permanent; another would be to prescribe a new local option program, perhaps requiring that programs meet certain service criteria.[96]

Local transit authorities complied with the interim rule in ways that did not necessarily ensure adequate service for disabled persons. The absence of service criteria or requirements for public participation, together with the self-certification process, meant that transit authorities had wide discretion. A GAO survey indicated that of eighty-four transit systems surveyed, only thirty of the eighty-three bus systems and six of the fourteen rail systems still intended to reach the level of accessibility previously required. Paratransit services, according to the study, seemed wanting: it cited waiting lists, long advance notice requirements, denials of request for service, shorter hours and fewer days of service, smaller geographical zones of service, priorities based on trip service, and inaccessibility of specialized transit.[97]

To redress these problems, Senators Alan Cranston of California and Donald W. Riegle, Jr., of Michigan succeeded in having Congress enact a measure that required the DOT to promulgate final regulations establishing "(1) minimum criteria for the provision of transportation services to handicapped and elderly individuals by recipients of Federal financial assistance . . . and (2) procedures for the Secretary to monitor recipients' compliance with such criteria."[98] The statute also required that organizations representing elderly and handicapped individuals be given an opportunity to comment on the proposed activities of the transit agencies. The version that originally passed the Senate, without deliberation or discussion, contained stronger language, requiring "minimum criterion for each recipient . . . to provide handicapped and elderly individuals with transportation

96. 46 Fed. Reg. 37491 (1981).

97. General Accounting Office, *Status of Special Efforts to Meet Transportation Needs of the Elderly and Handicapped* (GAO, 1982). Another study suggested much the same: Ecosometrics Incorporated, *Transition Planning for Accessible Mass Transit: Responses to DOT's 504 Regulation*, 2 vols., prepared for U.S. Department of Transportation (Bethesda, Md.: Ecosometrics, 1981).

98. 96 Stat. 2154.

services that such individuals can use and that are the *same as or comparable to* those which the recipient provides to the general public" (emphasis added). Because the "same or comparable" service formulation was dropped in conference committee, in part at the urging of the DOT, the department concluded that it was not obligated to pursue it.[99]

The interim rule was issued by July 20, 1981; the Cranston-Riegle amendment, enacted in December 1982, called for final regulations by June 1983. But the DOT did not even publish its notice of proposed rulemaking until September 1983. Quite obviously, in contrast to the Carter years, there was little pressure from the Reagan administration to meet the regulatory deadline in this policy area.

The political atmosphere had changed rather dramatically. The courts, through such opinions as *APTA* v. *Lewis,* largely took the steam out of the rights-oriented full accessibility approach. Consequently, the Reagan administration, whose philosophy rejected the full accessibility perspective in favor of local option, had considerable leeway in fashioning policy. The language of political dialogue about transportation changed from that of rights to one of resource allocation. As the various groups within the disabled community fought to protect their particular interests, the unity that had prevailed on the transportation issue during the rights era evaporated. The White House and the DOT felt little pressure from disability groups, perhaps with the notable exception of the PVA, to return to the full accessibility approach. With the rights battle over transportation largely lost in federal courts, disability groups focused their attention on other areas of policy in an attempt to thwart administration cutbacks in support. Indeed, the Reagan administration had the various groups scrambling when it announced in 1981 that the Department of Justice and the Bush task force planned to review and revise the section 504 guidelines. Each group attacked the planned revisions from its own perspective; the administration decided not to revise the guidelines largely because of the cumulative opposition.[100] But the narrowing judicial interpretations of section 504, combined with the administration's reduced enforcement effort, led many to conclude that the victory was mostly symbolic.

99. 48 Fed. Reg. 40685 (1983).

100. Vice-President Bush explained the administration's change of position in letters to leaders of handicapped groups, for example, in a letter to Robert J. Funk, Disability Rights Educational Defense Fund, March 21, 1983. The executive director of the Bush task force, Boyden Gray, was influenced by a long-time friend, Evan Kemp of the Disability Rights Center. Interview with Evan Kemp, March 27, 1986.

ASSERTING WHITE HOUSE CONTROL

Just as its predecessor sought to strengthen presidential control over the regulatory processes of its agencies and department, so the Reagan administration attempted to create an effective mechanism to stem the flow of what it perceived to be unnecessary rules. Soon after assuming office—on February 17, 1981—President Reagan issued Executive Order 12291, "to reduce the burdens of existing and future regulations, increase agency accountability for regulatory actions, provide for presidential oversight of the regulatory process, minimize duplication and conflict of regulations and insure well-reasoned regulations."[101] Under the terms of the order, agencies can take action only if the potential benefits outweigh the social costs. They are to choose the least costly alternative in selecting among regulatory objectives and are to set priorities for the purpose of maximizing net benefits. Agencies are to follow these requirements "to the extent permitted by law." The director of the OMB and the Presidential Task Force on Regulatory Relief were given authority to designate proposed or existing rules as "major" rules, to prepare uniform standards for measuring costs and benefits, to express approval or disapproval of regulatory impact analyses and rules of the administrative agencies, to make agencies respond to those views, and to set schedules for review and revision of existing major rules. If disagreements exist about a proposed regulation and the OMB requests a period of consultation, then the agency can be required to withhold publication of the notice of proposed rulemaking or final rule.

Not long before beginning his second term, Reagan further extended his regulatory grasp with Executive Order 12498.[102] The OMB's authority now takes hold even earlier in the regulatory process than under the previous executive order and includes "pre-rulemaking actions" by the agencies. Those activities are defined as "any important action taken to consider whether to initiate, or in contemplation of, rulemaking, publication of advance notices of proposed rulemaking and all similar notices, publi-

---

101. 3 C.F.R. 127 (1981). For each "major rule"—those likely to have an effect on the economy of $100 million or more, or which are likely to result in a major increase in costs or prices or significant adverse impacts on "competition, employment, investment, productivity, innovation, or on the ability of United States-based enterprises to compete with foreign-based enterprises"—an agency has to prepare a regulatory impact analysis, including a description of the potential costs and benefits of the proposed rule, its potential net benefits, and alternative approaches that might substantially achieve the objectives at a lower cost.

102. The Bush Task Force, after declaring its mission accomplished, began phasing out its operations during Reagan's first term.

cations and requests for public comment; and developments or dissemination of . . . documents that may influence, anticipate, or could lead to the commencement of rulemaking proceedings at a later date."[103] Executive agencies subject to the order are required to submit to the OMB each year a "draft regulatory program" noting all significant regulatory activities (including pre-rulemaking ones); upon review, the OMB director can remand agency proposals for revision. Agencies can appeal their disagreements with the OMB to a cabinet council or other forum the president may designate. However, once the OMB issues the "administration's regulatory program" for the year, agencies cannot take actions not provided in it unless the OMB approves or a court requires them to do so.

The Carter and Reagan strategies for exerting presidential control differ in subtle but important ways. The Carter mechanism left implementation largely to the agencies; it was the agencies that determined what constituted a "major" rule and thus merited review. Under the Carter system, RARG's influence was essentially limited to the notice and comment period after the agency had published its proposed rule. Ultimately, its authority was largely advisory, with the agency free to ignore its judgment. Moreover, the Carter approach, unlike Reagan's, did not require that decisions be based on a cost-benefit criterion; although such an analysis had to be conducted, agencies did not have to choose cost-effective options if they provided some justification for their decision.

The Reagan apparatus firmly established the OMB as the gatekeeper of the regulatory process; it can determine which rules are major. Thus it was the OMB and the Task Force on Regulatory Relief that identified both the HEW guidelines and the DOT full accessibility regulations as warranting review and modification. Indeed, the task force and the OMB's Office of Information and Regulatory Analysis later pointed to the suspension of the DOT regulations as a Reagan administration achievement that saved $2.2 billion—though no supporting data were provided to support that figure.[104]

Further bolstering the OMB's power is its authority, if it faults an agency's regulatory analysis, to block a rule until its concerns are satisfied or until the president overrules its objections. Its influence can be felt before either the notice of proposed rulemaking or final rule is promulgated. Indeed, the Reagan regulatory overseers can make their views known to the

103. 50 Fed. Reg. 1036–38 (1985).
104. Presidential Task Force on Regulatory Relief, "Reagan Administration Achievements in Regulatory Relief: A Progress Report," August 1982, p. 11.

agency concerned without ever offering a public submission to the rule-making docket. Conceivably, in dealings with agencies, the White House staff or the OMB could act as a conduit for interested parties without disclosing the nature, substance, or even existence of those contacts. Commented one DOT official, the OMB "never leaves tracks or footprints." If that is indeed true, then openness, which rulemaking is supposed to promote, is being subverted.

The impact of their respective regulatory mechanisms on the implementation of section 504 highlights the differences between the Carter and Reagan approaches. In the Carter administration, HEW, and then the Department of Justice, was charged with enforcing section 504; neither was under any obligation to consult with RARG. In the Reagan administration, in contrast, the activities of the Department of Justice in enforcing section 504 are subject to OMB review. Not long after the DOT's publication of the interim final rule, the Department of Justice, with the approval of the OMB, suspended that part of the section 504 guidelines pertaining to mass transit.[105] It cited the *APTA* decision, which it said raised questions about the legal basis of the HEW guidelines. Moreover, the department stated that suspension would eliminate any conflict and confusion between the section 504 full accessibility guidelines and the DOT's interim final rule. It would continue to review DOT regulations, but on a case-by-case basis.

Given these pronounced changes in administration policy, it is perhaps all the more striking that many of those engaged in this revisionary effort were involved in drafting the original HEW guidelines and the 1979 DOT regulations. At Justice, the section 504 unit was led by John Wodatch—the same attorney who had directed HEW's work in the Office of Civil Rights seven years earlier. When HEW was split into the Department of Education and the Department of Health and Human Services in 1980, authority for coordinating section 504 was originally vested in the latter. But, believing that the civil rights perspective embodied in the section 504 guidelines could best be institutionally preserved in the Department of Justice, Senator Cranston and handicapped groups urged the administration to shift responsibility. By executive order, President Carter did so in the waning months of his term.[106] As a consequence, Wodatch and his unit moved to the Civil Rights Division of the Department of Justice, where they functioned in much the same way as they had at HEW.

---

105. 46 Fed. Reg. 40687 (1981).
106. 45 Fed. Reg. 72995 (1980).

At the DOT, those very same careerist attorneys who had crafted the 1979 full accessibility regulations were charged with fashioning the new rules. The presence of Robert Ashby and Neil Eisner probably had a moderating influence at a time when it was well understood that the preferred alternative to the 1979 regulations was one that called for the federal government to withdraw as much as possible.[107]

ONCE MORE INTO THE BREACH

Once more, Ashby set about to review sets of comments, this time on the interim final rule. The responses were fairly predictable. Most disability groups opposed the provision, supporting either full accessibility or the delineation of criteria that would ensure comparable service for disabled people. Many institutions charged with providing services for handicapped persons, such as state vocational rehabilitation agencies, tended to favor a service criteria approach. Disability groups also supported requirements guaranteeing their participation in the decisionmaking process. Some expressed concern that the criterion for the financial level of effort (3.5 percent of section 5 funds) was too vague or too low, or an inappropriate basis for determining compliance given that operating assistance funds under section 5 would be phased out under Reagan administration proposals. Not surprisingly, most transit authorities supported the interim final rule.

Based on these comments, the DOT's Office of Assistant General Counsel for Regulation and Enforcement drafted a notice of proposed rulemaking.[108] Its objectives were to establish minimum criteria for the provision of transportation for elderly and handicapped persons, ensure public participation in the process, and create a mechanism so that the department could monitor compliance. Both the Department of Justice and the OMB approved the DOT proposal, which was published on September 8, 1983. But it was not until the spring of 1986 that the DOT published its final rule.

The department received 650 comments in response to the proposed rules and did not complete reading and analysis of them until March 1984. In addition, in order to satisfy the cost-benefit requirements of the executive orders, the DOT staff undertook case studies in several urban areas

---

107. Within the DOT, there had always been relatively few who had been committed to finding a solution to the transportation problems of disabled persons; some had their jobs redefined or were even dismissed as a result of the reduction in force initiated by the Reagan administration in 1982. Others, like Martin Convisser, transferred to divisions that did not deal at all with the problem.

108. 48 Fed. Reg. 40684 (1983).

and hired a consultant to use a computer model to predict nationwide effects of different approaches. Those projects were not finished until November 1984. After Secretary of Transportation Elizabeth Dole (Drew Lewis's successor) chose among various policy options consistent with the proposed regulations, the final rule was drafted and circulated within the department. In the fall of 1985 the regulations were sent to the Department of Justice for review; once that agency signed off on the regulations, the OMB still had to approve them.

The labyrinth of the new regulatory system not only complicated the work of DOT officials, but also confused various affected interests. Distressed by the delays, the Maine Association of Handicapped Persons filed suit in federal court, seeking an order that the secretary of transportation issue final regulations forthwith. But the complaint did not name officials in the OMB and the Department of Justice, without whose approval the final regulations could not be published. The suit was thus directed against a party that could not, on its own, provide the remedy. In December 1985 the court directed Secretary Dole to transmit the regulations to the OMB and the Department of Justice for their review within ten days of the court order and to urge those agencies to consider and respond to the final regulations on an "urgent basis." Moreover, the DOT secretary was to report to the court every fifteen days as to the progress of the OMB and Department of Justice review.[109] Within the DOT, those engaged in the rulemaking proceeding wished that the court could have found some way to ensure that these other agencies discharged their duties promptly—perhaps by setting a deadline for the publication of the final rules. Executive Order 12250, which transferred section 504 enforcement to the Department of Justice, did not specify any time limit for that agency's consideration of rules. Although Executive Order 12291 mentions a thirty-day time period for OMB evaluation of a final rule, it provides that the agency may, at its discretion, extend review indefinitely. Thus, the court order notwithstanding, DOT officials were concerned that delays would not be eliminated, that the prospect for even further negotiations among the three agencies was still at hand. But the fact that the DOT had to report to the court about OMB and Department of Justice progress may have spurred them to complete their tasks.

109. Memorandum of Decision and Order on Cross Motions for Summary Judgment, *Maine Association of Handicapped Persons* v. *Dole*, Civil No. 85-0083 P (D. Me. December 3, 1985).

As a result of the court order, the DOT sent the rules to the OMB before the Department of Justice had approved them, departing from the usual procedure. In fact, the OMB did not officially approve the regulations until after Justice had done so. Neither of the oversight agencies attempted to block or significantly change the rules, as they have in other policy areas, and officials in the DOT found the outside input generally useful. Nevertheless, the review effort added about a year to the effort, counting the periods for evaluating both the proposed and final rules.

The final rule, issued in May 1986, sought to provide local authorities with discretion as to how best to meet the needs of their disabled population. Asserting the difficulty of forcing the diverse circumstances across the country into a "single, made-in-Washington mold," the DOT decided that recipients of federal financial assistance can fulfill their obligations under the rule by choosing either (1) special service (for example, dial-a-van, taxi vouchers); (2) an accessible bus system (either scheduled or on-call); or (3) a mixed system (that is, having both special service and accessible bus components). Whatever the type of service selected, authorities have to satisfy six service criteria: (1) all persons who by reasons of handicap are physically unable to use the recipient's bus service for the general public must be eligible to use the service for disabled persons; (2) service has to be provided to a handicapped person within twenty-four hours of requesting it; (3) restrictions based on trip purpose are prohibited; (4) fares must be comparable to fares charged the general public for the same or similar trips; (5) service for handicapped persons must operate throughout the same days and hours as the service for the general public; and (6) service for disabled people must be available throughout the same service area as service for the general public.

The rule established a limit on the amount of money a transit system is required to spend to meet these services. That cap is calculated by taking 3 percent of the recipient's average operating costs over the current and two previous fiscal years. The DOT estimated that the amount would be more than that required under the 1981 interim rule, but far less than that compelled by the 1979 full accessibility regulations. If the transit authority cannot meet the six criteria for the type of service it chooses without exceeding the limit on required expenditures, then it may modify its service to keep its expenditures within the limit, after consulting through a public participation process. In part, to assure that service was delivered, the DOT required authorities to submit their plans for approval before putting them into effect. Recipients are to work with the public, soliciting the views of disabled people.[110]

The Department of Transportation has thus returned to an effective mobility standard—but with more detailed criteria than those found in the 1976 or 1981 interim regulations. Policy has surely changed, though, from the 1979 full accessibility rules. The retrofitting of subway facilities and vehicles is no longer required at all. Local authorities have a choice of how to meet their obligations. Even if a recipient chooses to comply through bus accessibility, not every new vehicle has to be equipped to serve wheelchair users. There is no requirement that 50 percent of a recipient's bus fleet has to be accessible, as there was in earlier rules. Further, the regulations explicitly provide for a cost cap to limit the amount that authorities have to spend. And so has ended, at last, a tortuous series of rulemaking proceedings.

Transbus: The Failure of Technology Forcing

For a dozen years, the Department of Transportation sought to write rules and regulations providing for some kind of transit for disabled people. However, these efforts to address the needs of the disabled rested not only on its regulations, but also on Transbus—a vehicle at first conceived to breathe new life into the ailing mass transit industry, though later viewed as the way to assure barrier-free transportation for those confined to wheelchairs. Indeed, for the DOT, Transbus was very nearly the perfect solution, which in large measure would both enable the government to fulfill its transit obligations to the disabled population and relieve it of the task of creating complex regulations resented by the transit community and local governments. Transbus was to be a technological fix—the union of commercial purpose, technological development, and social objectives. Millions of dollars were spent on research and testing. But in the end Transbus, the embodiment of DOT's commitment to the disabled, was abandoned. Reflecting upon the Transbus saga, one top DOT official wondered, "I do not know how all of us brilliant people could go through years of a rather constructive effort of this kind and come up as sterile as we have."[111]

110. 51 Fed. Reg. 18994–19038 (1986).
111. *Oversight of the Urban Mass Transportation Administration's Technology Development and Equipment Procurement Programs (Bus and Rail Rolling Stock)*, Hearings be-

Need for a New Bus

In the late 1960s public use of mass transit was declining. With a prosperous economy and inexpensive gasoline, automobiles were clearly the preferred mode of transportation. Beyond that, the uncomfortable buses then in existence could hardly have been expected to stem the disaffection with mass transit, let alone attract new riders. No new major design changes had been introduced in nearly a decade. A 1968 report of the National Academy of Engineering recommended that a new bus be built, with low floors, easier entry, improved appearance, better safety, and greater reliability.[112]

In 1972 the Urban Mass Transportation Administration awarded identical contracts, totaling about $28 million, to General Motors, Rohr-Flxible, and American Motors General, charging each company with the task of designing an attractive, easily maintained, fuel-efficient bus that would lure new passengers. The notion was that bus manufacturers would create their own designs for a wide-door low-floor bus (twenty-two inches off the ground rather than the standard thirty-four), and after testing the consulting firm of Booz-Allen Applied Research would draw up composite specifications, incorporating the best aspects of each design.

In essence, the DOT—or more precisely, UMTA—set out to remake the bus industry by determining the design or performance specifications. Previously, the bus industry had operated much like the automobile sector, developing and marketing its own vehicles. The assumption was that because UMTA, through its capital assistance program, paid 80 percent of the cost of new vehicles for public transit authorities, it could determine bus procurement policy. It could use that authority to force technology and thus induce manufacturers to create buses that were consistent with the government's vision.

A Bus for All Purposes

Meanwhile, in 1973 Congress enacted section 504 of the Rehabilitation Act. In August 1974, in appropriating UMTA's budget for fiscal 1975, Congress attached a rider forbidding the expenditure of funds for the pur-

---

fore the Subcommittee on Oversight and Review of the House Committee on Public Works and Transportation, 96 Cong. 1 sess. (GPO, 1979), p. 596. (Hereafter *Bus Hearings*.)

112. National Academy of Engineering, *Design Performance Criteria and Improved Nonrail Urban Mass Transit Vehicles* (Washington, D.C.: NAE, 1968).

chase of buses unless they were designed to meet the mass transportation needs of the elderly or handicapped. Even earlier, in 1970, Congress had passed the Biaggi amendment, declaring that "special efforts" should be made to ensure that elderly and handicapped individuals could use public transit. The DOT, which was reluctant to do very much in response, recognized that politically it would have to take at least some steps to satisfy these laws. The new bus project, known as Transbus, seemed to be at least one answer. After all, its low floor would provide access to individuals confined to wheelchairs. To UMTA officials, advancing Transbus as the vehicle for the disabled was, at the time, an inspired idea. Transbus was presumably in the DOT's future anyway; thus there appeared to be no cost and only benefit in promoting Transbus as the vehicle that would solve the mobility problems of the disabled. But, as will be shown, although the benefits were immediate, the costs were cumulative.[113]

In early January 1975, UMTA administrators announced a federal policy for introducing Transbus nationwide, even though the testing program was not finished. UMTA indicated that it would develop a performance specification based on the prototypes and that, barring unforeseen problems, it would require a low-floor bus plus a ramp or lift device to accommodate wheelchair users. The agency expected completion of Transbus prototype testing in August 1975; the performance specifications would be developed concurrently, and the buses were to be in service by late 1977 or early 1978.[114]

A day after the announcement, UMTA administrator Frank Herringer traveled to New York, where amid much fanfare at special ceremonies at City Hall, he introduced Transbus to the Big Apple. He declared, "We have set out to improve passenger comfort and safety, maintain economy of operation and maintenance and above all to make urban transportation accessible to all Americans, especially the elderly and the handicapped. Transbus designs have accomplished these goals." He added that the "special designs for boarding persons confined to wheelchairs on Transbus is a big first step toward improved mobility."[115] Not long after, in the preamble to its proposed rules for the elderly and handicapped, UMTA seemed to

113. This formulation was first used by Wallace Sayre in relation to government reorganization.
114. UMTA, "Policy for Introducing Transbus into Nationwide Service," January 8, 1975.
115. *DOT News,* January 9, 1975.

reiterate that commitment to Transbus, noting that it was perhaps on the "verge of providing a solution to the level-changing problem on at-grade vehicles."[116]

In fact, Transbus was not as imminent as UMTA's statements indicated. Herringer believed that his announcement would make it clear that Transbus was the only vehicle that could satisfy DOT policy. But at the same time that UMTA set forth its view about Transbus, it declared that in the interim it would fund the manufacture of other vehicles—"high-floor, two-axle buses incorporating styling and design changes consistent with the Transbus."[117] Herringer assumed that, in fact, manufacturers would not develop other models, given that they could expect the government to pay for them for only the few months' interim duration. However, manufacturers interpreted the interim policy as indicative of UMTA's own uncertainty about the feasibility of Transbus.

General Motors, the major manufacturer, gambled that Transbus would never see the light of day and decided to go into production with its own "advanced design bus," RTS-2. The company had already invested several years in designing such a prototype. GM claimed that it would ultimately produce a bus with a twenty-four-inch effective floor height, ten inches lower than the stationary floor height available before the introduction of the RTS. The bus would have two front-door eight-inch steps with an eight-inch step to the ground. Transbus specifications, in contrast, included a floor no more than twenty-two inches off the ground—a fourteen-inch step into the bus, plus one eight-inch step inside—one less step. GM believed that its advanced-design bus was an attractive alternative to Transbus and that the government would turn to RTS-2 once it became apparent that Transbus was not working. Of course, once it decided to go ahead with RTS-2, GM had little incentive to participate in the Transbus effort.

Transbus in Trouble

Meanwhile, tests of the Transbus prototype revealed serious problems. DOT Secretary William Coleman, who had assumed office in early 1975, went to Miami to observe some test runs only to find that "you could only

116. 40 Fed. Reg. 8315 (1975).
117. Ibid.

get one wheelchair on each bus, and the lift didn't work. So I said to Her-ringer, 'How in the hell can you say you're solving the problem of the handicapped?' What I saw didn't do it."[118]

In June 1975 UMTA Administrator Herringer left to become general manager of San Francisco's BART system. His successor, Robert E. Pa-tricelli, soon had to respond to those manufacturers who argued that Trans-bus was not a viable project. UMTA's final regulations pertaining to the elderly and the handicapped, issued in April 1976, backed away from UMTA's commitment to Transbus. Alluding to its discussions with GM about the advanced-design bus, UMTA noted that "substantial questions have arisen about the costs and benefits of a mandated 22-inch floor height requirement. One bus manufacturer [GM] wants to discuss the possibility of a 29-inch floor, with a kneeling feature [a device reducing the effective first-step height from ground level] to lower the floor five additional inches."[119] Accordingly, UMTA decided to hold a public hearing on May 5, 1976, and to accept written comments submitted before May 14, 1976, before reaching a decision.

At the end of July, Patricelli announced a new policy, effectively scrap-ping Transbus. Concluding that "it was not appropriate or feasible to man-date the 22-inch floor Transbus design," the UMTA administrator declared that henceforth all new transit buses purchased with federal grant funds and advertised for bid after February 15, 1977, had to have effective floor heights of not more than twenty-four inches; in other words, some com-bination of "kneeling feature" and lowered floor height had to be twenty-four inches or less. In essence, UMTA had accepted GM's view that its advanced-design bus was an appropriate substitute for Transbus.

Patricelli claimed that the twenty-four-inch effective floor height largely fulfilled the purposes of the Transbus program as originally conceived: "To bring into commercial use a new generation of transit buses that would provide better and more attractive transit service; and to encourage com-petition in the supply industry by providing equal opportunity to the three transit bus manufacturers to produce advanced design buses."[120] For Patri-celli, the needs of transit generally were of primary importance; the con-cerns of the disabled could only be considered in the context of the broader purposes of mass transit policy.

The switch to an effective floor height of twenty-four inches was based

118. *Los Angeles Times,* March 9, 1980.
119. 41 Fed. Reg. 18236 (1976).
120. "UMTA Policy Statement on Transbus," July 27, 1976, p. 1.

upon UMTA's finding that it was technically feasible. The agency noted that two manufacturers had announced their intention to produce interim or advanced-design buses within a year, and a third believed it could do so within eighteen months. Transbus, on the other hand, could not be introduced for another three to five years. A variety of other problems militated against continued development of Transbus. Testimony from manufacturers and APTA suggested that necessary components of the twenty-two-inch floor design were not yet proven or production-ready; the estimated capital and operating costs of the interim buses were lower; the low-floor bus would be less fuel efficient, would offer fewer seats, and would "cause a wasteful discarding of some of the new tooling already developed for advanced design buses"; as a matter of general policy, federal regulatory mandates should be limited when the market was properly responding; and APTA "strongly" opposed a federally mandated low-floor bus. UMTA concluded that "the marginal additional benefits in going from an effective 24-inch floor height (with kneeler) to a 22-inch floor height do not merit the substantial additional costs involved in any such Federal mandates imposed at this time."[121]

In the aftermath of the Patricelli announcement, Flxible decided to proceed with the development of its own version of the advanced-design bus—the 870. For its part, AM General brought an ultimately unsuccessful legal suit challenging UMTA's authority to fund acquisition of the interim advanced-design buses.[122]

If there was any one group that was disturbed, indeed bitter, about the decision to abandon Transbus, it was the activists in the disabled community. When UMTA pronounced that Transbus was a key part of its solution to providing transportation for the disabled, it transformed the vehicle from a project with commercial promise to a symbol of the federal government's commitment to provide fully accessible transit to the physically disabled. At the same time, UMTA created a constituency of disabled

121. Ibid., p. 6.
122. The so-called Houston consortium, consisting of the Houston Transit System, San Antonio Transit System, Dallas Transit System, Alameda–Contra Costa Transit District, Long Beach (California) Public Transportation Company, and Brockton (Massachusetts) Transportation Authority, sought to purchase the interim buses. The only bidder, GM, won a contract for its RTS-2. AM General charged that UMTA, by concurring in the specifications for buses presented by the consortium, had violated the Urban Mass Transportation Act's prohibition against "exclusionary" specifications. In the end judgment was entered in favor of the defendants. *AM General Corporation* v. *Department of Transportation*, 433 F. Supp. 1166 (D.D.C. 1977).

people who were dedicated to ensuring Transbus's success. For them, Transbus represented the marriage of technology and social purpose; it was the means of assuring what they thought to be fundamental rights. As one Transbus advocate, Sieglinde Shapiro, stated, "Just like the black citizens of this country who fought to get a seat in [the] front of the bus, we have had to fight to get on the bus."[123]

Even before UMTA officially sounded the death knell for Transbus, representatives of various disability groups lashed out at what they perceived to be a slackening of DOT interest in Transbus. John Lancaster of the Paralyzed Veterans of America and Richard Heddinger of the National Paraplegia Foundation, for example, blasted UMTA in House hearings early in 1976. A consortium of organizations, led by Disabled in Action of Pennsylvania, banded together to form the Transbus Group. The group, representing the disabled and elderly, had a roster of 13.3 million members nationwide. The Transbus Group sought to ensure that the original Herringer decision was implemented; it pressed its cause in discussions with DOT officials, before congressional committees, and, perhaps most significantly, in court. With the aid of the Public Interest Law Center of Philadelphia, the Transbus Group filed suit about six weeks before Patricelli's decision, seeking to require that federal funds allocated to local transportation authorities be used to purchase the twenty-two-inch low-floor vehicle.[124] In the end, the court ruled the case moot after DOT Secretary Brock Adams, who assumed office in 1977 with the Carter administration, reinstituted the Transbus mandate.

A New Life for Transbus

Five months after UMTA effectively scrapped Transbus, the Carter administration took the reins of power. Circumstances in the early days of the new presidency led Secretary Adams to reexamine and ultimately reverse the Patricelli decision. The fervor of the disability groups pressing HEW Secretary Joseph Califano to sign the section 504 regulations impressed the DOT head; he was sympathetic to those who argued that they had a right to enter society's mainstream. Moreover, Adams believed that

123. David C. Hackney, "Transbus as Last Hope," *Mass Transit,* vol. 6 (January–February 1979), p. 16.
124. *Disabled in Action of Pennsylvania* v. *Coleman,* 448 F. Supp. 109 (E.D. Pa. 1978).

government could spur technology by mandating requirements that manufacturers would have to satisfy if they wanted its support. He was not convinced that Transbus could not work. Further, pressure was mounting; not only was there a lawsuit in place, but also Senator Harrison A. Williams planned to introduce a bill mandating full accessibility.

In February 1977 Adams announced that he was reviewing the Transbus policy, the DOT would hold a public hearing in March at which all interested parties could participate, and he would make a decision no later than May 27.[125] He did so after weighing the views of manufacturers, APTA, individual transit authorities, DOT staff, groups representing the disabled and others, the record on which Patricelli based his decision, the transcript of the March public hearing, and written material submitted to the docket.

The Adams "Transbus mandate," announced on May 19, 1977, required that all procurements approved by UMTA and issued for bid after September 30, 1979, meet specifications that included a stationary floor height of not more than twenty-two inches, an effective floor height including a kneeling feature of not more than eighteen inches, and a ramp for boarding and exiting. The DOT secretary asserted that a review of the history of the program convinced him that simply encouraging Transbus would not result in its introduction in the short term or even in the long run. A mandate, however, would "provide the necessary federal leadership in the marketplace to allow transit bus manufacturers to plan investments and tooling costs around certain minimum performance and design characteristics. This, in turn, . . . [would] permit low-bid procurements that . . . [would] assist in the maintenance of a viable and competitive bus manufacturing industry based on a predictable federal policy."[126]

Suggesting that judicial and congressional pronouncements—such as the 1970 Biaggi amendment and section 504 of the Rehabilitation Act of 1973—would not countenance any needless delay in providing accessible transit, Adams declared that even apart from such concerns it was his responsibility to ensure such transportation services. "We cannot deny . . . [mobility-impaired] people the rights that so many others enjoy when it is within our ability to accord them such rights." The advanced-design bus, he argued, was not an adequate alternative because it was not accessible to the disabled without a wheelchair lift; and not only were the wheel-

125. 42 Fed. Reg. 9654 (1977). I discussed Adams's decision with UMTA analyst Douglas Gurin, May 24, 1984.

126. *Congressional Record* (June 23, 1977), p. 20535.

chair lifts, in his view, expensive and inefficient, but they also were re-garded as "degrading" by the disabled.[127] The low-floor bus, in contrast, could use a ramp.

Adams emphasized that in his judgment Transbus had been technolog-ically and economically feasible for some time. Although recognizing that Transbus might be more expensive, he concluded that the costs were not "unreasonable in light of the substantial benefits to all bus riders which Transbus will provide."[128] For the period before Transbus took effect, Adams decided to leave in place the interim policy on accessibility; that is, manufacturers had to continue to offer optional wheelchair lifts, and local transit authorities had to either buy buses with lifts or provide special ser-vices for elderly and handicapped persons. To do everything possible to assure early purchases of substantial numbers of the vehicle, the DOT an-nounced that it would encourage the creation of groups to make initial procurements of Transbuses from each manufacturer through advertised low-bid competitions; to help defray start-up production costs, the DOT agreed to make progress payments in connection with these initial pur-chases.

Adams's Transbus mandate satisfied Senator Williams, who moved to strike that part of his proposed legislation mandating accessible transit. In a letter to Adams, Williams outlined several steps he thought would facil-itate implementation of the Transbus decision, including the involvement of the disabled and the elderly communities, the creation of a monitoring system, active oversight by the Senate Committee on Labor and Human Resources, and the submission of periodic progress reports to the com-mittee.[129]

If the Adams announcement heartened Senator Williams and, of course, the disabled and elderly groups, it was unsettling to the manufacturers who had focused their energies on the advanced-design buses. General Motors supported an amendment introduced by Representative E. G. (Bud) Shu-ster, a Republican from southwestern Pennsylvania, that would have forced the DOT secretary to reassess the Transbus program and report to Congress by January 1, 1979. That expected reevaluation injected such uncertainty that a consortium of three cities backed away from plans to buy 530 Transbuses before the DOT deadline. Disability organizations, particularly the Transbus Group, were outraged, and branded GM the vil-

127. Ibid., pp. 20535, 20536.
128. Ibid., p. 20536.
129. Ibid., p. 20534.

lain. Declared Sieglinde Shapiro, "GM is the foe. . . . GM has been actively working to undermine the intent of the U.S. Transportation Department, congressmen and the will of the people."[130] The Transbus Group secured the support of such friends as Representatives Mario Biaggi and Claude Pepper, who met with DOT officials to reach a compromise that would preserve the Transbus program. Secretary Adams met as well with representatives of GM. In the end, an agreement was achieved; GM withdrew its opposition to the bus, while the DOT decided to extend Transbus's development time and to permit manufacturers to choose between a ramp *or* wheelchair option—thus satisfying GM, whose bus had the lift feature. With that compromise, the Shuster amendment was deleted.

Apart from these skirmishes within Congress, in the fifteen months following the Adams announcement the DOT engaged in an intensive review of Transbus, seeking public comment about various aspects relating to procurements and specifications. It was, in the words of UMTA administrator Richard Page, "the most thorough review . . . ever afforded a bus specification." Among the comments were those questioning the desirability of a ramp requirement—especially in communities with few curbs. UMTA decided, as noted above, to allow either a ramp or a front-door wheelchair lift, claiming that wheelchair technology was maturing.[131] In affirming the Transbus mandate in September 1978, Page noted that the three cities—Los Angeles, Miami, and Philadelphia—that earlier had backed away from the project would request bids under the specification on an order for 530 buses. "We expect the first consortium to advertise for bids within a month," Page declared. "In order to attain the earliest possible implementation of the Transbus mandate, the department is fully prepared to make progress payments to the winning bidder," he continued.[132]

The Manufacturers Fail to Bid

But in fact no bids were received from any manufacturer on the bid opening date, May 2, 1979. AM General had already dropped out a year before, after losing its suit that sought to prevent its competitors from marketing their advanced-design buses. It charged that uncertainty about bus requirements led to its decision to withdraw from Transbus. In early 1979,

130. Hackney, "Transbus as Last Hope," p. 18.
131. 43 Fed. Reg. 41988 (1978).
132. "DOT Reaffirms Transbus Mandate and Issues New Specification," *DOT News,* September 14, 1978.

Grumman, which had purchased Flxible from Rohr in January 1978, announced that it would not bid on Transbus. "Accessibility is not the real issue," declared Grumman/Flxible President Thomas J. Bernard.[133] Flxible cited business and technical reasons for its decision: fourteen of the specifications were allegedly impossible to meet; the specifications required a commitment to manufacture a product that was not yet designed at a price that could not be reasonably determined; Flxible did not make all the components of a bus, and the companies that manufactured tires, axles, transmissions, and other major components were not committed to supply them; the proposed Transbus would cost significantly more to buy and to maintain; and important questions of passenger safety remained unanswered.

General Motors also declined to bid and stated that accessibility was not the issue.[134] The company asserted that among its technological concerns were adverse impacts from the federal tandem rear axle and low-floor component, space limitations, significantly greater fuel consumption, and shorter component service life. GM further criticized the low-bid procurement process under which DOT planned to award Transbus contracts. The low-bid process, in its view, inhibited innovative research and development. Moreover, the procurement policies seemed to present what GM thought was an irreconcilable dilemma. Although initial contracts would be awarded solely to the lowest bidder, UMTA asserted that it might award future contracts on the basis of a life cycle cost evaluation; but GM argued that a lower-quality bus, designed to satisfy the strict low-bid requirement, would be inherently different from the higher-quality vehicle designed to meet the life cycle standards. Thus a bus manufacturer would have to have two designs, one for the initial Transbus contract and the other for future ones—and with those different contracts, two expensive engineering programs. The risk, GM concluded, was too great.

The End of the Line

Reacting to the decisions of the companies' effective withdrawal, Adams declared that he was "deeply disappointed." "In doing so," he continued, "they [the bus manufacturers] have acted against the transportation needs of all Americans, particularly the elderly and the handicapped."[135]

133. *Bus Hearings*, p. 99.
134. Ibid., pp. 238–40.
135. Statement of Secretary of Transportation Brock Adams on Transbus, May 2, 1979, Washington, D.C.

Chagrined that manufacturers would not bid, UMTA administrator Richard Page later voiced his frustration.

In view of the record of accomplishment of American industry and U.S. society in winning world wars and introducing new cars, building new airplanes, and all of the range of sophisticated technology . . . I find it hard to believe that General Motors Corp. or the Grumman Flxible Corp. or any other corporation which builds buses or trucks or rail cars could not find a way to produce a product that is already available in Western Europe within the space of 5 years.[136]

In light of the failure to bid, Adams called for an independent scientific review of the Transbus procurement requirements and specifications. The DOT engaged the Mitre Corporation, a nonprofit engineering consulting firm, in mid-June to make an assessment. The following month, not long before leaving office, Adams announced that the National Research Council (NRC), the principal operating agency of the National Academy of Sciences and the National Academy of Engineering, had, at his request, created a panel that would evaluate the Mitre findings. Mitre completed its work in July and the NRC, in late August.

Those reports, much to the disappointment of Transbus supporters, concluded that the decisions of the U.S. bus manufacturers not to bid were reasonable and understandable business judgments.[137] Both agreed that Transbus as specified would have entailed significant financial risk, given such factors as its smaller tires and unproven tandem axles. Although the vehicle as defined could not be procured, Mitre and the NRC panel concluded that in concept Transbus would represent a major advance over the previous generation of buses. The advanced-design bus, which would be less expensive than Transbus, would also offer substantial improvements over the older vehicles then in service. Both reports shared the view that the Transbus mandate should be delayed while the DOT reexamined its options with respect to the project. They differed sharply, however, in their assessment as to when an improved Transbus could be produced, with Mitre asserting that from a technical perspective it could be available within five years, and the NRC panel determining that insufficient evidence existed to make such a judgment.

136. *Department of Transportation and Related Agencies Appropriations for Fiscal Year 1980*, Hearings before a Subcommittee of the Senate Committee on Appropriations, 96 Cong. 1 sess. (GPO, 1979), p. 523. I benefited from a discussion with Page on this and other issues, May 12, 1983.

137. The Mitre Corporation, *Transbus: An Overview of Technical, Operational and Economic Characteristics*, MTR-79 W00332 (McLean, Va.: Mitre, 1979); and National Academy of Sciences, *NRC Transbus Study* (Washington, D.C.: NAS, 1979).

The Transbus evaluations confirmed what was already known—that the project was in desperate straits. Even before the NRC study was completed, UMTA announced that it was deleting the original effective date of September 30, 1979, for Transbus procurement requirements until some future time to be specified later—thus quietly putting Transbus to rest.[138] In addition, in the summer of 1979, the project's most important advocate, Secretary Brock Adams, left office. His successor, Neil Goldschmidt, was not inclined to resurrect the venture.

Conclusion: Two Administrative Approaches

The administrative process took two routes. One involved the development of regulations—based on either the full accessibility or the effective mobility standard—requiring state and local governments to provide some measure of transportation for the disabled. The other concentrated on forcing technology to produce a vehicle that would accommodate all categories of riders. In both cases, the policy course was rocky and uncertain. I consider each in turn, in an effort to understand how various elements of the administrative process contributed to the outcome.

Evaluating the Regulatory Process

Bureaucracies are generally thought to be forces of stability, slow to alter direction. But over a period of twelve years, the Department of Transportation shifted back and forth between the conceptions of full accessibility and effective mobility. In assessing these changes, what can be said in conclusion about what influenced the result—about the factors affecting decisionmaking, the impact of rulemaking, and the extent of presidential control of agency policymaking?

FACTORS AFFECTING DECISIONMAKING

That the DOT would have devoted much attention to devising policies for the disabled in the first place could not have been predicted. Organizations—the professionals within them—generally resist the imposition of policies that would divert them from what they conceive as their mission. Certainly, the DOT's program experts and planners, as well as its natural

138. 44 Fed. Reg. 47343–44 (1979).

constituency, the transit operators and industry, opposed the efforts to devise a comprehensive transportation policy for disabled people, particularly one based on the full accessibility conception.

A variety of factors—internal and external—affected the course of policy. Prominent among the former were the interests of the political leadership (principally the DOT secretary) and the entrepreneurial abilities of young attorneys in the general counsel's office and generalists in the policy offices who assumed pivotal roles in the rulemaking process. The technical experts—the planners and engineers—did not have central policymaking duties. External factors—congressional action, judicial rulings, and the involvement of another bureaucracy, HEW, charged with coordinating governmentwide enforcement of section 504—were vitally important in affecting the shifting interplay of forces that constituted agency decisionmaking. Those outside elements influenced the course of policy by spurring agency action, by providing an opportunity for those within the DOT to press for their preferences. In a broader sense, the administrative response reflected, if somewhat belatedly, the changes in the larger political environment—the increasing concern in the body politic with costs rather than rights. For each regulatory period—for instance, the creating of the special efforts regulations in 1976, or the full accessibility proceedings of 1979—the weight of one factor over another, internal or external, depended upon the totality of the circumstances.

To the extent that there was any interest in providing transportation for the disabled, however limited, in the late 1960s and early 1970s, it was due to a sympathetic political leadership and broad-gauged bureaucrats in the policy office at the secretarial level. But this issue was not of the highest priority for the political leadership, whose active and continuous involvement was necessary if anything significant were to be done. Thus concerned bureaucrats in the policy office could not overcome the resistance of the transit professionals in the operating bureau (UMTA), who believed that the DOT's mission did not include supplying transportation for the disabled community. What moved UMTA to begin work on the 1976 "special efforts" regulations was the threat of legal suits brought by disability groups, seeking relief peripherally under the Biaggi amendment. It was external considerations—the desire to ward off judicially imposed decrees—that motivated UMTA. Bureaucracies seek to avoid uncertainties, such as those posed by outside forces. The DOT was no exception.

The 1976 regulations were crafted in a way that was sensitive to the department's transit mission. The potency of section 504 had not yet been felt or even foreseen. Ultimately, influence in the regulatory process shifted to UMTA lawyers, in part because most of the transit professionals did not seek a role for themselves, and in part because of the force of personality of UMTA chief counsel Sallyanne Payton. But even more important, the lawyers achieved dominance because of the legal significance of the regulations: it was their responsibility to ensure that UMTA would survive legal assault from the handicapped community. Whoever controls the writing of the regulations is bound to play a preeminent role in the setting of policy itself.

As for the 1979 full accessibility regulations, a chain of external forces would once again be an important element of the story. These included a congressional conference committee report mandating HEW to issue regulations pursuant to section 504—engineered by an alliance of OCR bureaucrats and congressional staffers, acting without direction from the leaders of either HEW or Congress; a presidential order vesting HEW with authority to coordinate the governmentwide effort; a judicial decision compelling the promulgation of regulations; and HEW guidelines requiring the DOT to adopt the rights-oriented full accessibility approach. The involvement of HEW, with its civil rights conception, fortified those in the DOT (especially at the secretarial level) who were sympathetic to that view. HEW thus spurred the shift in the balance of power within the DOT. The entrepreneurial skills of Martin Convisser, who was knowledgeable about matters of both substance and policy, facilitated the change. Secretary Brock Adams's strong commitment to the full accessibility conception, which general counsel Linda Kamm clearly communicated to the operating bureaus, was a critical element of the shift.

External forces were important too in the events leading to the suspension of the full accessibility regulations in 1981 and to the ultimate return to the effective mobility standard. The Reagan administration was philosophically opposed to the regulations and sought to review them. Judicial decisions ruling that section 504 did not require full accessibility stripped the regulations of much of their legal underpinnings and facilitated the DOT's policy change. Moreover, the near passage in 1980 of the Howard and Cleveland amendments, which would have modified the 504 regulations by providing an "effective mobility" option, signaled to the department that it would not meet with serious congressional opposition if it engaged in a similar effort through the administrative route.

IMPACT OF RULEMAKING

In the various rulemaking proceedings described here, the philosophical premises—effective mobility or full accessibility—were already clearly established before those processes were set in motion and were not changed fundamentally as a result of the process. How then did the rulemaking proceedings affect policymaking—that is, the gathering of data, the participation of the parties, and the allocation of decisionmaking responsibilities?

For information, the rulemaking process relied upon that provided by the parties involved (apart from that supplied by the agency), and thus the value of the data depended in large measure upon the capacity and willingness of those actors to produce the information. In this case, particularly in the full accessibility round, agency decisionmakers thought that the parties did not generate reliable information. Most DOT officials believed that the disability groups tended to underestimate costs, while APTA inflated them. For the most part, the disability organizations did not even have the resources to undertake the complex studies needed to address the various issues. Agency decisionmakers thus had to work with their own data, which were often incomplete and based on scattered and not always relevant research, supported by the DOT, at local sites. Studies mandated by Congress were finished after the DOT issued the full accessibility regulations and thus were of no use in the rulemaking deliberations.[139]

The rulemaking proceedings afforded the relevant actors an opportunity to participate in the policymaking experience. But the openness of that process—however desirable—was not without cost. When positions can be expressed only on the public record, it is not easy for the proponents to retreat from them, especially if the issues are highly visible and emotional and to do so would seem at odds with the strongly held views of constituent interests. In these situations, it is difficult for agency decisionmakers to know what compromise would satisfy those parties.

On the surface at least, the rulemaking process imposed a certain orderliness. It involved several stages: a notice of proposed rulemaking and a comment period preceded the issuance of the final regulations. Rulemakers had to address the criticisms submitted to the docket. But in practice the

139. In the proceedings culminating in the 1986 regulations, DOT decisionmakers claimed that because they were not laboring under the same time constraints as they were in the earlier round, they could undertake thorough studies before acting.

course of policy was not always the model of rational decisionmaking. Apart from inadequate information, an important constraint was that of time. In the 1979 proceedings, DOT officials did not have an opportunity to review all of the comments before writing the final rules; the pressure to meet imposed deadlines short-circuited the decisionmaking process.

A presumed virtue of the administrative process is that it gives a role to those agency personnel who, because of their substantive knowledge, are best suited to resolve the problems before them. They are presumably guided by policy set by politically accountable department heads. However, the need to satisfy legal requirements tended, at least in this rulemaking case, to shift ultimate influence away from professionals in the particular policy arenas and to lawyers who sought to immunize the regulations from judicial assault. In the case of transportation policymaking for the disabled, the attorneys—a most capable team—were not initially familiar with the technical complexities of the issues. But over the years they became knowledgeable about the matters before them.

PRESIDENTIAL CONTROL OF POLICYMAKING

A basic tenet of political theory is that the president is the policymaker for the executive branch—the departments and bureaus are responsive to his preferences. If he is to exert such direction, then he must communicate his views clearly and unambiguously and have mechanisms that enable him to control policy. In fact, in this case the policy course was confused and reflected the fragmentation among the White House and executive departments. It is arguable that neither Ford nor Carter resolved the tradeoffs between the rights and cost-benefit approaches, equity and efficiency, or full accessibility and effective mobility—thus contributing to the uncertain and inconsistent outcomes in the administrative process. Reagan, on the other hand, rejected the rights ethos in favor of the cost-benefit, effective mobility conception and could clearly make his preferences known to the executive branch.

But it is unlikely that Ford, given the general tone of his administration, could have imagined that his executive order seeking to assure nondiscrimination for the handicapped in federally assisted programs would lead ultimately to regulatory schemes that involved a potentially massive and costly affirmative effort. HEW Secretary Mathews believed that the regulations went beyond the intent of Congress and administration policy; bureaucrats in the Office for Civil Rights had taken control of the regulatory process away from the cabinet secretary, and, indirectly, the president.

During the Carter years, although the president strongly endorsed the cause of the disabled community and of a more active federal effort, he never publicly addressed the transportation issue. The administration did not speak with a unified voice and was seemingly at odds with itself. To be sure, DOT Secretary Adams was in essential agreement with HEW's full accessibility requirement. Indeed, as has been noted, the secretary and his staff used HEW to their benefit, claiming that they had no choice but to follow the directives of the department charged with coordinating the section 504 effort. But in the White House, the RARG unit disagreed with HEW's interpretation of the section 504 mandate. However, it could not impose its view; its role was essentially advisory and limited to submitting comments to the DOT rulemaking docket.

It was not until the Reagan administration that a mechanism was created so that the presidency could assert effective authority over agency rule-making activities. Influence shifted to the Office of Management and Budget as a result of an executive order requiring agencies to submit their proposed rules to the OMB for review before publication. That effort to centralize presidential authority, however, raises concerns: the absence of protection against undisclosed communications by interested parties, the White House staff, and the OMB could affect the integrity of the rulemaking process; by exerting greater influence, the OMB could erode the authority of department heads; and departments and agencies might feel compelled to make decisions that they would not ordinarily have reached.

Why Technology Forcing Didn't Work

Transbus—a project initially conceived to revitalize bus transport and later viewed as a solution to the mobility problems of the elderly and the disabled—met a dead end by 1980. Millions of dollars and years of effort had not achieved the intended result. How could that have happened?

Part of the answer lies with the federal government. Its view was that it could spur innovation and force technology by mandating requirements to which manufacturers would have to respond. If that vision was to be realized, then at the very least policy would have to be coherent and stable over time. But in fact, the direction was uncertain and the signals confused. Within a few years, the DOT mandated Transbus, but at the same time allowed federal money to be used to buy interim buses; then the Transbus project was dropped, only to be revived once again before meeting its demise. The period saw frequent shifts in regulations and specifications, not only with respect to Transbus, but also in other dimensions of transportation policy for the disabled. Constant turnover among the top officials—between 1968 and 1980 the DOT had six secretaries and UMTA eight full or acting administrators—made it difficult to chart a consistent course. For the bus manufacturers, such instability only increased the risks of Transbus.

Miscalculations contributed to the difficulties. By mandating Transbus, the government sought to force technology; but it did not anticipate the length of time it would take to create new components or to change the bus market. As Charles F. Bingman, former deputy administrator of UMTA, stated:

> I would have thought that they [the manufacturers] were able to change their products more swiftly, but I find they really cannot. They do need protracted periods of time after some front-end capital investment to make a legitimate return on that investment. You cannot change the bus market very quickly.[140]

Disagreements between the government and the manufacturers about the feasibility of specifications also created obstacles. UMTA rejected the claim that its specifications were not workable, arguing that they were in fact a distillation of the comments of the manufacturers and operators themselves. But one expert active in the disability movement, Dennis Cannon, while contending that the technical problems were not insoluble, concluded that "the specification created had many faults due to the attempt to satisfy everybody from transit operators to vehicle manufacturers."[141] The low-bid procurement policy—whereby a higher-quality product reflected in a higher bid was effectively penalized—created a disincentive for manufacturers to exceed minimum performance specifications. Conflicts among legitimate objectives were never fully resolved. UMTA sought to encourage standardization of equipment, believing that it would result in economies of scale, facilitate the replacement of parts, and ultimately increase large block purchases. But transit operators argued that uniformity failed to consider local differences between, for example, snow-stricken northern communities and the dry areas of the Sun Belt. Striking the appropriate balance between flexibility and standardization was not an easy task.

The government also did not fully appreciate the relationship between bus manufacturers and component suppliers. Because the bus market is

140. *Bus Hearings*, p. 606.
141. *Bus Hearings*, p. 362.

small, suppliers resist making special parts on the grounds that it would be unprofitable to do so. Thus manufacturers use tires, axles, and other parts designed for other sectors, such as the larger and more profitable truck market. Transbus would have involved the production of specially tailored components, but suppliers were reluctant to undertake such activity.

In retrospect, one decision that had a pivotal impact was the approval of federal funding for the interim advanced-design buses while Transbus was still being tested. That announcement made it feasible for GM (and later Flxible) to continue technological development of their own bus, which incorporated many of the advances of the Transbus research program. GM gambled that Transbus would not be built and that its model would prevail—a strategy that seemed a winning one when Patricelli effectively scrapped Transbus. Having then decided to make heavy capital commitments to the advanced-design buses, the manufacturers resisted Brock Adams's revival of the Transbus mandate. It was not in their financial interests to make the shift to Transbus.

To a considerable extent, the commitment to Transbus can be understood in terms of the desire to satisfy the needs of the disabled. Brock Adams would not have resurrected Transbus in 1977 unless he believed that it was the best means of resolving the mobility problems of the handicapped and the elderly. Transbus had become for the disability movement a bellwether of the federal government's commitment—anything less was viewed as a retreat. Thus the advanced-design buses, though they incorporated some of the features of Transbus, were deemed inadequate. In a sense, then, as former Administrator Patricelli observed, Transbus involved "a debate about social and economic policy rather than a failure of Federal technology development or procurement policy."[142] The attempt to satisfy at once a variety of social, economic, and technical concerns could only complicate matters. As Adams's general counsel, Linda Kamm, remarked, "In some measure that has been part of our problem. We have tried to accommodate all of these conflicting desires—the desire for local option, the desire of the elderly and handicapped groups to meet certain requirements."[143]

142. *Bus Hearings*, p. 578.
143. *Bus Hearings*, p. 421. I discussed Transbus with Kamm on September 28, 1982.

CHAPTER FOUR

The Judicial Process

GIVEN the confused signals emanating from Congress and the radical shifts in policy in the administrative process, it is not surprising that disgruntled parties would turn to the courts for support.

The judiciary's role differed from that of the legislative or administrative bodies. Its duty was not to set policy, to choose between the effective mobility or full accessibility approaches, or to ascertain the most suitable means of achieving one end or another. Rather, the courts were to interpret the law, to determine legislative intent (however unclear it seemed to be), and to decide whether administrative action was in keeping with the statutory meaning. In theory, the Supreme Court is the final arbiter of conflict, assuring uniformity of interpretation throughout the federal judiciary; but, because in practice the Court can review only a small fraction of cases, final authority is for the most part exercised by some 740 judges in district and appellate courts that are effectively autonomous, reaching judgments sometimes inconsistent with one another and with differing consequences for policy.

The Impact of Courts on Institutions and Policy

In the course of resolving conflicts among litigants, judges can affect policy in a variety of ways. A court's ruling can bear directly upon substance—for example, when it either mandates that specific steps be taken or holds that an agency is not required to undertake certain actions advocated by one or more of the parties. Judges can affect process, as they have in "hybrid rulemaking" cases, by imposing a wide range of procedural requirements on agencies engaged in informal rulemaking. Indirectly, the judiciary can influence outcomes by supporting or altering the balance of power among the various forces. The effects of judicial decisions reach beyond the relationships among agencies, Congress, and interest groups: they can change the relationships among competing factions within a bureaucracy, strengthen or weaken the president in his dealings with agencies, or bolster the influence of congressional staffs and subcommittees.

Examining the impact of the judiciary on other institutions, Martin Shapiro has propounded the concept of a new "iron triangle," consisting of agency, court, and interest group.[1] Congress creates a statutory right, but then withdraws. An interest group goes to court, seeking enforcement of the right. The judiciary interprets the right broadly and mandates the executive to implement it, regardless of the president's wishes. In essence, according to this view, court action effectively constrains presidential authority, even with respect to the executive branch. Another somewhat related perspective maintains that the judiciary is the instrument of interests seeking to advance their policy preferences. Thus subcommittee leaders and staff create legislative histories supportive of their positions—sometimes after the fact, buried in committee reports—for later judicial consumption.[2] In those efforts, the staff members and legislators may be allied with bureaucrats who are advocates for particular programs. Judicial decisions thus strengthen subcommittee government and the power of those bureaucrats.

In recent years, there has been much discussion about judicial activism. Judges, according to one conception, are viewed as usurpers of the electoral process, as unelected philosopher-kings seeking to enforce their vision on society.[3] The image is of jurists bending congressional statutes out

1. Martin Shapiro, "The Presidency and the Federal Courts," in Arnold Meltsner, ed., *Politics and the Oval Office* (San Francisco: Institute for Contemporary Studies, 1981), pp. 5–14. See also Shapiro, *The Supreme Court and Administrative Agencies* (Free Press, 1968). The term *iron triangle* was previously used to describe the relationship among agencies, congressional committees, and pressure groups.

2. See R. Shep Melnick, "The Politics of Partnership," *Public Administration Review*, vol. 45 (November 1985), pp. 653–60. Melnick's article is a natural extension of his *Regulation and the Courts: The Case of the Clean Air Act* (Brookings, 1983). See also Gary Bryner, "Congress, Courts and Agencies: Equal Employment and the Limits of Policy Interpretation," *Political Science Quarterly*, vol. 96 (Fall 1981), pp. 411–30.

3. See, for example, Nathan Glazer, "Towards an Imperial Judiciary," *The Public Interest*, no. 45 (Fall 1975), p. 104. Commentators have also questioned the capacity of courts in making social policy. See, for instance, Donald L. Horowitz, *The Courts and Social Policy* (Brookings, 1977); and Alexander Bickel, *The Supreme Court and the Idea of Progress* (Harper and Row, 1970). For a review of the literature on judicial intervention in social policy, see Robert A. Katzmann, "Judicial Intervention and Organization Theory: Changing Bureaucratic Behavior and Policy," Note, 89 *Yale Law Journal* 513–18 (1980).

of shape to assume the role of legislator and administrator. Another view maintains that the reality is more complex. Judges, according to this thinking, are faced with the inherently difficult task of interpreting vague and ambiguously worded statutes with often scant legislative histories. If courts are an active presence, it is in part because Congress has thrust responsibility upon them. Congress has vested jurisdiction in the federal courts in acts that cover over 300 subjects (not including a more commonly viewed source of judicial congestion—suits between citizens of different states).[4] Those duties may require judicial involvement in such minor matters as the odometer law, the Tuna Convention Act, and the Apple Barrel Act. The image is not of a grasping, overreaching judiciary, but of an overworked one that must somehow find the time to manage a diverse and complex caseload. Still another perspective maintains that courts not only have a duty to intervene actively in social policy, but also are competent to do so.[5]

As I examine the role of the judiciary in interpreting statutes that were the source of transportation policy for the disabled, I ask these questions: How did courts assess legislative histories, rules, and regulations? Did courts behave as imperial entities, seeking to impose their visions on the legislative and administrative processes? How did the judiciary affect the balance of power among the key players, and, in so doing, the course of policy?

Judicial Deference to Administrative Expertise

In the early 1970s the federal judiciary had a number of opportunities to impose its vision on legislative and administrative processes in the area of transportation for the disabled, but it acted with considerable restraint. The occasions stemmed from suits brought by disabled individuals and groups to prod the Urban Mass Transportation Administration and local communities to enforce the Biaggi amendment more vigorously and to introduce technological devices that assured accessible transportation.

4. The list was prepared by federal judge Charles Clark, chairman of the Judicial Conference Committee on the Budget, noted in "Congress and the Judicial Budget," *The Third Branch*, vol. 16 (August 1984), p. 5.

5. See, for instance, Abram Chayes, "The Role of the Judge in Public Law Litigation," 89 *Harvard Law Review* 1281 (1976); and Owen M. Fiss, "Foreword: The Forms of Justice," 93 *Harvard Law Review* 1 (1979).

As was described earlier, the initial administrative response to the legislative enactments of the early 1970s was limited. The helter-skelter way in which Congress passed those measures, the absence of deliberation, the fact that they did not emanate from the transportation committees, suggested to the Department of Transportation that there was little pressure to do more than the minimum. But for the disabled community, which had not been actively involved in securing passage of the legislation, those measures promised federal action. After all, the Biaggi amendment "declared to be the national policy that elderly and handicapped persons have the same right as other persons to utilize mass transportation," that "special efforts" be made in the planning and design of mass transportation services so that the elderly and handicapped can use them, and that all federal programs offering assistance in mass transportation include provisions implementing that national policy. Three years later, in the Rehabilitation Act of 1973, Congress pronounced that "no otherwise qualified individual in the United States . . . shall, solely by reason of his handicap be excluded from participation in, be denied the benefits of, or be subjected to discrimination under any program or activity receiving federal assistance."

The Disabled File Suit

To prod UMTA and local communities to act more vigorously, disabled individuals and groups filed lawsuits across the nation. These cases were not part of a coherent national strategy, but were geared toward particular circumstances in such cities as Baltimore, Minneapolis, and Philadelphia. They shared in common a view that section 16(a) of the Urban Mass Transportation Act—the Biaggi amendment—meant that *all* transit equipment and facilities purchased with UMTA grant assistance had to be accessible to *every* disabled person. UMTA, in the view of the disability groups, was responsible for guaranteeing that federal monies were used only for purchasing fully accessible equipment and facilities. They sought injunctions prohibiting authorities from buying or placing in service inaccessible equipment and facilities.

UMTA, for its part, argued that the measure did not require that all mass transit equipment purchased with UMTA grant funds had to be accessible to wheelchair-bound individuals. Rather, its duty was to ensure that "special efforts" were being made to provide handicapped persons with mass transit services they could use. Thus UMTA asserted that it fulfilled its obligations by issuing guidelines, supporting special studies and transportation planning, undertaking research and demonstration projects, requiring urban areas eligible to receive operating money to implement a program of half-fares during off-peak hours for elderly and handicapped persons, and funding capital projects relating to the transportation needs of elderly and disabled persons.

UMTA officials were hopeful that their interpretation would for the most part prevail. But they understood that the judiciary was not monolithic, that it consisted of individual district courts and appellate courts across the country. And they were thus concerned that some of the decisions would not support their position and they would be compelled to undertake actions that were not consistent with their policies. Conflicting judicial interpretations could complicate UMTA's implementation of the laws.

UMTA Responds with Regulations

As a means of controlling the process, UMTA chief counsel Sallyanne Payton determined that something had to be done to make it clear to the courts that the agency was serious about fulfilling its obligations. Thus UMTA decided to issue regulations pursuant to legislation, setting planning and service requirements, as well as equipment standards, and providing examples of satisfactory levels of "special efforts." It agreed to do so in October 1974, as part of an out-of-court settlement in a case brought by Disabled in Action of Baltimore against UMTA and Maryland and Baltimore transportation agencies.[6]

By and large, the UMTA strategy seemed to work. A report by the General Accounting Office, issued not long after the special efforts regulations took effect, showed that UMTA had won ten of the twelve lawsuits for which at least a lower court decision had been rendered. Of the other two, one was the Baltimore case that had been resolved out of court, and the other involved a temporary injunction against the purchase of buses until the court ruled on UMTA's motion for summary judgment.[7] In some sense, the disabled litigants had also achieved success; the threat of lawsuits had spurred UMTA to issue regulations that would at least begin to address some of their needs. And the very fact that UMTA would promulgate such regulations strengthened the claims of those who argued that the

6. Memorandum of Understanding, *Disabled in Action of Baltimore* v. *Hughes*, Civil No. HM-74-1069 (D. Md. October 30, 1974).

7. General Accounting Office, *Mass Transit for Elderly and Handicapped Persons: Urban Mass Transportation Administration's Actions* (GAO, 1977), p. 69.

Biaggi amendment was more than a statement of policy aspirations. In one case, for example, an appellate court ruled that were it not for the regulations, it would have denied relief to the plaintiffs.[8]

The Courts Weigh the Technology

At the same time that disabled litigants sought to enjoin authorities from purchasing inaccessible buses, they also, in effect, were asking courts to make judgments about the state of technology—about whether vehicles could be procured with lifts or ramps that would meet the needs of those confined to wheelchairs. Judges tended to take their cues from the policy statements and regulations set forth by the government. For example, in an early case, arising in Birmingham, Alabama, the court denied relief to a physically disabled woman after citing the "uncontroverted" affidavits of UMTA administrator Frank Herringer and a local operator, stating that there was no device "presently developed and proven reliable for use in a standard full-size urban transit bus which would make the bus fully accessible to plaintiff and her class."[9] Judges also took into account changes in the state of technology, citing the DOT's own pronouncements. In a matter in which the plaintiffs brought suit against the secretary of transportation to prevent the Southeastern Michigan Transportation Authority from buying inaccessible vehicles, the court concluded that the "technology which did not exist when *Andre* . . . and *Snowden* . . . were decided in the district courts now exists."[10] It did so after citing Brock Adams's revival of the Transbus mandate, promulgated not long before the case was decided.

UMTA understood that courts placed considerable weight on the government's statements about the state of technology and that they tended to defer to the agency because it seemed seriously committed to resolving the problems of providing transportation for mobility-impaired persons. The

8. *United Handicapped Federation* v. *Andre*, 558 F.2d 413, 416 (8th Cir. 1977).

9. *Snowden* v. *Birmingham–Jefferson County Transit Authority*, 407 F. Supp. 394, 398 (N.D. Ala. 1975), *aff'd* 551 F.2d 862 (5th Cir. 1977). In a case involving the Cuyahoga County Regional Transit Authority of Ohio (*Vanko* v. *Finley*, 440 F. Supp. 656, 660 n.3 [N.D. Ohio 1977]), the court stated that, in enacting the Biaggi amendment in 1970, "Congress was certainly cognizant of the technological and economic problems"—an assertion unsupported by the facts. The "special efforts" required could "only be defined by the state of mass transportation technology at any particular moment." Because the plaintiffs did not cite any evidence that a universally accessible transit vehicle was then technologically feasible, the court concluded that section 16(a) did not, in 1977, require universal accessibility.

10. *Michigan Paralyzed Veterans of America* v. *Coleman*, 451 F. Supp. 7, 11 (E.D. Michigan 1977).

government also recognized that courts might not be so accepting if they determined that UMTA's representations were not reliable. At a time when Transbus was in a precarious state in 1976, UMTA chief counsel Sallyanne Payton noted in a memo to the administrator that in each of the lawsuits the government had "relied heavily" on both the proposed special efforts regulations and the Transbus program. "Most courts," she noted, relied on the government's policies and "have viewed the problem simply as one of technology and have ruled in our favor because they believe after Transbus is available, each federally-assisted bus will be accessible." She warned that unless the government acknowledged its Transbus problem and offered a meaningful substitute while the matter was under review, the courts would be dismayed. She noted that "the courts could thus review UMTA as an agency that hinted strongly at a Transbus solution, but when problems developed . . . was unwilling to require an alternative solution. . . . Without those [substitute] requirements a court might well impose its own."[11] In fact, UMTA did confront its doubts about Transbus in the final "special efforts" regulations.

A notable attempt to use the courts to spur technology was guided by Disabled in Action of Pennsylvania, a group created in 1974. It sought to persuade local authorities to offer barrier-free transportation. It joined forces with the Public Interest Law Center of Philadelphia (PILCOP) to use the law to achieve its objectives. Their experience led these two groups to conclude that they would fare better if they geared their efforts toward federal rather than local policy. In that view, they were reinforced by the Paralyzed Veterans of America (PVA) and the American Coalition of Citizens with Disabilities (ACCD). The notion that those organizations might work together to affect federal policy was born in 1975 when James Raggio, a lawyer for PILCOP, was testifying before a committee and met John Lancaster of the PVA. When it seemed that UMTA was stepping back from its commitment to Transbus, the two groups put together a nationwide coalition of groups to fight for the low-floor vehicle. Those organizations, representing 13.3 million disabled and elderly members nationwide, formed the Transbus Group.

Even before UMTA administrator Robert Patricelli announced in July 1976 that the DOT would not require Transbus, the coalition filed suit against DOT Secretary William T. Coleman, Jr. Citing section 504 of the Rehabilitation Act of 1973, the Urban Mass Transportation Act,

11. *National Mass Transportation Assistance Act of 1977*, Hearings before the Subcommittee on Housing and Urban Affairs of the Senate Committee on Banking, Housing and Urban Affairs, 95 Cong. 1 sess. (Government Printing Office, 1977), pp. 489, 490.

the Federal-Aid Highway Acts, and various constitutional provisions, the plaintiffs claimed that federal funds could be used to purchase only the low-floor, wide-door Transbus. Alleging that Secretary Coleman had not complied with that mandate, they asked the court to enjoin him from refusing to comply with those provisions. The secretary argued that the statutory language was not mandatory, but simply stated a policy that "special efforts" should be used so that mass transit was available to the elderly and the disabled; moreover, he contended that it was solely within his discretion to determine the means by which that policy was to be discharged.

While the case was in progress, a new DOT secretary, Brock Adams, assumed office and in May 1977 revived the Transbus mandate; consequently, Judge Louis Bechtle ruled the Transbus Group's claims moot.[12] Adams knew of the suit when considering the Transbus matter, and his awareness that the court might have ruled in favor of the plaintiffs contributed to his decision to resurrect the low-floor vehicle.

For the Transbus Group, legal action was but one part of its efforts to secure full accessibility. Noting that the "courts are not a magically different instrument of change," PILCOP chief counsel Thomas K. Gilhool added that "in no case will singleminded use of the courts be effective. The use of litigation along with lobbying and bargaining promises to be effective. Our task is to use the courts not only for their own yield, but also for their effect in other arenas."[13] And to that end, the Transbus Group also lobbied in Congress, participated in DOT proceedings, and conducted demonstrations. In essence, Gilhool recognized that the judiciary—though of important strategic value—was generally reluctant to substitute its judgment for the presumed technical expertise of the agency, that more often than not restraint would be the order of the day. Disabled litigants were more likely to be successful to the extent that they pursued their causes under statutes that seemed more clearly to provide a remedy as a matter of right.

The Courts Deal with Transportation as a Right

The passage of section 504 of the Rehabilitation Act struck a responsive chord in disabled individuals, who viewed it as their civil rights statute. Coalitions were formed among diverse interests; the ACCD, an umbrella

12. *Disabled in Action of Pennsylvania* v. *Coleman*, 448 F. Supp. 111 (E.D. Pa. 1978).
13. Thomas K. Gilhool, "The Use of Courts and of Lawyers," in Robert Kugel and Ann Shearer, eds., *Changing Patterns in Residential Services for the Mentally Retarded* (Washington, D.C.: President's Committee on Mental Retardation, 1976), p. 155.

outfit, was created in 1974. Section 504 spurred the activities of fledgling groups such as Disabled in Action; it aroused the Paralyzed Veterans of America, whose younger Vietnam-era members were much affected by the example of the civil rights movement. The statute was not only a rallying force; it became an important prong of the legal arguments of those who sought to redress the wrongs suffered for so long by disabled people. At first, section 504 was almost of secondary importance, used for auxiliary support. The seemingly more specific transportation measure, the Biaggi amendment, was more critical to the legal argument. But section 504 soon became the linchpin of an ambitious affirmative action regulatory program that culminated in the 1979 DOT rights-oriented full accessibility regulations—an effort that dissolved not long thereafter. Paradoxically, the judiciary played a pivotal role in both the rise and fall of section 504. Indeed, contrary to the conventional wisdom, courts were not the engine that powered the rights ethos; they ultimately were less supportive of it than was either Congress or the bureaucracy.

To make the point, I will examine three pivotal cases. The first, *Cherry* v. *Mathews*, a district court case interpreting section 504, mandated the issuance of regulations and was a victory not only for disability groups, but also for the Office for Civil Rights of the Department of Health, Education, and Welfare and for congressional subcommittee government. The second, *Southeastern Community College* v. *Davis*, a Supreme Court decision holding that section 504 did not require major affirmative action, undermined the DOT's rights-oriented full accessibility regulations; and the third, *APTA* v. *Lewis*, an appellate opinion applying *Davis*, provided the basis for suspension of these regulations and the return to the effective mobility approach.

Cherry v. Mathews

Cherry v. *Mathews* was representative of section 504 litigation: a disabled individual, generally active in a group, brought suit, with the aid of a public interest organization, to change government policy.[14] James L.

---

14. Besides the cases involving PILCOP, other examples of such litigation include *Paralyzed Veterans of America* v. *Washington Metropolitan Area Transit Authority*, Civil No. 776-72, Final Consent Order and Dismissal (D.D.C. September 30, 1978). For an account by the prime mover behind the case, see Richard W. Heddinger, "The Twelve Year Battle for a Barrier-Free Metro," *American Rehabilitation*, vol. 1 (May–June 1976), pp. 7–10. Another such case was *Zukas* v. *Alameda–Contra Costa Transit District*, No. 678-0874BR

Cherry, a Kentuckian, suffered from a chronic, progressive neuromuscular disease and could walk only with the aid of leg braces and a cane. He was an active member of the Action League for Physically Handicapped Adults (ALPHA), a 200-member organization based in Kentucky and dedicated to promoting the interests of the disabled. Both individually and as a member of ALPHA, he had participated in efforts to assure that state and federal administrative agencies implemented laws affecting physically handicapped Americans.

Cherry, who was undergoing treatment at the National Institutes of Health in Bethesda, Maryland, had completed one year of law school while away from Kentucky. He hoped to return home and continue his studies at the University of Louisville Law School, but, he claimed, the law school and the public library were inaccessible to him. Convinced that legal action was the only effective recourse, Cherry secured the aid of the Institute for Public Interest Representation of Georgetown University Law Center (since renamed the Institute for Public Representation).[15]

Founded by the Ford Foundation and Georgetown University Law Center in 1971, the institute is a public interest law firm and law school clinical education program dedicated to providing legal services to groups and individuals who are unable to secure effective legal counsel on matters significantly affecting issues of broad public importance. Over the years, the institute has represented clients concerned with such issues as civil liberties and civil rights, environmental protection, corporate responsibility, health and safety, immigration policy, and the rights of the handicapped. Its first director, Victor Kramer, enjoyed a long and distinguished career in government and private practice before becoming a law professor at Georgetown in 1971.

After reviewing the case, Kramer determined that section 504 of the Rehabilitation Act of 1973 provided an apt basis for relief, on the grounds that it prohibited discrimination in any program receiving federal aid or assistance. Given that the Kentucky institutions were recipients of such support, they would presumably have to comply with the nondiscrimination statute. Bolstering Cherry's case, Kramer concluded, was the committee report on the 1974 amendments to the Rehabilitation Act, which declared that although section 504 "does not specifically require the issu-

(N.D. Calif. 1978). For a discussion of the relationship between the disability rights movement and lawyers, see Susan M. Olson, *Clients and Lawyers: Securing the Rights of Disabled Persons* (Westport, Conn.: Greenwood Press, 1984).

15. I am grateful to the institute for affording me access to the files on the *Cherry* case.

ance of regulations or expressly provide for enforcement procedures . . . it is clearly mandatory in form, and such regulations and enforcement were intended by this Committee and by Congress." The conferees declared that they "fully expect[ed] that HEW's section 504 regulations should be completed by the close of this year. Delay beyond this point would be most unfortunate since the Act was enacted over one year ago—September 26, 1973."[16] HEW had not issued those regulations by the time the Institute for Public Interest Representation entered the case in early 1975.

As a matter of strategy, the institute decided to file a petition requesting the secretary of HEW to issue a rule under authority of section 504 of the Rehabilitation Act of 1973. Cherry's lawyers sought a rule declaring that "the existence of architectural barriers in certain facilities is discrimination prohibited by the Rehabilitation Act"; defining "handicapped individuals to include those who suffer from mental impairment, all types of physical disabilities, and disabilities of incoordination and aging"; stating that "all types of facilities are covered by the rule"; and interpreting the act's "Federal financial assistance" phrase to include "direct grants for unspecified programs in the form of revenue sharing funds, grants to taxpayers in the form of tax expenditures, and any other scheme that operates to transfer value from the federal government to a recipient for the purpose of providing financial assistance."[17]

In an exchange of letters in the ensuing nine months, Martin H. Gerry, acting director of the Office for Civil Rights, replied that HEW was preparing regulations and would welcome Cherry's and Kramer's reaction during the comment period. Kramer responded that the secretary's failure to act on the petition, given the conference committee directive to issue rules by the end of 1974, constituted unreasonable delay in violation of the Administrative Procedure Act.[18]

On behalf of Cherry and ALPHA, Kramer and his colleagues filed suit in the U.S. District Court for the District of Columbia seeking to compel

16. *Rehabilitation Act Amendments of 1974*, S. Rept. 93-1139, 93 Cong. 2 sess. (GPO, 1974), p. 24; and *Rehabilitation Act Amendments of 1974*, S. Rept. 93-1270, 93 Cong. 2 sess. (GPO, 1974), p. 28.

17. Petition of James L. Cherry and the Action League for Physically Handicapped Adults for a rule, submitted to the secretary of HEW, June 3, 1975. The Administrative Procedure Act provides that "each agency shall give an interested person the right to petition for the issuance, amendment, or repeal of a rule." 5 U.S.C. sec. 553(e).

18. Letters of Martin Gerry, acting director, Office for Civil Rights, to Victor H. Kramer, Georgetown University Law Center, August 15, 1975, and February 17, 1976.

the secretary of HEW to promulgate regulations implementing section 504. The government, in documents prepared by the Department of Justice, countered that the "plain language of section 504 does not include a rulemaking requirement. . . . If Congress—as opposed to Senator Humphrey, Representative Vanik, the Senate Labor and Public Welfare Committee, and the Conference Committee, none of which have the Constitutional authority to adopt legislation—had intended to impose a rulemaking requirement, it would have done so. There is ample evidence that Congress knows how to impose such a requirement."[19] It is instructive that the OCR was not involved in preparing the government's case; the OCR, of course, had welcomed the opportunity to craft the regulations and was thus implicitly at odds with the Justice Department's position. In the course of the case, the ACCD, the American Council of the Blind, and the National Association of the Deaf moved to intervene in support of Cherry and the Action League for Physically Handicapped Adults. But the government succeeded in convincing the court that such intervention would only delay the proceeding and that the existing parties already fully represented the interests of the applicants.[20]

In mid-July 1976, the summer of an election year that pitted Gerald Ford against Jimmy Carter, District Judge John Lewis Smith, Jr., concluded that the HEW secretary was required to promulgate regulations implementing section 504. The court relied heavily on the committee reports on the 1974 amendments indicating that Congress contemplated swift implementation of section 504 through a comprehensive set of regulations. Judge Smith noted that the HEW secretary had already issued proposed regulations. Rather than declaring a date by which the final regulations would have to be promulgated, the court retained jurisdiction "to assure that no further unreasonable delays" occurred.[21]

On January 17, 1977, six months after the district court decision, and three days before turning over the department to the new administration, Secretary David Mathews stated that although the regulations had been prepared, he would not sign them, but would instead transmit them without

19. Points and Authorities in Opposition to Plaintiffs' Motion for Summary Judgment and in Support of Defendants' Cross-Motion for Summary Judgment, May 10, 1976, p. 3. On the role of Department of Justice lawyers, see Donald L. Horowitz, *The Jurocracy: Government Lawyers, Agency Programs and Judicial Decisions* (D.C. Heath, 1977).

20. Order of U.S. District Court for the District of Columbia, *Cherry* v. *Mathews*, April 27, 1976.

21. *Cherry* v. *Mathews*, 419 F. Supp. 922, 924 (D.D.C. 1976).

his signature to Congress for its consideration. Mathews, as noted earlier, was concerned that the regulations were so sweeping in scope that they may have gone beyond what Congress intended. Accordingly, he sought congressional guidance. On the day of the announcement, anticipating that the disability groups would be displeased and mindful of the district court order, Mathews met with representatives of the Institute for Public Interest Representation, the American Council of the Blind, the National Association for Retarded Citizens, the Children's Defense Fund, and the American Coalition for Citizens with Disabilities.

The HEW secretary could not mollify the litigants in the *Cherry* case. A day later, the plaintiffs obtained a temporary restraining order from Judge Smith enjoining "defendant F. David Mathews from further delaying the promulgation of regulations implementing section 504. . . ."[22] On January 19, 1977, Mathews unsuccessfully sought a stay in the district court of the temporary restraining order issued the previous day. But on the same day that the district court denied his motion, an emergency panel of the U.S. Court of Appeals issued an order staying enforcement of the temporary restraining order, pending appeal. The secretary contended that if he were required to sign the regulations, he would be precluded from raising important legal issues—whether it is within the discretion of a cabinet officer to confer with Congress for a short period of time before final promulgation of regulation, and whether his decision to seek further congressional advice amounted to an "unreasonable, arbitrary or capricious delay."[23] The appellate court decision meant that Mathews could leave office the next day with the matter left to incoming Secretary Joseph Califano to resolve.

The new HEW secretary announced that he would review the section 504 effort—much to the consternation of the disability groups—but promised to issue regulations within a few months (sometime in May, at the latest). The legal wranglings continued, ending only when Califano signed the regulations. In a "Dear Joe" letter, Victor Kramer wrote that he "was delighted to read . . . that you signed the section 504 regulations, which were the subject of our *Cherry* suit." Responding, Califano stated that "I join with you in the hope that these regulations will contribute to the real-

22. January 18, 1977, Order of District Court of District of Columbia.

23. Motion of the Secretary of Health, Education and Welfare to Stay Injunctive Order of the District Court Pending Appeal, *Mathews* v. *Cherry*, January 19, 1977.

ization of equal opportunity and independence for all our handicapped citizens."[24]

The district court decision was a victory for disability groups. But its impact went beyond that. The decision affected the internal workings of HEW—the relationship between a bureau and the cabinet head. It strengthened those within the OCR who had championed the regulations and weakened the authority of the HEW secretary who was charged with promulgating them. Further, the reliance of the court on the language of the committee reports indicated that legislators and staff could further their policy preferences by using low-visibility mechanisms and engaging in retrospective legislative history. As was pointed out earlier, it is doubtful that those who enacted section 504 of the Rehabilitation Act of 1973 anticipated that it would lead to the regulations that the court mandated. Substantively, the court's decision affected the course of policy—leading first to the HEW regulations and then to guidelines mandating the rights-oriented approach for a wide range of government programs. Ultimately those guidelines resulted in the DOT's full accessibility regulations.

In the aftermath of *Cherry,* other courts called on to interpret section 504 in the transportation context also pointed to the "legislative history" of the 1974 amendments to the Rehabilitation Act as indicating that Congress contemplated implementation of section 504 through regulations and that the law required an affirmative remedy. The courts determined that the DOT's 1976 special efforts regulations, then in existence (and nominally based on section 504), offered affirmative relief of "substantial scope."[25] But, in essence, these jurists determined that the affirmative remedy that

24. Letters from Victor H. Kramer to Joseph A. Califano, Jr., April 29, 1977; and from Joseph A. Califano, Jr., to Victor H. Kramer, May 23, 1977.

25. *Lloyd* v. *Regional Transportation Authority,* 548 F.2d 1277, 1281 at 1283 (7th Cir. 1977). In this case, arising in Chicago, the court followed *Cherry.* An appellate panel adhered to *Lloyd* in *United Handicapped Federation* v. *Andre* at 415. In committing itself to issue regulations that afforded some affirmative action, albeit not full accessibility, UMTA seemed at least tacitly to accept the view that the mere absence of invidious and overt discriminatory practices was not sufficient. In fact, in an early case that antedated the regulations, a court in Alabama ruled that section 504 had not been violated where wheelchair-bound individuals were allowed to ride a bus, even though they could not do so unless they arranged for someone to help them board and leave the vehicle. *Snowden* v. *Birmingham–Jefferson County Transit Authority,* 407 F. Supp. at 397. Given the subsequent advances in wheelchair lift technology, it is doubtful that a court would reach the same result today.

section 504 envisioned did not require full accessibility.[26] They did not go nearly as far as the OCR did in its regulations and governmentwide guidelines. Indeed, in fashioning those guidelines, the OCR proceeded as if those transportation cases never existed.

Southeastern Community College v. Davis

The Supreme Court dealt a severe blow in 1979 to the program advocates, legislators, committee staffs, and disability groups for whom section 504 was a central part of their policy aspirations. Although the matter before the Court did not involve a transportation case, the section 504 holding had a direct impact on that policy area. From the perspective of section 504 proponents, the facts of the case before the Supreme Court did not augur well for an expansive interpretation; the remedy sought called for the expenditure of substantial funds, which arguably might not have resolved the basic problem.

The case centered around Frances B. Davis, a woman who suffered from a serious hearing disability. Enrolled at Southeastern Community College, a North Carolina state institution receiving federal funds, she hoped to progress to the school's Associate Degree nursing program. Completion of that course of study would have made her eligible for state certification as a registered nurse. In the interview part of the application process, it became apparent that she had difficulty understanding the questions posed to her. Even with a hearing aid, Davis could not discriminate among sounds sufficiently to understand normal spoken speech. Her lipreading skills were essential to effective communication.

Southeastern College denied her admission to the program. The school concluded that her hearing impairment could interfere with her safely car-

26. Alluding to the 1976 special efforts regulations, and noting that they were promulgated in part under the authority of section 504, one court stated approvingly that they did "not require a full and immediate solution to the problem. What they do require is that special efforts are being taken to ensure that the mobility handicapped will be provided with services equivalent to the rest of the community." Bartels v. Biernat, 427 F. Supp. 226, 232–33 (E.D. Wisconsin 1977). In still another case involving section 504, but primarily based on section 16(a) of the Urban Mass Transportation Act, the court specifically rejected the contention that section 504 or the regulations promulgated under it required that all buses had to be accessible to persons in wheelchairs; Vanko v. Finley, at 660–61. Although "vague plans for the indefinite future and second-rate transit for the mobility handicapped" were unsatisfactory, "instantaneous conversion to a transportation system that is comparable in every minute detail" was not required either. Ibid. at 666.

ing for patients. Lipreading would supposedly be impossible in many situations, such as an operating room, intensive care unit, or postnatal care unit, in which all doctors and nurses wear surgical masks. She would be disadvantaged in circumstances where the doctor could get the nurse's attention only by vocal means.

Davis filed suit in the U.S. District Court for the Eastern District of North Carolina, alleging violation of section 504 and of the equal protection and due process clauses of the Constitution.[27] She argued that she was an "otherwise qualified individual" within the meaning of section 504, and thus had been wrongly subjected to discrimination. But, after a bench trial, the district court ruled differently. In its opinion, "otherwise qualified, can only be read to mean otherwise able to function sufficiently in the position sought in spite of the handicap, if proper training facilities are suitable and available."[28] The court ruled that Davis's exclusion from the nursing program was not discriminatory in the context of section 504, because her disability would prevent her from "sufficiently" performing her duties.

On appeal, the U.S. Court of Appeals for the Fourth Circuit reversed the lower court's decision in view of administrative regulations promulgated by HEW while the case was still pending.[29] Under those regulations, the court noted that handicapped persons "otherwise qualified" for postsecondary and vocational educational services are those "who meet the academic and technical standards requisite to admission or participation in [a federally funded] education program or activity."[30] The regulations, the court observed, define "technical standards" as "all nonacademic admissions criteria that are essential to participation in the program in question." It thus concluded that "the college must reconsider [Davis's] application for admission to the nursing program without regard to her hearing disability." The lower court had erred in taking Davis's handicap into consideration in determining whether she was "otherwise qualified" for the program rather than restricting its inquiry to her "academic and technical qualifications." Moreover, the court stated that section 504 mandated "affirmative conduct" on the part of Southeastern to modify its program to

27. Both the district court and the court of appeals dismissed those claims and Davis did not seek Supreme Court review of those rulings.

28. *Davis* v. *Southeastern Community College*, 424 F. Supp. 1341 at 1345 (E.D.N.C. 1976).

29. *Davis* v. *Southeastern Community College*, 574 F.2d 1158 (4th Cir. 1978).

30. 45 C.F.R. 84.3(k)(3).

accommodate the disabilities of applicants, "even when such modifications become expensive."[31]

Southeastern Community College appealed to the Supreme Court.[32] The potential significance of this case—the first time the Court would interpret section 504—was well understood by the wide range of parties affected. Twenty-seven states through their attorneys general filed a friend of the court brief urging reversal of the court of appeals decision. They were joined by the American Council on Education, the nation's largest association of colleges and universities. Because those institutions had an obligation to comply with section 504, and "to bear, without any federal assistance, the enormous financial and other burdens associated with its administration," they obviously had an important stake in its interpretation. They stated that they were

> concerned that a one-sentence prohibition with no particular legislative history is being transformed by administrative excess and judicial inventiveness into a tool of oppression not contemplated by Congress. For example, the Department of Health, Education and Welfare . . . in regulations implementing the basic prohibition of section 504 has excised key statutory language and has imposed affirmative action requirements on entities receiving federal funds where Congress with apparent deliberation placed none.[33]

Many disability groups urged that the Court uphold the court of appeals.[34] The United States also filed on the side of Davis. The briefs urging the court to uphold the appellate decision claimed that although the legislative history of section 504 was sparse, the committee reports accompanying the 1974 amendments to the Rehabilitation Act provided a highly authoritative aid to the proper construction of section 504. Those reports stated that Congress intended not only to prohibit discrimination, but also to require affirmative action; they declared, moreover, that Congress intended

31. *Davis* v. *Southeastern Community College,* 574 F.2d at 1160, 1161, 1162.

32. *Southeastern Community College* v. *Davis,* 442 U.S. 397 (1979). Southeastern Community College had unsuccessfully sought a rehearing in the court of appeals.

33. Brief of the American Council on Education on petition for a writ of certiorari to the U.S. Court of Appeals for the Fourth Circuit, in the Supreme Court of the United States, *Southeastern Community College* v. *Davis,* No. 78-711, October Term 1978, pp. 2–3.

34. By the time the case had been appealed to the Fourth Circuit, it had already begun to attract attention. The Disability Rights Center and James Cherry—of *Cherry* v. *Mathews*—filed a friend of the court brief in the appellate court. On review in the Supreme Court, the National Association of the Deaf Legal Defense Fund handled Davis's case. Many disability rights groups filed friend of the court briefs. Only one state, California, which has perhaps the most politically sophisticated disabled community, offered a brief supporting affirmation of the court of appeals ruling.

that the secretary of HEW would issue regulations governing the implementation of section 504 and assume responsibility for coordinating the statute's enforcement. The brief of the U.S. government departed from the appellate court's instructions to Southeastern Community College to reconsider Davis's application without regard to her hearing disability. The solicitor general reasoned that under section 504 a recipient of federal funds need not ignore an applicant's handicap; it must only make efforts, where practicable, to adjust its programs and provide the educational assistance necessary to permit qualified handicapped persons to participate.[35]

Just seven weeks after oral argument, a unanimous Supreme Court overturned the court of appeals ruling. Justice Powell, speaking for the Court, began with an examination of the plain meaning of the language of section 504 itself. The terms of the statute indicated that the mere possession of a handicap was not an acceptable basis for assuming an inability to function in a particular context; but that was not to say that an individual did not have to meet legitimate physical requirements in order to be "otherwise qualified." An "otherwise qualified" person was one who was able to meet all of a program's requirements *in spite of* his handicap. Drawing upon HEW's own interpretation, the Court sought to highlight the difficulties of interpreting "otherwise qualified" to include persons who were qualified except for their handicap. Under such literal reading, a blind person meeting all the qualifications for driving a bus except sight could be said to be "otherwise qualified" for the job of driving.[36]

Moreover, the Court ruled that section 504 did not require Southeastern to undertake "affirmative action" such as providing Davis with individual supervision whenever she attended patients directly, dispensing with certain required courses, or training her to perform some but not all of the duties a registered nurse is licensed to discharge. An interpretation of the regulations that mandated "extensive modifications" and required "substantial adjustments in existing programs beyond those necessary to eliminate discrimination against otherwise qualified individuals," the Court maintained, "would do more than clarify the meaning of section 504." "Instead," the Court declared, it "would constitute an unauthorized extension of the obligations imposed by that statute." The Court continued:

35. Motion of the United States for Leave to File Brief of Amicus Curiae and Brief for the United States as Amicus Curiae, *Southeastern Community College* v. *Davis,* No. 78-711, October Term 1978, p. 23.
36. *Southeastern Community College* v. *Davis* at 407 n. 7.

Neither the language, purpose, nor history of section 504 reveals an intent to impose an affirmative action obligation on all recipients of federal funds. Accordingly, we hold that even if HEW has attempted to create such an obligation itself, it lacks the authority to do so.[37]

Rejecting the government's claim that committee reports to the 1974 amendments offered authoritative guidance about the scope of section 504 and indicated that section 504 requires affirmative action, the Court stated:

These isolated statements by individual Members of Congress or its committee, all made after the enactment of the statutes under consideration, cannot substitute for a clear expression of legislative intent at the time of enactment. Nor do these comments, none of which represents the will of Congress as a whole, constitute subsequent legislation such as this court might weigh in construing the meaning of an earlier enactment.[38]

Undercutting HEW's view that section 504 compelled affirmative action, the Court concluded, was the agency's position for the first three years after the section was enacted, when it maintained that Congress had not contemplated the issuance of regulations. It altered its view only after having been enjoined to do so by the district court in *Cherry* v. *Mathews*.

Finally, the Court conceded that it was not suggesting "the line between a lawful refusal to extend affirmative action and illegal discrimination against handicapped persons always will be clear." Technological advances might qualify handicapped persons for useful employment "without imposing undue financial and administrative burdens upon a State."[39] But in the case before it, the Court determined that Southeastern's unwillingness to make "major adjustments" in its nursing program did not constitute discrimination.

The Supreme Court decision was a significant defeat for the disability organizations, bureaucrats, legislators, and committee staffers who hoped that section 504 would be viewed as more than a nondiscrimination statute. The unanimous Court had determined that section 504 did not require "affirmative action" or "major modifications," that it could not impose "undue financial and administrative burdens upon a state." The ruling seemed to undercut the DOT full accessibility regulations that envisioned expensive structural alterations of subway transit. Those rules, after all, were explicitly crafted to conform to HEW's section 504 guidelines—which were based on an interpretation of the legislative history that the Supreme

37. Ibid. at 410, 411–12, footnote omitted.
38. Ibid. at 412–13 n. 11, citations omitted.
39. Ibid. at 412.

Court firmly rejected. The DOT did cite two other statutes, section 16(a) of the Urban Mass Transportation Act of 1970 and section 165(b) of the Federal-Aid Highway Act of 1973, as authority for the regulations. But the preamble to the regulations mentions only section 504 and makes clear that the DOT felt bound by the HEW guidelines and evaluated alternatives in terms of consistency with them.

American Public Transit Association v. Lewis

For the American Public Transit Association, a trade association representing the interests of transit operators, the *Davis* decision provided an opportunity to use the judiciary to strike down the full accessibility regulations. Not long after those rules were issued, APTA, on behalf of itself and eleven municipal transit systems, brought suit to prevent the implementation of DOT regulations governing provisions for handicapped persons in federally assisted mass transportation programs. APTA challenged the regulations on a number of grounds: first, they were illegal and exceeded statutory authority; second, they were procedurally deficient under section 553 of the Administrative Procedure Act because the DOT did not consider all relevant issues, options, and comments during the rulemaking process; and third, the regulations were arbitrary and capricious in that they failed to recognize limitations on available technology, imposed greater costs but would result in fewer benefits to the handicapped than alternative approaches, and failed adequately to consider diversity in local conditions.[40]

The record before the court was unusually comprehensive, consisting of materials relating not only to the legal questions, but also to the policy questions as well. Thus, it included, for example, studies about wheelchair lift technology and excerpts from a Congressional Budget Office report. Barry Cutler, APTA's lawyer and himself the father of a disabled child, believed that the regulations were of little benefit to most handicapped persons; he was determined to educate the court about what he thought were the practical consequences of the DOT rules.[41] Supporting APTA's position were the National Association of Counties and the American Associa-

40. Peripherally, the plaintiffs also alleged that the DOT failed to consider adequately the environmental impact of the regulations; the court agreed, ordering the DOT to file an environmental impact statement on or before September 1, 1980.

41. Interviews with Barry Cutler and Robert Batchelder of APTA, October 14, 1981, and October 29, 1981. Cutler generously afforded me access to the full record in the case.

tion of State Highway and Transportation Officials. On the other side, a joint amicus brief backing the DOT was filed on behalf of numerous associations of the disabled.

In February 1980 Judge Lewis Oberdorfer of the U.S. District Court of the District of Columbia held that the regulations did not exceed statutory authority and were not procedurally defective and that the DOT's decision to issue them was not arbitrary and capricious.[42] The court reached its ruling by considering, apart from section 504, the DOT's statutory authority, such as the Urban Mass Transportation Act and the Federal-Aid Highway Act of 1973. It assumed that each of these statutes had guided the DOT in crafting its regulations, given that the department had cited them. Judge Oberdorfer reasoned that Congress delegated to the secretary of transportation broad authority to establish terms and conditions for grants for transportation facilities generally and, beginning in 1970 (with the Biaggi amendment), for the handicapped in particular. "These statutes and their legislative history," the court ruled, "reflect a consistent Congressional charge to the Secretary of Transportation that he attach conditions to grants made from appropriated funds which will, to the extent feasible, make transportation available to handicapped persons." Accordingly, the court concluded that statutory authority existed for the regulations independent of section 504. Judge Oberdorfer conceded that if the regulations rested solely on section 504, *Southeastern Community College* v. *Davis* "might create serious doubts about their validity."[43] But then for reasons that are not altogether clear, the court went on to suggest that section 504, although perhaps not independently justifying the regulations, did "buttress" the secretary's authority under the Urban Mass Transportation Act and the Federal-Aid Highway Act.

The court fully recognized that Congress, in enacting these two laws, may not have contemplated a costly regulatory program. "The wisdom of the choice [between full accessibility and effective mobility], and indeed the question whether it is the choice Congress intended, is not free from doubt," the court declared. But, Judge Oberdorfer continued, "it is completely feasible for Congress to reverse or revise that choice, by withholding or conditioning appropriations, and by directly legislating." The court stated that "Congress has the Secretaries' decisions before it and may decide they have wrongly decided, because they misjudged cost-benefit fac-

---

42. *APTA* v. *Goldschmidt*, 485 F. Supp. 811 (D.D.C. 1980).
43. Ibid. at 822–23, 826.

tors or because of fiscal policy or even political considerations. If so, Congress can revoke or amend the regulations."[44] In essence, the court sought to shift the battleground to Congress: if APTA sought a change in policy, then it would have to take its case to the legislature. That, in fact, it did in 1980 when Congress came close to passing the Howard and Cleveland amendments, which would have legislated changes in the regulations.

As to the other challenges, the court rejected the claim that the regulations were procedurally defective under section 553 of the Administrative Procedure Act. The court determined that DOT's "section-by-section" analysis accompanying its final rules reflected "both a careful consideration of the various alternatives and an adequate basis for the ultimate decision." With respect to the claim that the regulations were arbitrary and capricious because they failed to recognize limits on existing technology, the court ruled that an agency may impose requirements premised on future advancements. Finally, Judge Oberdorfer refused to assess independently whether the regulations in fact imposed fewer benefits to the handicapped at greater costs than alternate approaches. "Judicial review of DOT's final decision on this issue is an extremely limited one," the court concluded. "DOT's ultimate cost-benefit determination, as reflected in the regulations, is an exercise of its special expertise and is entitled to great deference."[45]

APTA appealed the district court ruling to the U.S. Court of Appeals for the D.C. Circuit, essentially reiterating its basic arguments. By the time the appellate panel, consisting of Judges Abner Mikva, Harry Edwards, and George MacKinnon, rendered a decision in May 1981, much had changed in the political environment. Congress had come close to passing legislation that would have provided an alternative to the full accessibility regulations, and the Reagan administration, which rejected the affirmative action premises guiding HEW and the DOT, had assumed office. The DOT, under the leadership of Secretary Drew Lewis, could only have welcomed the opinion of the D.C. Circuit, which reversed the lower court decision and remanded the case for further proceedings.

A unanimous court, in an opinion written by Judge Mikva, began its inquiry by examining whether the rules were a valid way of enforcing section 504 of the Rehabilitation Act of 1973—"the moving force" behind the full accessibility regulations. Noting that at some point a transit system's

44. Ibid. at 824–25.
45. Ibid. at 827, 830.

refusal to take modest affirmative steps to accommodate handicapped persons might well violate section 504, the panel determined that the DOT rules did not mandate "only modest expenditures." The regulations, the opinion stated, required "extensive modifications of existing systems and impose[d] extremely heavy financial burdens on local transit authorities." Reciting various cost estimates, the court suggested that the DOT's figures were "almost certainly too low." The regulations, Judge Mikva concluded, envisioned "the kind of burdensome modifications that . . . [the Supreme Court in *Southeastern Community College* v. *Davis*] held to be beyond the scope of section 504."[46] If section 504 and the HEW guidelines were the only underpinnings for the 1979 regulations, their validity could not be sustained.

Unlike the district court, which justified the regulations based on the DOT's authority to enforce section 16(a) of the Urban Mass Transportation Act and section 165(b) of the Federal-Aid Highway Act, the appellate panel declared that it could not fulfill its judicial obligation "by relying on the formal citation of additional authority." The court reasoned that when an administrative decision is based on inadequate or improper grounds, a reviewing court may not presume that the administrator would have made the same decision on other valid grounds. Quoting approvingly from other opinions, Judge Mikva wrote that a court "usurps the position of the proper decisionmaker when it 'rummages through the record' . . . to find an alternative basis for the administrator's action; 'a court, if it sustains a decision by recourse to reasons outside those specified, opens the door to the improper substituting of the court's judgment . . . in place of that of the agency . . . with responsibility.'"[47] Thus the court concluded that its task was to determine whether it was likely that the DOT's decision to promulgate the 1979 regulations was affected by its mistaken reliance on section 504 and the HEW guidelines.

Observing that the 1976 regulations did not mandate "mainstreaming" or full accessibility, the court stated that "if the HEW Secretary had not implemented guidelines enforcing section 504 inconsistent with DOT's 1976 regulations, it is quite possible that the latter would still be in effect."

The primary reason DOT rescinded the newly promulgated 1976 regulations and replaced them with the regulations at issue in this appeal was the perceived

46. *APTA* v. *Lewis*, 655 F. 2d 1272, 1278, 1278 n. 12 (D.C. Cir. 1981).
47. Ibid. at 1278–79.

need to follow HEW's section 504 guidelines. Every aspect of the rulemaking procedure points to those guidelines as the moving force for change.[48]

To support its claims, the court noted that the DOT, in its own regulations, indicated that it felt bound by the HEW guidelines. It added that the department had denied requests from transit systems that regulations be waived on the ground that such a step would be inconsistent with the guidelines.[49]

In reaching their decision, the judges did not hold that because the secretary of the DOT followed HEW's section 504 guidelines, he could not have determined that the regulations carried out other statutes. Rather, they simply stated that events "strongly suggest that he did not do so," and therefore they remanded the case to give the secretary an opportunity to explain whether the regulations were based on statutes other than section 504.[50]

In a concurring opinion, Judge Edwards commented that the government's position was ambiguous, claiming at one time that section 504 alone could support the regulations and at another that all three statutes were relied upon in devising the rules. Because of that absence of clarity about the statutory basis for the regulations, Edwards concluded that it made "good sense" to remand the case for further explication. But he added that he expressed no opinion on the "extremely complicated question" of whether the regulations exceeded the permissible scope of section 504 by imposing on transit authorities a requirement of "affirmative action" as opposed to one of "non-discrimination." The application of section 504 to public transportation systems, he continued, raised significantly different questions than those considered in *Southeastern Community College* v. *Davis*. "In considering the accessibility of public transportation to 'otherwise qualified' handicapped persons, it is much more difficult," Judge Edwards asserted, "to avoid 'discrimination' without taking some kind of 'affirmative action.'"[51]

The opinions of the district and appellate courts differed not only in their reasoning and conclusions, but also in the audience to which their messages were directed. Whereas the former's decision was addressed to Congress, the latter's opinion was aimed at the new secretary of transportation,

48. Ibid.
49. Ibid. at 1278, 1280.
50. Ibid. at 1280.
51. Ibid. at 1281.

Drew Lewis. The appellate ruling bolstered the secretary's position, providing him with wide latitude as he set department policy on transportation for the disabled. The court surely knew that it was unlikely that the DOT secretary, given the philosophical views of the Reagan administration, would seek to find independent justification for the 1979 full accessibility regulations. The more probable outcome was that he would use the decision as a means to scrap the regulations, by concluding that they did not enforce other statutes. Indeed, the court must have been aware of that possibility; it noted that

> the Presidential Task Force on Regulatory Relief has included both the regulations at issue in this appeal and the HEW guidelines in its list of regulations scheduled for review and possible modification. . . . Our disposition of this appeal does not limit or restrain that process.[52]

The change in administrations and secretaries in 1980 may very well have had a profound impact on the consequences of the remand; if Brock Adams, for example, had still been secretary, then it is quite possible, given his support for the full accessibility principle, that he would have attempted to justify the 1979 regulations on grounds independent of section 504.

In the aftermath of the ruling of the court of appeals, the DOT, as expected, suspended the full accessibility regulations. In their place, the department resurrected a modified version of the 1976 "special efforts" regulations. The court decision not only eviscerated the impact of section 504 on agency decisionmaking; it also profoundly affected the politics of disability groups. As long as section 504 seemed to offer a civil rights premise (with a strong affirmative action component), it served to unify diverse groups representing various disabilities; each could support the demands of the others without financial consequence to its own cause. If a right to a benefit exists, it stands independent of the state of the treasury. But the judiciary's rejection in *Southeastern Community College* and *APTA* of the rights premise transformed the terms of the public debate; the language of rights was supplanted by the politics of resource allocation. The fleeting and always loosely bound coalition disintegrated as groups competed with one another for a piece of the finite budgetary pie. As a result, the judicial decisions, by indirectly diminishing the potency of the disability coalition, served to lessen the pressure on the Reagan administration to maintain and

52. Ibid. at 1280 n. 14. Judge Mikva, who wrote the opinion, had been a member of Congress and was very familiar with the intricacies of the legislative and administrative processes.

create federal programs for disabled persons. A few groups, such as the Paralyzed Veterans of America, continued to press their cause in federal court, generally with those cases that were already under way before the *APTA* ruling. But the litigants soon realized that the lower courts were interpreting section 504 in a highly restrictive way in light of *Southeastern Community College* and *APTA*. Even when a court sought to find some way to grant relief pursuant to section 504, it was not likely to involve retrofitting of subways—an important element of the full accessibility approach.

The *APTA* Aftermath: The Limits of Relief

Two cases are evidence of the difficulty of securing fundamental affirmative relief in the post-*APTA* era. In the first one, the appellate court rejected full accessibility; in the second, though the court seemed disposed to grant some relief, the remedy fell far short of that needed to achieve full accessibility. The limits of such relief suggested to at least some litigants that they would have to find other forums than the federal judiciary to press their claims; they would have to redirect their energies toward state courts and legislatures.

Rhode Island Handicapped Action Committee v. *Rhode Island Public Transit Authority*

In 1981 the Rhode Island Public Transit Authority (RIPTA) operated a fleet of 267 public buses running along fixed routes; of these, 53 were equipped with wheelchair lifts. Ridership on the fixed-route system by wheelchair users was low: 488 one-way trips in 1980 and 605 in 1981. Apart from these fixed-route activities, RIPTA subsidized private paratransit services, the twelve largest of which provided nearly 1 million one-way trips in 1981 to elderly and handicapped persons, only a portion of whom were wheelchair users.

When RIPTA announced that it planned to purchase forty-two new buses without wheelchair lifts, two advocacy groups for the disabled, the Rhode Island Handicapped Action Committee (RIHAC) and the Rhode Island Paraplegia Association, as well as three handicapped persons, filed a class action suit. The plaintiffs alleged that RIPTA and other state and federal defendants violated section 504 of the Rehabilitation Act of 1973,

section 16(a) of the Urban Mass Transportation Act (the Biaggi amendment), the Fifth and Fourteenth amendments, and a state statute express-
ing a policy of assistance to the disabled. The disability groups asked that
the forty-two new buses that RIPTA was about to purchase be equipped
with wheelchair lifts.

In the course of a nine-day trial, many disabled riders and nonriders of
the public transit and paratransit systems, RIPTA officials, representatives
from other transit authorities, and experts on the problems of the disabled
debated the merits of paratransit and accessible fixed-route transportation.
RIPTA sought to demonstrate that it had not only subsidized an extensive
paratransit service, but also operated some wheelchair-accessible routes,
constructed wheelchair ramps at various bus shelters, and provided free
rides and priority seating for the handicapped and special services for the
blind. It stipulated that its expenditures for those with impaired mobility
exceeded 3.5 percent of its funding under section 5 of the Urban Mass
Transportation Act, thus satisfying one illustration of satisfactory "special
efforts" contained in the DOT interim regulations promulgated after the
APTA decision. Those regulations required transit authorities to "certify
that special efforts are being made in their service area to provide transportation that handicapped persons, including wheelchair users and semiambulatory persons, can use."[53] RIPTA argued that it met the requirements
of those regulations and thus did not violate section 504 in not spending
additional funds for installation of lifts on the forty-two new buses.

The disability groups introduced evidence that tended to show that the
Rhode Island system was discriminatory because it was often inconve-
nient, some of its existing special equipment did not work properly, and
RIPTA was not responsive to their needs. They alleged that RIPTA could
make significant improvements at relatively little cost.

Federal District Judge Raymond Pettine, using a two-step test, held that
RIPTA and the state defendants had violated section 504 of the Rehabilitation Act. First, he examined whether the requested relief would consist
simply of "modifications" to existing programs or the beginning of new
service. Having determined that only the former was involved, the court
held that the remedy sought did not violate the strictures in *Southeastern
Community College* v. *Davis* against major affirmative changes. Next the
court conducted a cost-benefit inquiry, reasoning that if the price of equipping the buses with lifts and providing other relief was reasonable and not

53. 49 C.F.R., sec. 27.77 (1982).

"undue" relative to the benefits realized, then RIPTA's failure to buy such additional devices was an act of discrimination in contravention of section 504. Deciding that the cost was reasonable, Judge Pettine ordered RIPTA to purchase the forty-two buses, complete with wheelchair lifts and with two wheelchair bays per bus; maintain no more than a 15 percent reserve ratio (number of lift-equipped buses held in reserve in case of breakdown compared with those in use); repair the kneeling feature of its buses; provide a locking device on each lift-equipped bus to secure electric wheelchairs; and offer some wheelchair-accessible weekend and evening services.[54]

In reaching its decision, the district court found that its interpretation of section 504 was broader than that contained in the DOT's 1981 interim regulations. Judge Pettine argued that he was obligated to follow the statute before the regulation. Conceding that the 3.5 percent expenditure figure that the DOT had offered as an illustration fulfilling its requirement might in some situations satisfy a recipient's duties under section 504, the court determined that such was not necessarily always the case. The 1981 regulation merited little deference because it was not a contemporaneous interpretation of the statute, was the third set of regulations issued in five years, differed dramatically from the 1979 regulations, and was a short-term measure issued without notice and comment.[55]

On appeal, the U.S. Court of Appeals for the First Circuit reversed Judge Pettine's ruling. Chief Judge Levin H. Campbell, speaking for a unanimous panel, stated that while the Supreme Court in *Southeastern Community College* v. *Davis* did "not rule out the possibility of some affirmative relief in gray areas, its central message remained that section 504 does not impose the duty to engage in affirmative action. . . . We are unable to square the [court's] . . . language with an order imposing a duty on RIPTA to spend $320,000 on controversial lifts for its new buses." Holding that primary guidance must come from the regulations promulgated by the federal agency responsible for overseeing the federal monies being used by the state or local agency, Judge Campbell wrote that the district court should have deferred to the DOT's determination that the 3.5 percent expenditure levels complied with section 504. Dependence upon the responsible federal agency to flesh out the requirements of section 504 and the other pertinent statutes, the appellate court maintained, was "far

54. *Rhode Island Handicapped Action Committee* v. *Rhode Island Public Transit Authority*, 549 F. Supp. 592 at 607, 616 (D.R.I. 1982).
55. Ibid. at 609 n. 5.

preferable to a post hoc, case-by-case cost-benefit analysis undertaken by individual district courts around the nation."[56] Citing a critique of the judicial role in an influential book, Judge Campbell observed:

> Commentators have pointed out that judges are not selected nor are they trained as administrators, and the judicial process is not structured as an organ of governance. . . . If judges eschew the DOT regulation and are themselves to have the last word in this area, they will be doing so totally without legal standard or guidance, since none whatever is provided in the statute. Instead of administering the rule of law, they will be engaged in making personal policy assessments indistinguishable from those made by administrators in executive agencies.[57]

Concluding that primary guidance must come from the federal regulations and that some deference is also due the policy choices of state and local agencies, the court limited its review to the more "usual" role of disapproving actions found to be illegal, arbitrary, or capricious. Determining that the defendants' behavior withstood such a challenge, the appellate panel reversed Judge Pettine.

Dopico v. Goldschmidt

The second case began while the 1979 DOT regulations were still in effect. The plaintiffs—Disabled in Action and several disabled persons—filed class action suits on behalf of all wheelchair users in New York City against local and federal transit officials.[58] They alleged that the local officials had failed to use federal mass transit funds to make the "special efforts" required by law toward making transportation services in New York City available to the elderly and the handicapped. They further charged that the federal defendants—DOT and UMTA officials—continued to approve and fund the local programs, even though they should have known of the failure to engage in the "special efforts."

The plaintiffs based their claims principally on section 16(a) of the Urban Mass Transportation Act, section 165(b) of the Federal-Aid Highway Act, section 504 of the Rehabilitation Act of 1973, the 1976 "special ef-

---

56. *Rhode Island Handicapped Action Committee* v. *Rhode Island Public Transit Authority,* 718 F.2d 490 at 496–97 (1st Cir. 1983).

57. Ibid. at 498. He cited Horowitz, *The Courts and Social Policy.*

58. I am grateful to the lawyer for the plaintiffs, Aileen Meyer, of the firm of Winthrop, Stimson, Putnam and Roberts of New York City, for affording me access to the record.

forts" regulations and the 1979 full accessibility regulations, and section 315 of the Department of Transportation and Related Agencies Appropriations Act of 1975. The last made fiscal year 1975 funds for the purchase of subway cars and buses available on the condition they were designed to meet the needs of the elderly and the handicapped.[59] The disability groups sought substantial relief that, among other things, would have required the court to appoint a special master with wide-ranging duties. The master would determine the amount of funds not spent or misspent on "special efforts" and monitor and report to the court on the implementation until the system was accessible. Moreover, the disability groups sought to compel the expenditure of "special efforts" funds.

Judge Edward Weinfeld of the Southern District of New York, in a thorough opinion, dismissed the complaint against the local transit officials for failure to state a claim upon which relief could be granted. He ruled that the statutes upon which the disability groups depended either did not give them the right to sue or did not allow the kind of remedy they sought. In determining whether Congress intended these statutes to give disabled individuals the right to sue, the court sought to answer such questions as whether there was any indication of legislative intent, explicit or implicit, either to create such a remedy or to deny one, and whether it was consistent with the underlying purposes of the legislative scheme to imply such a remedy. Judge Weinfeld noted that the legislative history was "virtually barren" with respect to whether the Biaggi amendment was intended to create or deny a private right of action. But, noting that the statute bears upon "complex matters involving an interrelated maze of governmental decisions at many levels," the court reasoned that implying a private cause of action would not be "consistent with the underlying purpose of the legislative scheme, would upset the delicate balance of administrative and local decisionmaking, and would risk the possibility of inconsistent results in different areas of the country."[60]

Reviewing the legislative history of the Biaggi amendment, Judge Weinfeld declared that it did not "unequivocally create a substantive right."

59. 88 Stat. 768, 781 (1974). The plaintiffs also sought redress of alleged violations of their right to equal protection of the laws under the federal Constitution, contending that the local defendants purposefully and invidiously discriminated against wheelchair users. That claim was not the linchpin of the plaintiffs' case and was quickly dismissed by both the district and the appellate courts. Measured by the appropriate test—rational relation—the defendants' actions were judged constitutionally unobjectionable.

60. *Dopico* v. *Goldschmidt*, 518 F. Supp. 1161 at 1172 n. 42, 1173 (S.D.N.Y. 1981).

Showing an awareness of the process by which it was enacted, he added:

> Section 16 of the Act was added in 1970 as a floor amendment; it did not appear in either the House or Senate committee reports. . . . It was adopted with little discussion in the House and none in the Senate. Indeed, it was presented in the Senate as part of an entire slate of amendments to the Act, most of which involved funding programs and none of which merited discussion. . . . In determining if the statute creates a right, the Court must be guided by the entire law and not just a single sentence. The UMT Act is designed to "assist" and "encourage" states and localities to develop various mass transportation programs via federal grants. And Section 16 itself, contrary to plaintiffs' view, does not unequivocally create a substantive right. Rather, it merely declares a "national policy" of equal access to mass transportation facilities for the elderly and handicapped and instructs that "special efforts" should be used to that end. Finally, it provides that all federal programs assisting in the area of mass transportation "should" implement this policy. Moreover, the section was meant to continue the existing general policy of removing barriers to the elderly and handicapped. Thus, [quoting from a Supreme Court decision in another case] "nothing suggests that Congress intended the Act to be something other than a typical funding statute."[61]

Similarly, with regard to section 165(b) of the Federal-Aid Highway Act of 1973, the court stated that it was "merely one part of a massive funding statute"; although it identified an area mandating various kinds of benefits for the elderly and the handicapped, its "focus was not on creating rights." Judge Weinfeld also concluded that when Congress amended the section in 1974, adding a provision virtually identical to section 16(a) of the Urban Mass Transportation Act, it did not create substantive rights.[62]

The court rejected the claim that the Appropriations Act of 1975 created rights simply because it prohibited the secretary of transportation from expending funds for the purchase of equipment for the fiscal year ending 1975 unless it was designed to meet the needs of the elderly and disabled.

The court did concede that section 504 supports a private right to sue,[63] but nevertheless it dismissed the case because the disability groups were seeking "massive relief involving extraordinary expenditures" that would amount to the "'kind of burdensome modifications that the *Davis* Court held to be beyond the scope of section 504.'"[64] Judge Weinfeld said:

---

61. Ibid. at 1177, footnotes omitted.

62. Ibid. at 1178.

63. The question of whether a private right of action existed under section 504 was not decided by the Supreme Court until 1984. In a unanimous decision, the Court ruled that it did. *Consolidated Rail Corporation* v. *Lee Ann LeStrange Darrone*, 465 U.S. 624 (1984).

64. *Dopico* v. *Goldschmidt* at 1175, 1176, quoting *APTA* v. *Lewis*, 655 F.2d at 1278.

Courts are not "super-agencies" with the power or expertise to exercise their own scientific judgment; neither are they necessarily qualified to interject themselves in the midst of competing policy considerations to ferret out the "best" ultimate policy. Thus, the standard of review in this kind of case is properly limited to ensuring that the administrative agency has complied with all the procedural requirements the statutes and regulations impose.

The competing policy and technical factors presented in this case are staggering. . . . It is properly the role of the administrative agency to assess the route to take, not the court. . . .

Moreover, perhaps the single overriding factor here that counsels against a court assuming an active role is the very practical nature of the problems presented. These problems do not lend themselves to rigid application of general rules. The agency must consider not only the needs of the general population but also the conflicting interests of different groups within the handicapped community. For example, some individuals prefer escalators, other[s] elevators; blind persons want gates on subways. The handicapped community includes, besides those in wheelchairs, the deaf, blind, and mentally retarded. A court, besides not being equipped with the expertise of an agency to oversee such affairs, cannot properly consider all these competing concerns when only the class of wheelchair users is before the Court.[65]

Judge Weinfeld ruled that the federal transportation officials had not made funding decisions that were "arbitrary, capricious, an abuse of discretion, or otherwise not in accordance with law."[66]

The disability groups appealed to the U.S. Court of Appeals for the Second Circuit. Judge Jon Newman, author of the majority opinion, affirmed several aspects of the lower court ruling, but, most significantly, rejected its conclusion that section 504 did not permit any of the relief that the plaintiffs sought. Reasoning that the situation did not involve "an all-or-nothing choice of remedies," the court stated that "if ordering relief based on the 1979 regulations would exceed the mandate of section 504, then more modest relief must be fashioned within the limits of *Davis*." The *APTA* decision, in the appellate court's view, only sketched the "outer limits in the mass transportation context of the limitations laid down by the Supreme Court in *Davis*. The key issue, therefore, is whether *Davis* not only proscribed forcing 'massive' restructuring of transportation programs, but in fact prohibits *any* possible prospective relief in this setting." To that question, the court answered no—section 504 required "at least

65. Ibid. at 1189, footnotes omitted.
66. He granted a summary judgment in favor of the federal defendants. A summary judgment can be granted only when the parties do not dispute the facts of the case in affidavits or other evidence in the record.

'modest affirmative steps' to accommodate the handicapped in public transportation."[67] Judge Newman asserted that the lower court's focus on the "massive" restructuring needed to comply with the 1979 full accessibility regulations obscured the fact that the plaintiffs charged violations of the 1976 "special efforts" regulations as well; and unlike the ill-fated 1979 requirements, no court had ruled that the "special efforts" regulations went beyond the intent of section 504. The appellate court reversed the part of Judge Weinfeld's ruling dismissing the complaint under section 504, and sent the case back to the lower court for consideration of the merits of the plaintiffs' claims and for the determination of appropriate relief.[68]

Turning to the States

Although the Second Circuit ruling offered some hope of relief under section 504, disability organizations recognized that it was far less than the 1979 regulations envisioned.[69] For example, massive structural alterations of the subways to make them accessible was obviously beyond the scope of section 504, given the ruling of the Supreme Court in *Southeastern Community College* v. *Davis*. In the future, relief under federal law seemed limited; the 1981 interim regulations were evidence of the abandonment of the full accessibility conception at the national level. Disability groups had to seek other means to pursue the full accessibility objective. Increasingly, they came to focus their efforts on state laws and to pursue their claims in state courts.

In New York, the Eastern Paralyzed Veterans Association sued in state court, claiming that under the laws of New York State the transit authorities could not undertake renovations without ensuring that such plans included provisions to make New York City subways accessible to the disabled. A

67. *Dopico* v. *Goldschmidt,* 687 F.2d 644 at 650, 652 (2d Cir. 1982).

68. In his opinion, Judge Newman also disputed the district court's grant of the motion for summary judgment of the federal defendants. Concluding that some question existed as to whether the record before the court was the full record that had been before the federal agencies, the appellate court sent the case back to allow determination of the completeness of the administrative record. Only after that was the district court to consider the merits of the federal defendants' motion for summary judgment. (Ibid. at 653–54.) Judge Richard Cardamone dissented from the majority in its reversal of the district court's grant of summary judgment for the federal defendants, arguing that he was satisfied that the full administrative record was before the court. (Ibid. at 654–55.)

69. Interview with Arlene Battis, attorney, Paralyzed Veterans of America, December 5, 1984.

state court upheld the veterans' group, thereby forcing transit authorities to reach some accommodation. The New York subways were badly in need of renovation; but transit officials did not want to bear the cost of making every station accessible. A period of intense negotiations among disabled groups and state and local officials ensued. On July 20, 1984, the state legislature enacted legislation, contingent in part upon the adoption of a resolution by the board of the New York City Transit Authority, providing for the "reconstruction, rehabilitation, alteration, or improvement of transportation terminals and stations in accordance with [the new law], and . . . the procurement of accessible buses in accordance with [the new law]."[70] Five days later, the board adopted such a resolution. The resolution (and therefore the legislation) were to take effect only upon the final settlement and dismissal of the existing lawsuits in federal court, including the *Dopico* case. On September 24, 1984, the veterans' group agreed, subject to the approval of the court, to dismiss the actions; the case could be reinstated only if the legislation were modified or repealed so as to diminish any of the substantive obligations of the authorities in the eight years following the effective date of the new law.[71]

The new law—in essence, the settlement agreement—provided for the creation of a New York City Transportation Disabled Committee, an eleven-member body comprised of state and city officials and members of the New York City transportation-disabled community. The committee was charged with overseeing the law's implementation. With respect to buses, it was agreed that 65 percent of the vehicles in the regularly operated fleet were to be accessible to transportation-disabled persons. In addition, fifty-four subway stations—designated as "key" stations—were to be structurally altered so that disabled individuals could use them. The "key" station concept was a compromise much like that found in the 1979 DOT regulations, which relieved the authorities of making every station accessible.

The New York experience—the use of state laws and courts to achieve ends not obtained through the federal judiciary—promises to be a model for interests representing disabled persons in other communities throughout the nation. The success of disability organizations is likely to depend not only upon the substance of state laws and judicial rulings, but also on the political strength of those groups in particular states and cities.

70. Chap. 498 of the Laws of 1984 of the State of New York.
71. Settlement Agreement, in Civil Actions No. 82 Civ. 7270 (M Ec), 80 Civ. 4562 (EW) and 80 Civ. 4862 (EW) in the U.S. District Court for the Southern District of New York, September 24, 1984.

The Courts and Transportation Policy for the Disabled

The federal judiciary has affected the course of transportation policy at various junctures. The concern that judges might impose an unwanted solution prompted UMTA to develop the 1976 effective mobility "special efforts" regulations. A district court decision mandating the secretary of HEW to promulgate section 504 regulations led to the rights-oriented full accessibility guidelines imposed upon the DOT. But in the end, a Supreme Court ruling assessing the scope of section 504 undermined the full accessibility approach; and a decision of the U.S. Court of Appeals for the D.C. Circuit, applying the Supreme Court's reasoning, facilitated the DOT's suspension of the 1979 regulations.

In interpreting statutes, the courts quite obviously affected the power relationships among the institutions and actors involved; support for one—for example, entrepreneurial congressional staffers—tended to be at the expense of another—for instance, the president. *Cherry* v. *Mathews,* mandating the issuance of regulations, bolstered the subcommittee staffs responsible for the language in the committee reports upon which the court depended. That decision also increased the leverage of the Office for Civil Rights in its dealings with the HEW secretary and the administration, which argued that the legislative history of section 504 did not require the promulgation of regulations. The Supreme Court's holding in *Southeastern Community College* v. *Davis* was, of course, a blow to those who had benefited from *Cherry,* as well as those within the DOT who championed the full accessibility regulations. The lower court and appellate rulings in the *APTA* case showed an acute understanding of institutions, though each was directed at a different target—Congress or the DOT secretary.

Regardless of whether a court is conscious of how its rulings will affect the relationships among political actors, it is inevitable that the interpretation given to particular laws will shape the relative influence of the key players and institutions. For example, consider the case of a president who has resolved the trade-off between rights and costs in favor of the latter. To the extent that judges interpret vaguely and broadly worded laws as creating rights, requiring affirmative action, or providing for private forms of action to enforce those rights, they tend to reduce presidential control and to fortify the rights-oriented bureaucrats and congressional staffers who crafted the statutes. When a court mandates the issuance of regulations, an agency has little choice but to obey, even though the president might oppose such action. But the judiciary generally facilitates presidential authority over policy to the degree that it reads those statutes as discrete statements of general policy or mere declarations of a desire to help a particular group or achieve a specific goal. In other words, presidential control is maintained to the degree that courts vest it with the responsibility to set priorities and make trade-offs among various goals embodied in statutes— for instance, between the objectives of preventing discrimination against disabled people in mainline transit and improving mass transportation generally. Such was the case in the post-*Davis*, post-*APTA* period, which marked the reassertion of presidential control.

This is not a story of judicial imperialism. Courts were the instruments used by all the parties—sometimes bolstering one side, then the other. The judiciary did not seek to impose procedural requirements on agencies. It did not substitute its views for the technical judgments of the agencies, but generally deferred to the administrators. Judges did not involve themselves in the details of public administration, as they have in some other areas of social policy—for example, civil rights, education, environmental regulation, and penal reform.[72] Moreover, the record of decisions presented here belies the commonly asserted view that the politics of rights is synonymous with judicial activism. On balance, courts were less attached to a rights-based approach to policymaking than was either Congress or the bureaucracy.

In interpreting statutes, the courts made conscientious efforts to understand the legislative histories. Some courts gave credence to the retrospective histories found in committee reports. But that was not a matter of overreaching—in some sense, the courts could not be faulted for accepting too uncritically the language of those reports, for believing that they were an expression of the congressional will. That the courts gave weight to those reports does raise questions about the value that should be afforded to materials other than the statutes themselves—such as committee reports and the *Congressional Record*. Such concerns are important, for how judges assess legislative histories affects their interpretation of statutes and ultimately the course of policy.

72. See Colin S. Diver, "The Judge as Political Powerbroker: Superintending Structural Change in Public Institutions," 65 *Virginia Law Review* 43 (1979).

CHAPTER FIVE

Searching for Solutions

TRANSPORTATION policy for the disabled has been far from coherent. For all the activity, there has been uncertainty and vacillation—constant shifts in direction that have confused state and local governments, the transit community, and disabled groups alike. Should one have expected anything else, given the nature of the system? How can the result be explained? To understand what could account for the outcome, it is necessary to examine both policy and process—that is, both conceptual and substantive development as well as the operations of institutions. Thus the answer might have to do with problem definition, the internal life of the institutions involved, or the interplay among those institutions. It may be that particular institutions are not working; perhaps each institution is faithful to its own interests and incentives, but in ways that have unfortunate side effects for the system as a whole. Or that vacillation may be the product of an open, responsive system, of the painful process of selecting among contending justifiable purposes, values, and claims.

I seek in this conclusion to review why there have been so many twists and turns. To the extent that institutions are part of the answer, as the thrust of this work would suggest, it is appropriate to inquire whether organizational structures and incentives can be altered so that processes and outcomes are more coherent. And in so doing, it behooves one to keep in mind the costs of such changes, which include both the difficulty of reshaping organizational dynamics and the danger of weakening the values that are embedded in those institutional processes. If those defects—vacillation and confusion—are products of the system's virtues, then one must decide whether to endure them if to do otherwise might do harm to those values.

In large measure, policy confusion resulted from a failure to define the problem precisely and to choose between two different approaches—the rights-oriented full accessibility conception and the transit-oriented effective mobility approach. Decisionmakers generally neither engaged in serious debate about the consequences of pursuing a particular approach nor compared the ramifications of favoring one conception over the other.

In part these conceptual ambiguities reflected changing notions in the political climate about the balance to be struck between competing values, about what was in fact possible, about normative judgments as to what should be done. In the late 1960s and early 1970s, a popular view was that technology forcing could be easy and cheap, if government merely asserted its commitment. That was also a time when the language of rights was not only firmly rooted, but also could still be used effectively in political discourse to achieve particular ends. Conceivably, the right to transportation might have been defined as an entitlement to a particular level of services that provided equivalent mobility, if not full accessibility. But the civil rights analogy of the 1960s bears with it the elimination of the stigma of "separate but equal," and the complete integration that full or equal accessibility requires. In the American culture, rights tend to be viewed as absolutes, overriding considerations of cost effectiveness. A great premium is placed on the protection of rights. Thus there is benefit in having one's demands—for example, the right to equal accessibility—classified as being entitled to such protection.

Those claims can come from a variety of sources. Although interest groups are usually assumed to be the sources of rights-oriented legislative activity, that was not true in the case presented here. Legislative entrepreneurs spearheaded the section 504 effort; after its passage, coalitions of highly ideological groups were formed, held together principally by their rights perspective.[1] Whatever their point of origin, the technology-forcing and rights-oriented rhetoric of the 1960s provided support for the full accessibility approach. By the late 1970s the growing concern with costs and the economy, combined with disillusionment with some of the Great Society programs, helped produce a more conservative mood, which may have facilitated the move back toward effective mobility. In some sense,

1. In this case, policy origination owes little to "interest group liberalism." See Theodore S. Lowi, *The End of Liberalism: The Second Republic of the United States,* 2d ed. (Norton, 1979). On the role of interest groups, see, for example, Kay L. Schlozman and John T. Tierney, *Organized Interests and American Democracy* (Harper and Row, 1986); Terry M. Moe, *The Organization of Interests* (University of Chicago Press, 1986); Andrew S. McFarland, *Common Cause: Lobbying in the Public Interest* (Chatham House, 1984); and Jack L. Walker, "The Origins and Maintenance of Interest Groups in America," *American Political Science Review,* vol. 77 (June 1983), pp. 390–406.

what was involved was the uneasy, never finally resolved, tension between the values of equity and efficiency. A settled popular consensus, in such a circumstance, may be slow to emerge and perhaps always elusive. To the extent that this conflict exists, one should not expect policymaking to be smooth, although one might still hope that it is deliberative.

To conclude that the problem of providing transportation for the disabled was not well defined begs the more fundamental question of why it was not better conceived. In part, the relatively open, pluralistic system, which allows competing policy premises to exist, did not provide satisfactory means to choose among them. Americans pride themselves in allowing, indeed encouraging, a competition of ideas and premises. They want a system that is flexible enough to allow changes from one approach to another, from one political administration to another. But at the same time they seek stability. Change should result from reasoned deliberation, which is essential to the making of intelligent decisions. Institutions are to help clarify choices and resolve differences. The process is not necessarily expected to be tidy, nor are outcomes always to be free of ambiguity. Indeed, it would perhaps be unusual if government did not reflect to some degree societal ambivalence about how to address problems. But over time, Americans tend to believe, institutions can help make sense of the complexity and confusion and guide participants in determining what can or cannot be done. Thus, although Congress has generally been viewed as slow to act—dependent upon the formation of a consensus achieved after the often laborious process of bargaining and compromise—its behavior is nonetheless generally thought to be deliberative. The executive branch, with its superior resources for assembling information, is perceived as being equipped to design policy. Separate bureaucracies, staffed with professionals, are guided by doctrines and expertise that presumably give consistency and predictability to their activity. The judiciary's task is to interpret the laws, consistent with the legislative history and traditional modes of statutory analysis. Government is more likely to be criticized because it is cumbersome, rather than because it is erratic. But in this case, at least, institutions were often not up to the tasks before them.

A wide range of institutions were engaged in the effort to devise policy, including a host of congressional committees, a variety of agencies within the executive branch, and all levels of the judiciary. With no opposition, the legislature passed several measures. Three cabinet-level departments conducted apparently comprehensive rulemaking proceedings consistent with the spirit of the Administrative Procedure Act. The judiciary conscientiously sought to make sense of the legislative histories and statutory ambiguities. But although these institutions may have agreed that something should be done, there was no consensus within and among them as to how the problem should be defined. The institutional processes did not function in ways that contributed to the clarity of thought necessary for coherent policymaking.

Congress produced statutes that were the product of almost no deliberation; major policy changes were made of which the membership was generally unaware. The executive branch was for much of the time the victim of its own fragmentation, with factions competing against one another; the Executive Office of the President, for much of the period, was either not aware of the policy conflicts or had not developed the means to resolve them.

In this case, the conflict of policy approaches was compounded by, if it did not actually originate in, the fragmentation of national institutions, which has seemingly increased in the past few decades. The legislature, already divided into committees, is apparently now further fragmented by the proliferation of staff units, with the attendant opportunities for individual entrepreneurship. On the executive side, policymaking has become confused as functionally specialized bureaucracies compete with agencies having cross-cutting responsibilities. Careerist program specialists, who provided stability over time, now act with less authority. They have been superseded to some extent by individuals in other agencies charged with coordinating governmentwide efforts. These individuals cannot be expected to have much depth about particular programs, and their departments do not have to bear the costs of the directives issued to others, however worthwhile and necessary those directives may be. The involvement of bureaus with cross-cutting duties may be fitful, but it is nonetheless consequential. To be sure, such efforts presumably could make policy more uniform across agencies and could inject broader values than the concerns of individual bureaus and program experts. But those activities are not without potential costs.

Given the vagueness of the statutes, the absence of deliberation, and the seeming confusion in the legislative and administrative processes, it is not surprising that the many courts across the nation did not always reach judgments consistent with one another—thereby exacerbating the problems of formulating coherent policy. Differences within each of the branches of government were at least as important as differences among them in frustrating development of a stable policy; the price of all this activity was prolonged uncertainty and some loss of government's credibility, not to mention the absence of a policy that firmly addressed the needs of disabled people.

In view of the fragmentation within each branch, it is perhaps wishful thinking to even contemplate that some more stable, reasoned pattern among those institutions could be achieved. But recognition of the realities of the policymaking process need not lead to an unconditional acceptance of them; to simply acquiesce is to resign oneself to inconstant policies that ultimately affect the lives of the individuals with worthy needs. To the extent that this and other case studies may suggest structural weaknesses, consideration of possible institutional remedies, however limited, is in order. Accordingly, I turn briefly to each institution—legislative, administrative, and judicial.

The Legislative Process

Apart from its customary tasks, Congress from time to time provides leadership reserve for those issues that the president chooses not to initiate, matters not on his program.[2] That capacity makes it more likely that the legislative-executive relationship will give expression to a wide range of values and approaches and that the public policy agenda will be a full one. At the same time, though, it must be recognized that the legislature is generally limited by its organization and resources in its ability to assume the leadership role in gathering and assessing large amounts of information and initiating complex pieces of legislation. In this case, much of the confusion can be traced to the legislative process itself. The congressional structure is fragmented, divided into authorization and appropriation committees and subcommittees with cross-cutting jurisdictions and differing, sometimes incompatible, policy approaches. The absence of effective formal consultative or coordinating devices means that Congress is often not aware of the conflicts among committees and thus does not make deliberative trade-offs among various alternatives. Consequently, congressional outcomes can be confusing and thus difficult for the administrative process to implement.

The legislative process itself provides points of opportunity for legisla-

2. See John R. Johannes, *Policy Innovation in Congress* (Morristown, N.J.: General Learning Press, 1974); and Arthur Maass, *Congress and the Common Good* (Basic Books, 1983).

tive entrepreneurs to push through measures and achieve policy objectives without close congressional examination, hearing, or discussion. Amendments can be added on the floor to bills only tangentially related to them. If drafted in an apparently noncontroversial way, those proposals may not be the object of scrutiny as legislators concentrate on the larger issues before them. Through such low-visibility devices as committee reports, members of Congress and their staffs can further their policy goals, unnoticed by the whole house. They may, as the case study described, compel the executive to take steps not contemplated in the legislation itself, often causing confusion in the administrative process.

The substantive objectives of those using these devices may be worthwhile. Certainly the goal of addressing the concerns of people with disabilities is both desirable and necessary. Those taking advantage of opportunities to advance their preferences in ways that are generally unnoticed might feel that such methods are not only the most expeditious avenue of resolving legitimate problems, but also at times the only viable means to achieve their purposes. Against rather strong odds, these legislators move important, legitimate issues onto the government agenda. But at the same time, the means employed could ultimately encourage haphazard decisionmaking and may in the end prove counterproductive. The cumulative effect of such efforts could be a grab bag of programs that ill serve the targeted population. Worse still, perhaps, those activities may give the illusion that the legislature is being responsive and perhaps relieve its members of a felt need to act more coherently.

The structural characteristics of Congress do not merely impede coherent policymaking, they frustrate institutional responsibility. For if the legislature is to be judged institutionally responsible—whatever the substantive merits of its decisions—then, at the very least, the whole chamber must be aware of the actions of its parts. But, as I have shown, the legislative process can operate such that the whole is not conscious of the activities of its parts. Staffs may go about their business, unobserved by the whole house, and achieve policy objectives not envisioned in the legislation itself. If these congressional characteristics make deliberative behavior less likely and make it difficult for the legislature to act with collective responsibility, what, if anything, can be done?[3] There are no obvious panaceas, especially given the complexity of the legislative process, to impel

3. I recognize, of course, the difficulties of imposing major congressional reforms. See Roger H. Davidson and Walter J. Oleszek, *Congress Against Itself* (Indiana University Press, 1977).

improved behavior. But to the extent that institutions can always do better, there is always something to be said for considering such proposals, however limited their effect is likely to be.

A central obstacle is fragmentation. Elimination of overlapping jurisdictions would seem to be one answer.[4] Perhaps for some issue arenas, such a step would be possible; doing away with overlapping jurisdictions could lead to a more efficient decisionmaking process and to less confused outcomes. But because issues cut too many ways, it may be difficult to organize committees in a single dimension. Moreover, multiple committees with differing approaches, sharing authority over particular subject areas, could ensure that the full range of values, purposes, and interests is represented in formulating policy. Both the House and Senate have procedures for multiple referrals of legislation to various committees,[5] and various means to try to keep track of intrabody activities—for example, computers, staff, and the *Congressional Record*. Although there is some evidence that the referral system is being used with increasing frequency, it is obviously not foolproof; much still slips through the cracks of the legislative labyrinth. The same is apparently true with respect to information mechanisms that in theory would keep committees apprised of the work of their counterparts and make the whole house conscious of differing and competing approaches so that it could choose among them.

The extent to which such devices will work is open to question. Much depends upon the willingness of committees and legislators to keep their colleagues abreast of measures that touch upon mutually shared policy interests. In some instances, members of Congress, in an effort to avoid turf battles, might draft legislation so that those overlapping policy ramifications are obscured: they may have little incentive to draw attention to their proposals if to do otherwise would invite jurisdictional conflict. Legislators recognize that the multiple referral system, in enlarging the number of actors and interests, can complicate policymaking by increasing the opportunities for delay and veto: however, to the degree that a referral process becomes routinized and a congressional norm, legislators might find it more difficult to evade.

4. The "jurisdictional quandary," as Gilbert Y. Steiner put it, is found in other areas of social policy. See Gilbert Y. Steiner, *The Children's Cause* (Brookings, 1976), pp. 250–51; and Steiner, *The State of Welfare* (Brookings, 1971), pp. 328–30.

5. See Roger H. Davidson, "Subcommittee Government: New Channels for Policy Making," in Thomas E. Mann and Norman J. Ornstein, eds., *The New Congress* (Washington, D.C.: American Enterprise Institute, 1981), pp. 120–22.

Also troublesome are amendments, tacked on to larger and sometimes unrelated bills, which escape congressional scrutiny because legislators tend to focus on the more prominent matters at hand. It is tempting to argue that such amendments should not be allowed; such a position might be especially justifiable for those measures that proceed from a dead-of-night posture. But at the same time it is important to consider the benefits of the amendment process. It can afford an opportunity to legislators, particularly those in the minority, to raise issues that the majority might not ordinarily address and to bring to the floor matters upon which the committee of jurisdiction did not act. The need, therefore, is to strike a balance between conflicting concerns—the need to preserve fluidity and flexibility in the legislative process yet inhibit passage of peripheral amendments drafted in calculated obscurity. One means of doing so is to provide that tangentially related or nongermane amendments could be considered only if a majority of those present so agreed. A similar majority could reject rulings of the chair holding an amendment tangential or nongermane.[6] Of course, separating what is tangential from what is relevant is not necessarily a simple task. But having attention thus focused on the amendment would presumably make it more likely that legislators would concentrate on its merits rather than rush to quick judgment.

Also meriting attention are such low-visibility mechanisms as committee reports used to make policy not contemplated in the plain language of the legislation itself. The legislative workload is so heavy that it would be unrealistic to expect members of Congress to read all of the reports with care. Their constituents tend to evaluate them, after all, on the basis of such things as their votes on bills and on how well they deliver services for the district, not on their scrutiny of committee reports removed from their policy bailiwicks. But the absence of such examination provides the opportunity for those who wish to shape policy through committee reports. To ban such reports would be extreme and unwise; administrators look to them for guidance, especially when the statutes are poorly drafted. If the improper use of committee reports is to be addressed, then much depends ultimately on self-discipline—on the willingness of committee members and their staffs not to proceed beyond the legitimate contours of the legis-

6. The House already has a rule about germaneness. Nongermane amendments were most recently a concern of the Temporary Select Committee to Study the Senate Committee System. See *Report With Proposed Resolutions,* Committee Print, Temporary Select Committee to Study the Senate Committee System, 98 Cong. 2 sess. (Government Printing Office, 1984), pp. 15–16.

lation or to use the reports to engage in retroactive legislative histories. Such restraint, though, can only be exercised effectively to the extent that legislative staffs do not have incentives to engage in furtive activities. Their principals can remove those incentives, but they are likely to do so only if such behavior is against their interests. Staffers who are rewarded by their employers for such entrepreneurial efforts cannot be expected to stop them.

Apart from changes in procedures that might facilitate more coherent policymaking, the legislature must be prepared to assume responsibility for its actions. When Secretary David Mathews asked key congressional leaders for guidance as to whether the proposed HEW regulations were consistent with the legislative intent of section 504, he received none. In a system involving the interaction of legislative and executive processes, it is incumbent upon each, where appropriate, to respond to the queries posed by the other branch. That is particularly so when the proposed actions of one are based on an apparent directive from the other.

The Administrative Process

Examination of the administrative process raises questions about aspects of rulemaking.[7] The rulemaking process is, at least on the surface, structured in a way that would seem to aid in formulating policy approaches and making specific regulations consistent with them. After all, it presumably generates information from a wide range of sources, encourages representation from the full spectrum of viewpoints, and promotes rationality and order through the notice and comment and review procedures. But, as noted in the case study, data secured from the affected parties, especially for the 1979 proceedings, tended not to be reliable, reflecting the self-interest of the participants. Time pressures in the 1979 round meant that regulations were sometimes written before all the comments in the docket were assessed. Rulemaking can deprive agency deci-

---

7. The concern here is with rulemaking and policy formulation. For analyses of the application of rules, see Robert A. Kagan, *Regulatory Justice: Implementing a Wage-Price Freeze* (Russell Sage Foundation, 1978); and, more generally, Eugene Bardach and Robert A. Kagan, *Going by the Book: The Problem of Regulatory Unreasonableness* (Temple University Press, 1982); and Christopher K. Leman, "The Forgotten Fundamental: Successes and Excesses of Direct Government," in Michael Lund and Lester Salamon, eds., *The Tools of Public Policy* (Washington, D.C.: Urban Institute, forthcoming).

sionmakers of information to the degree that its public aspects lock the concerned parties into rigid positions. It is not easy for representatives to offer compromises in the open without risking complaints from their constituents, particularly when the issues are highly visible and stir strong emotions. As a consequence, agency officials may not be sure of what the parties would really be willing to accept. The absence of informal negotiation makes virtually impossible the bargaining needed to resolve satisfactorily the differences among the parties. To deal with this problem, agency officials might engage in discussions with interested persons before the rulemaking process begins, so that the government might better understand the compromises that the parties might find tolerable.[8] The agencies could create informal task forces or advisory committees to offer counsel about the way problems should be defined and addressed; such a flexible give-and-take might well provide a secure foundation for the rulemaking proceedings.

Deserving further study are recent proposals for "negotiated rulemaking"—direct negotiations among directly affected parties, resulting in regulations embodying a group consensus.[9] Presumably the process would facilitate the bargaining often needed to reach an agreement that would satisfy the various interests, and it would secure political support for the regulations from the groups involved in the negotiations. Clearly, if the negotiated regulation process is to work, these groups must accept the policy premises underlying the negotiations, because they either agree to them or, given the political realities, conclude that they have no choice but to arrive at a common solution. In the case of the 1979 full accessibility regulations, where strong, fundamental disagreements existed, the negotiated regulation process would probably not have been appropriate.[10]

Examination of the administrative process also raises questions about presidential control of policymaking, at least in executive departments and agencies. It is a fundamental tenet of the U.S. constitutional system that the president is the chief executive, that he sets broad policy. But the ex-

8. Some agencies, such as the Federal Communications Commission, already undertake such inquiries; see Ernest Gellhorn and Glen O. Robinson, "Rulemaking 'Due Process': An Inconclusive Dialogue," 49 *University of Chicago Law Review* 201, 249 (1981).

9. See Philip J. Harter, "Negotiating Regulations: A Cure for Malaise," 71 *Georgetown Law Journal* 2 (1982).

10. Before the negotiated regulation process could even begin, there would also have to be some resolution of such basic questions as which parties could participate, who should set policy, what the role of government should be, and how the matter of ex parte contacts would be addressed.

ecutive branch is so far-flung and uncoordinated that various parts are often in conflict. For all its presumed abilities to secure data and design complex policies, the executive in this case was as fragmented as the legislature. For instance, during the Carter years, the White House Regulatory Analysis Review Group was at odds with HEW and the DOT. Which spoke legitimately for the presidency? If policy is to be coherent and responsibility is to be fixed, then some means must be found to assert control. The president, as the one elected official with a national constituency and the authority to supervise the execution of many statutes at once, is most suited to the task.[11] Recent administrations have used various mechanisms to gain some measure of control. The Carter presidency did not always achieve its purposes because its mechanism, RARG, was largely advisory. The Reagan instrument has exerted tighter control, but it has not provided safeguards against the use of Executive Office staff, in the White House or the Office of Management and Budget, as conduits for parties seeking to influence agency rulemaking proceedings. Under Reagan's executive orders, White House staff or the OMB can make their views known to the agency before the publication of the notice of proposed rulemaking without public comment. Indeed, the OMB can generally forestall the issuance of a rule until its objections are met or the president overrules it. Thus the public might never know what the position of the White House staff was, how affected parties influenced it, or the extent to which the agency changed its policy because of Executive Office intervention.

Although the efforts to centralize authority are necessary, the devices used should be consistent with the spirit of the Administrative Procedure Act and statutory mandates. Conversations between Executive Office staff and affected parties and discussions between the Executive Office and agency officials should be summarized and made public.[12]

Mechanisms to centralize control are not absolute remedies. Courts may

11. This view is set forth in Peter L. Strauss, "The Place of Agencies in Government: Separation of Powers and the Fourth Branch," 84 *Columbia Law Review* 573, 662–66 (1984); Lloyd N. Cutler and David R. Johnson, "Regulation and the Political Process," 84 *Yale Law Journal* 1395, 1461–63 (1975); and Commission on Law and the Economy of the American Bar Association, *Federal Regulation: Roads to Reform* (Chicago, Ill.: ABA, 1979), p. 73. For a more cautious view of the Cutler argument, see Stephen Breyer, *Regulation and Its Reform* (Harvard University Press, 1982), pp. 359–60.

12. I deal here only with the issue of presidential control over agency behavior; my concern is not with specific aspects of the executive orders, which raise other legitimate questions. To address some of the problems discussed in the text above, the OMB agreed in June 1986 to fuller disclosure of its role in reviewing proposed regulations. See *Washington Post*, June 17, 1986, p. A21.

interpret statutes as commands to agencies to act against the president's policy preferences. Moreover, whether the executive speaks with one voice is likely to depend not only upon the use of control mechanisms, but also upon the president's ability to convey his views clearly and unambiguously. Ford and Carter did not explicitly resolve the conflict between rights and costs—thus exacerbating the difficulties of formulating and implementing coherent policy. Ronald Reagan did, and in so doing sent clear signals throughout the administration about the kind of approach he would find acceptable.

The Judicial Process

Tocqueville's view—that in the United States political disputes often become judicial ones—is as apt today as it was nearly 150 years ago. But in the case presented here, the judiciary was not an imperial one, pressing its policy preferences and adding procedural requirements for agencies to follow. Belying the charge that courts are insensitive to the intricacies of policymaking, judges showed themselves quite capable of appreciating the problems of other institutions and of learning from experience. Contrary to the oft-stated critique leveled by opponents of judicial activism, courts did not impose the rights ethos; indeed, they were less supportive of it than was the bureaucracy or Congress. Courts were less the eager participant than a means used by all sides to push their ends. Judicial rulings reinforced one institution, then another. The way judges interpreted statutes—whether the laws were said to have created rights (particularly to affirmative action) or were simply discrete statements of general policy—affected the relative capacity of the political actors to shape the course of events.

However conscientious the judiciary was in discharging its duties, this account nevertheless raises questions about statutory interpretation, specifically the assessment of legislative histories.[13] How judges analyze legislative history can influence the direction of policy in important ways,

13. The relationship between statutory interpretation and legislative history deserves a book-length treatment of its own. Some recent additions to an already considerable literature call for a greater understanding of the legislative process. See Richard A. Posner, *The Federal Courts: Crisis and Reform* (University of Chicago Press, 1985), especially pp. 261–93, 317–40; and Frank H. Easterbrook, "Foreword: The Court and the Economic System," 98 *Harvard Law Review* 4 (1984).

affecting the balance of power among the various actors. In determining whether section 504 required the promulgation of regulations, some lower courts placed considerable weight on a conference committee report issued a year after the passage of the statute in connection with legislation that in no way altered the measure. The report erroneously asserted that in enacting section 504 Congress intended that regulations should issue. In fact, the authors of the committee report had engaged in ex post legislative history; it is fair to say that few legislators even thought about section 504, let alone whether regulations were called for.

It is understandable that courts would accept the committee report in interpreting the meaning of the statute, that they would presume that a document emanating from the legislature accurately represented its position. But if those reports are in fact not always reliable, what is the judicial recourse? One option would simply have the plain language of the statute guide the courts. However, legislation is often unclear; and the legislative history, as embodied in part in committee reports, can provide legitimate direction about how statutes should be administered. A preferred alternative, more measured in nature, would look to committee reports, but go beyond them; if the reports assert what the legislators intended in enacting a particular measure, then the courts should examine the relevant committee hearings, debates, and votes. The judiciary should be particularly wary of retroactive legislative histories.[14]

The courts especially need to be apprised of the way Congress has changed in the last fifteen years.[15] By and large, judges learned about the legislative process a generation ago in college and law school. Their conception is based on the textbook view then prevailing—of tight congressional committee discipline. Influenced by that perspective, they have tended to accept the language of committee reports as reflective of the legislative will. But the decrease in discipline and the growth in staffs and legislative activity have widened entrepreneurial opportunity, free of whole house control and sometimes exercised in ways inconsistent with congres-

14. For a useful survey of statutory construction and legislative histories, see Norman J. Singer, *Sutherland Statutory Construction*, Sands 4th ed., vol. 2A (Callaghan, 1984), pp. 277–419.

15. Analyses of the changes in Congress include Thomas E. Mann and Norman J. Ornstein, eds., *The New Congress* (Washington, D.C.: American Enterprise Institute, 1981); Lawrence C. Dodd and Bruce J. Oppenheimer, eds., *Congress Reconsidered*, 3d ed. (CQ Press, 1985); and James L. Sundquist, *The Decline and Resurgence of Congress* (Brookings, 1981).

sional intent.[16] If they were cognizant of these changes, courts would be better equipped as they interpret statutes.

Some Final Observations: The Effect on People and Policy

This account of institutional processes is not simply an academic exercise. It is not just a saga of inconstant actions and indirection. What happens in the legislative, administrative, and judicial processes affects people—in this case, individuals with disabilities, with legitimate needs. It is thus appropriate to discuss the effect of those federal efforts on the population they were presumably designed to serve and to offer some thoughts about the future in light of the past.

On one level, governmental activities, however incoherent and piecemeal, raised the political consciousness of the disabled community. The passage of section 504 of the Rehabilitation Act of 1973 suggested that federal policy would go beyond the therapeutic or medical model, which focused on particular physical and mental difficulties of individuals; with section 504, disabled people could appeal to a rights approach, premised on the view that the state was obligated to eliminate discrimination, indeed undertake affirmative steps, to ensure that the disabled could enter society's mainstream. Federal legislation and regulations heightened awareness at the state and local level of the transportation problems of physically disabled individuals; though the level of compliance with those regulations varied across the nation, at least some steps were being taken, even if they fell far short of what was needed.[17]

16. Some judges are already raising questions about the uses of legislative history. In one case, Circuit Court Judge Antonin Scalia disputed reliance on a committee report in interpreting the 1985 amendments to the Equal Access to Justice Act: "I frankly doubt that it is ever reasonable to assume that the details . . . set forth in a committee report come to the attention of, much less are approved by, the house which enacts the committee's bill. And I think it time for courts to become concerned about the fact that routine deference to the detail of committee reports . . .[is] converting a system of judicial construction into a system of committee-staff prescription." *Hirschey* v. *Federal Energy Regulatory Commission*, 777 F. 2d 1 at 7–8 (D.C. Cir. 1985).

17. On this point, see General Accounting Office, *Status of Special Efforts to Meet Transportation Needs of the Elderly and Handicapped* (GAO, 1982); and Ecosometrics Incorporated, *Transition Planning for Accessible Mass Transit: Responses to DOT's 504 Regulation*, 2 vols., prepared for U.S. Department of Transportation (Bethesda, Md.: Ecosometrics, 1981). DOT officials themselves also stated in the course of interviews that compliance was spotty, in part because of inconstant policy directions.

But if those federal activities raised expectations, they also led to disappointment. The lack of coherence meant that state and local governments were uncertain about what to do. Given its complexity, devising transportation policy for disabled people requires considerable time before it can be fully implemented; during this period, there must be a sense of consistency. At minimum, if objectives are to be achieved, there must be guidance from federal policymakers—from the legislature and the bureaucracy, with its skilled professionals. Such support was not forthcoming; what emerged were mostly confused signals from a fragmented Congress and inconsistent direction from the Department of Transportation, sharing responsibility with the Department of Health, Education, and Welfare. The consequence was shifts back and forth between two different approaches—the transit-oriented effective mobility and rights-oriented full accessibility conceptions. The effect on state and local bodies was perhaps predictable: if the federal thrust kept changing, then those governments had little incentive to devote their energies to devising programs to satisfy soon-to-be outdated requirements. Whatever efforts they made risked a short life as policy shifted. Moreover, the absence of clarity impeded technological development because the transit industry could not determine with reasonable certainty whether the federal government would adhere to its existing pronouncements or would soon change them. Not surprisingly, local governments and the transit industry urged the Department of Transportation in its most recent rulemaking proceeding to chart a firm and certain course.[18] Moreover, the disabled community has been quite understandably concerned as a consequence of these radical twists and turns.

Addressing concerns about process—legislative, administrative, and judicial—will not by itself resolve the substantive problem of providing transportation for disabled persons. That matter is most complex, raising basic questions of efficiency and equity.[19] Since the late 1960s, the federal government has devoted more of its efforts to the problems of disabled

18. DOT, "Nondiscrimination on the Basis of Handicap in Programs Receiving Federal Assistance from the Department of Transportation," Docket no. 56b (1983–86).

19. On this point, see two excellent discussions: Sandra Rosenbloom and Alan Altshuler, "Equity Issues in Urban Transportation," *Policy Studies Journal*, vol. 6 (Autumn 1977), pp. 29–40; and Alan A. Altshuler with James P. Womack and John R. Pucher, *The Urban Transportation System: Politics and Policy Innovation* (MIT Press, 1979), pp. 252–316. Rosenbloom and Altshuler argue that three main concepts of equity uneasily coexist and compete for priority within the field of urban transportation: fee for service, equality in service distribution, and distribution according to need.

people, an obviously positive development. But it has had difficulty choosing between two conceptions—effective mobility (assuring that disabled individuals can get where they need to go) or full accessibility (facilitating the integration of disabled persons into the rest of the population). It has had trouble determining the mix it wants of these two approaches. The regulations issued in 1986 point to a return to effective mobility. Assuming that the political climate of budgetary restraint persists, they are likely to be in place for some time. Under the terms of the regulations, the locus of decisionmaking will shift to state and local governments. As those bodies proceed, they should perhaps keep in mind that what is needed is a *policy* that firmly sets goals, not simply a grab bag of *programs* resulting from political accidents and back-door approaches.[20]

Devising appropriate policy, determining who should qualify for particular services, is hard, given the wide range of disabilities and circumstances.[21] It makes sense to review the experiences at the state and local levels under previous federal regulations and to examine the response of disabled individuals to various programs. In choosing means, decisionmakers should concern themselves with how best to deliver services, the degree of discretion that should be afforded to local transit authorities, the mix of fully accessible and specialized transit, and the utility of other means of support such as transportation vouchers or income supplements.[22] Policymakers should look not only to the Department of Transportation, but also to social service agencies engaged in providing transit assistance, and should find some way to coordinate activities across de-

20. Daniel P. Moynihan first taught me about the perils of programs without policies when I was a graduate student. See his essay, "Policy versus Programs in the 1970's," in Moynihan, *Coping: On the Practice of Government* (Viking Press, 1975), pp. 272–84. Gilbert Y. Steiner also examines programs without policies in *The Children's Cause*, pp. 206–38. On the difficulties of devising policy, see Lawrence D. Brown, *Politics and Health Care Organization: HMOs as Federal Policy* (Brookings, 1983).

21. For two different views, see Dennis Cannon and Frances Rainbow, *Full Mobility: Counting the Costs of the Alternatives* (Washington, D.C.: American Coalition of Citizens with Disabilities, 1980); and David Lewis, "Transportation for Handicapped Persons: From Policy to Administration," *Specialized Transportation: Planning and Practices*, vol. 1 (March 1982), pp. 1–18.

22. Sandra Rosenbloom, "Federal Policies to Increase the Mobility of the Elderly and the Handicapped," *Journal of the American Planning Association*, vol. 48 (Summer 1982), pp. 335–50; Michael Fix and Ronald Kirby, "Providing Public Transportation to the Disabled: The Search for a Stable Policy," paper presented at the conference of the Association of Public Policy Analysis and Management, October 24, 1985; and John R. Meyer and José A. Gómez-Ibáñez, *Auto Transit and Cities* (Harvard University Press, 1981), pp. 230–53.

partments and programs.[23] If these concerns are to be satisfactorily addressed, then there must be an institutional willingness and capacity to do so—at the federal, state, and local levels. At bottom, that means working toward the development of a stable environment populated by program experts, in which institutional processes would interact and incentives would be provided for industry to make technological advancements.[24] It is essential, as well, for the consumer groups to participate in the decision-making process.[25] The evisceration of the rights ethos that unified these groups and the competition among them for budgetary resources makes coalitional politics less likely, at least in the immediate future.

Government efforts need not and should not be based upon the haphazard passage of legislation, on measures that pass unobserved, on ever-shifting policy directions. It is incumbent upon institutions to respond in a more coherent way to citizens with disabilities, to those who seek access to society so that they can contribute to it to the fullest extent possible.

23. American Public Welfare Association, "Recommended Strategies to Improve Specialized Transportation" (Washington, D.C.: APWA, 1983).

24. Program experts themselves can bring continuity and stability; on this point, see Martha Derthick, *Policymaking for Social Security* (Brookings, 1979), pp. 58–62, 158–82; and Barry G. Rabe, "When the Federal System Works: Federalism and the Management of Federal Programs in Health Care and Education" (Ph.D. dissertation, University of Chicago, 1985).

25. Frank Bowe, former leader of the American Coalition of Citizens with Disabilities, writes eloquently about policy for disabled people in *Rehabilitating America: Toward Independence for Disabled and Elderly People* (Harper and Row, 1980). See also Harlan Hahn, "Paternalism and Public Policy," *Society,* vol. 20 (March–April 1983), pp. 36–46. On the value of including and relying upon consumer groups in the policymaking process, I learned much from a discussion with Itzhak Perlman, January 13, 1984.

Index